"What a wonderful book! A deep dive into the wounded, wonderful, witchy female in every woman. *Heal Your Witch Wound* is a delightful brew of illumination and insight."

— **Marianne Williamson**, American Author, Spiritual Leader and Political Activist

"Annalise calls us into rallying around the resurrection of the feminine soul, and the healing of the feminine wound in a poetic, sensual swirl of literary delights while revealing a different side of feminism, a quiet, sacred remembrance waiting within us all."

— **Alexandra Roxo**, Author of *"F*ck Like a Goddess: Heal Yourself. Reclaim Your Voice. Stand in Your Power."*

"*Heal Your Witch Wound* contains the marvelous intimation that books are not just objects in space but events in time – that books happen, which I really dig."

— **JF Martel**, Canadian Writer, Filmmaker and Podcaster

ANNALISE OATMAN, LCSW

HEAL YOUR WITCH WOUND

*A Magickal Depth Approach to Reclaiming
Creative and Intuitive Potency
and Reawakening the Feminine Soul Voice*

Publishing Services provided by Paper Raven Books

Printed in the United States of America

First Printing, 2021

Cover design by Maria Levene, marialevene.com

Paperback ISBN= 978-1-7371405-0-4

Hardback ISBN= 978-1-7371405-1-1

Dedicated to all weird, wild, wise, vulgar and misfit women,
and to those who seek to understand them.
Dedicated especially to the kind, brave, hilarious women
who loved me into being.
Dedicated to Water women, Spring women,
Tree women, Secret saint women,
Professional love-maker women,
Daemon-muse women,
Doomed-to-be-an-artist women,
Keeper-of-the-land women,
and to the women and little girls
who suffer this very moment.
May they find solace.
Dedicated to the maenads
and to the women
who are unknown poets
and ever-unfolding stars
of the first magnitude.

Because Pan is dead,
the oracles are silent.
-Plutarch

I want to unfold.
I don't want to stay folded anywhere,
because where I am folded, there I am a lie.
-Rainer Maria Rilke

TABLE OF CONTENTS

INTRODUCTION

The genesis of this book can be traced to 2015, when I had a series of experiences that upended my understanding of mental health, womanhood, and even reality. It seemed I'd begun to drink the bewitching water of a deeper well, and there was no telling what effect it would ultimately have on me. The phrase *feminine mysteries initiation* kept coming to me, though I had no idea what that meant.

A book was starting to happen to me. And no one had ever prepared me for the helpless transpersonal meaning and magick that can seem to erupt across our lives when we engage deeply in the creative process. When we create from what the French poet Jean Cocteau called 'the poetic instinct,' it is as if we are caught up in a larger magick that outstrips us and must be allowed. From this strange state of being, we are granted a sort of second sight, and the world seems to flash her timeless, mythopoetic dimensions with the regularity of passing butterflies.

Simultaneously, I was undergoing a spontaneous integration process, bringing buried parts of myself home for good. I had the distinct sense of having unearthed a soulful, wakeful femininity. It was not the heartless, pink femininity packaged and sold to me by popular culture. It was a deep, ancient, blood-hot femininity that carried the fragrance of magnitudes and ancient lineages. No one had prepared me for that either. And so I knew I needed to write about it.

Coincidentally, the strange occurrences of 2015 took place while I was in the process of becoming a mental health clinician. It was as if life conspired to show me a much more psychedelic, lunar side of womanhood, reality, and healing to prevent me from finishing grad school with an understanding of these things that was only lab coat-deep. For that reason, much of Part I of this book attempts to adumbrate the shape of what is missing, and then details the feminine ecology of psyche I was in the process of dreaming back. After that, the book becomes a sort of psychopomp, gently guiding the reader into her own initiation waters.

This book was titled *Heal Your Witch Wound*, but it could just as well have been called Follow Your Butterflies, Calling Moonchild's Name or The Silence of the Oracles. And while the concept of the witch wound does figure largely in this book, its starring role is really an invitation into a more ancient mystery hall.

Mystery schools are typically about initiating someone into secret, sacred teachings. So, into what mysteries will the reader be initiated in these pages? Well, this would be no mystery initiation if I gave them all away here, would it? You might think of it as an initiation into the mysteries made accessible to us by lunar consciousness. The holy mystery of love is at the center of everything revealed here, the fulcrum from which this book spins. And if this book was added to the mysteries of the Catholic church, it would be the mystery wherein a woman becomes Virgin (or one-unto-herself) or (in the case of any artist woman) a priestess of the Real.

The word 'mystery' is also important because when strange and anomalous things happen all we can really do is tell the story. We must resist the temptation to reify these experiences into complex systems of esoteric belief. It seems we *must* approach the mysteries as mysteries in order to have a real relationship with them at all. Once ossified into concepts or dogma, the living mystery recedes like the fog of hot breath on a window. And so, the best invitation into the realm of mystery is story. Story freed from the clamps of overzealous explanation. It is especially important that women tell their stories as a catalyst for the reemergence of each other's feminine consciousness.

Due to the confessional nature of some passages of this book, its emergence has felt like an initiation into life as a porn star of the heart and soul (despite the classical admonition that psychotherapists remain as close to a perfect blank slate as possible). Maybe some inner penchant for exhibitionism goads me to flash the pussy of the deepest human truth and vulnerability. Or maybe I knew, intuitively, that to begin a career of writing in my own voice, out of my own musculature, I would need to first tell a secret story or two to break the seal.

Maybe it's also to do with my own imbalances that I want to welcome you to my country, its clime, its caverns, and bring you in with a lantern. Or maybe it's to do with the monthly confessions of my Catholic upbringing. Out with it! Every. Last. Little. Thing. A confession of what it really feels like to be a human woman. I've tried to remain aware of my imbalances and impulses, of the reactionary nature of my inner rebel. I've tried not to exhibit only for exhibition's sake.

The primal longing beneath my writing is to illuminate, with the deepest blood-honesty, the embodied, living truth of each moment with a soft candle (or with a Thoric lightning bolt, as the case may be). And the wordless faith underneath it all is that writing can deepen the love, intimacy, and kindness of this world. For that reason, a sensitive reader may be able to tell that this book tried to squeeze itself into some sort of classic self-help shape, sighed, and then offered the dark, raw side of life in the same breath as the brighter stuff. There is a vacillation between academically influenced writing and a weirder, more poetic voice. It remains something of a mystery how much of the poetic voice is my own soul, and how much is the voice of this book itself, which begged to be born.

You may also notice the undersigned does not exactly hold her pen with an 18th century lightness. There's more of that vulgar, flowery, empurpled style to come because this book is about reaching amorously towards the filthy gorgeousness of the feminine soul voice.

HOW TO READ THIS BOOK

Some books serve as catalysts for processes of deep transformation, and even for times of amped up synchronicity. This book is designed to be one of those. In other words, it is designed to be a magickal object.

Bits of my story (in the style of a weird, philosophical memoir) are braided into a process for the reader to follow. The process blends ritual with numerous invitations to self-discovery through writing, embodiment, and relationship with the mysteries. I highly recommend you follow the steps in order, as I've carefully ensured you are prepared to go deeper with each chapter, and that you pause and seek support if needed along the way. For that reason, don't use the book as an oracle (randomly turning to a page to see what wisdom it has for you) until after you've completed the process.

The process offered here is very much informed by my clinical training, but also by my intuition and creativity, and by my own experiences in the mystery matrix of a female bodysoul. I consider the approach to be a "magickal depth" approach in that it uses concepts from depth psychology but applies them in an unabashedly magickal way.

Writing practice is integral to the process offered here. This can be done in a regular notebook journal, or in a fancier

Book of Shadows. I recommend acquiring a special journal just for this process. As an aside, I (coincidentally) discovered Pauline Oliveros *roughly two weeks after* I decided to name this book's journaling process "Deep Listening." She created a practice of radical attentiveness she called "Deep Listening," which transcends the lines between music, personal growth, and spiritual practice.

Such are the strange occurrences that befall one on the artist's path. Due to my discovery of Oliveros, I've decided to change the name of the writing practice to Oceanic Listening. Think of it as a practice of sinking into your depths, all the way down to the underwater cave where you can hear the mermaid of your soul speaking, and where you can write down her voice. You may find that when you write from the depths, the line between writing, listening, and music begins to dance as if viewed from underwater.

Women's journals are sanctums of explosive power because they can serve as secret places where the feminine soul voice is safe and invited to emerge. They are also surefire places to find hope, solace, ideas, resilience, excitement, possibility, and a sense of what's next. In a journal, real art and real magick can be made in three minutes flat, using only a pen and paper.

Use the Oceanic Listening questions as an opportunity to hear your deepest self, your soul, speaking. Your internal listening will *need* to be deep in this practice. This is because the voice of the soul is often much softer than the surface-level running dialogues that can dominate our internal world.

To help the reader get still and "drop in," several practices are offered or suggested in these pages which are influenced by classic meditation, and/or which involve a Deep Imagination element. For that reason, I would like to acknowledge and thank India, the birthplace of meditation and Tantric yoga (possibly the first tradition to ever use guided imagery as a way to communicate with the gods).

Use this book as an altarpiece, if you feel so moved. When songs are mentioned, listen to them if or whenever you can. Randomly choose a reference, or another writer, or thought leader mentioned here, and take that as an invitation to explore deeper in the vein of that person's work. Keep following the breadcrumb trail from there.

After our scene has been laid in the first two chapters, you will be drawn into your own Oceanic Listening at the end of the following two chapters. We'll get into meatier process steps in chapters 4-8 before cooling down again with some gentle, easy journal prompts and processes in chapters 9-13. Finally, some questions for your Oceanic Listening practice are sprinkled throughout chapter 14. Perhaps, by then, you will have become adept enough at hearing your own soul voice that you won't even need to pick up a pen.

DISCLAIMERS & PRECAUTIONS

Please ensure you are seeing a therapist regularly before you read this book if you have ever been diagnosed with bipolar I or II, any personality disorder, or psychotic disorder, or even if you currently meet criteria for a mood disorder. I must invoke here the ancient proverb that one person's medicine is another person's poison. Interacting with the magnitudes is no joke.

If you are a current or former client, please be advised before proceeding that there is some self-revelation of a semi-sensitive nature in this book. Should you choose to continue anyway and stumble on a passage that you find upsetting or disturbing in any way, please bring it up in session or contact me for a booster session.

Another disclaimer of sorts: If there is any fundamental flaw in this book as far as its faithfulness to feminine mysteries, it is that it gets too abstract, intellectual, airy. Any time you feel you are getting too cerebral in these pages, put this book down and dance, walk, writhe, or smear your hands around in freshly spilled paint. Make a mess. Don't be sorry. Run to the window and shout, "Mooooon chiiiiild!"

Lastly, I don't really know anything. This book was loved into being because it had to be.

A QUICK WORD ON WOMXN V. WOMEN AND GENDER

I began writing this book believing that "womxn" was the most inclusive spelling of "women," even when extended beyond myself. The word was originally created as an intersectional term, designed to indicate the inclusion of those traditionally left out of white feminist discussions, i.e., Black women, women of color, trans women, and nonbinary people.

However, thanks to a great article (*Why 'Womxn' Isn't Exactly the Inclusive Term You Think It is* by Cassie Barradas) and my explorations of the experiences of the people the term purports to include, I was reminded that, of course, nonbinary people do not identify as falling on either side of the gender binary. Therefore, having "womxn" applied to them feels dysphoric and weird. Furthermore, trans women are women. They do not need a special designation to signal their inclusion. So, this book uses the terms "woman" and "women" throughout. I wrote this book with women in mind, specifically women in their 20s and 30s. However, I wholeheartedly and graciously welcome a broader audience. I hope this book will be helpful, powerful, and transformational for anyone who feels drawn to it, regardless of gender. The book does reference "masculine" and "feminine" energies/arcana (more on that later). Whatever words you want to use to describe those energies, we each contain a unique blend of both, regardless of gender. Therefore, the *feminine mysteries* are an aspect of our humanity.

FINALLY, A QUICK WORD ON MAGIC V. MAGICK

Magick with a 'k' first appears in Aleister Crowley's *Thelema*, to distinguish occult magick from performance magic. I use it here because what I am referring to is certainly closer to occult magick than it is to performance magic. Though not even the classical definition of occult magick is perfect for what I'm referring to either because it is not as simple as directly causing change to occur in conformity with the will. I am referring to a process by which humans seem to be able to participate in and even invite, to some degree, acausally connected events. You'll know what I mean. So now, let's drink from the cup of forbidden knowledge.

PART I

DECLINING FEMALE HAPPINESS AND THE LOST MYSTERIES

CHAPTER ONE

THE PARADOX OF DECLINING FEMALE HAPPINESS

———•◦•———

WHAT WE DON'T LET OUT TRAPS US. WE THINK, NO ONE ELSE
FEELS THIS WAY, I MUST BE CRAZY. SO WE DON'T SAY ANYTHING.
AND WE BECOME ENVELOPED BY A DEEP LONELINESS, NOT
KNOWING WHERE OUR FEELINGS COME FROM OR WHAT TO DO
WITH THEM. WHY DO I FEEL THIS WAY?
— SABRINA WARD HARRISON

The sound of silverware clanking on white ceramic dishes marries the hum of several vibrant lunchtime conversations. Where am I? When am I? It appears I've entered some fancy-ish, metropolitan-seeming restaurant somewhere in America. As if picking up a smell in the air, I sense that a historically noteworthy American president is in office, and also that great women's movements are underway. Blearily, I walk up to the second level of the restaurant and it is filled with women, and women only, all dining in freshly pressed women's business suits.

Clearly, they are all successful, but in a worldly, patriarchal kind of way. In other words, they've been granted entry to play the "boy's game," even taking on masculine qualities, ways of dressing, thinking, feeling, and speaking, in order to be considered worthy. They sit looking smart and eating salads with balsamic vinegar dressings and sipping decadently on afternoon champagnes.

I drift to a table in the far back, which is located right beside a window where I can look out and see other women marching down the street with colorful protest signs. My heart swells. I know my mother is insinuated in all of this, though I can't be sure exactly how. It's something I pick up like another fragrance on the electrically charged air.

A cadre of professionally successful women have colonized the large, round table. They invite me to sit. But instead of introducing myself, or saying anything normal at all, I pronounce the word, "Anandamayi." One of the other women responds, as if knowing exactly what I'm talking about, "Filled with light," and I respond, "Joy-permeated. Ma."

And this was how Anandamayi Ma, the great Indian saint, appeared to me in a dream, except not in form. Rather, her name was placed into the center of the dream like a single stone on the surface of a lake, gently disrupting the apparent completeness of this image of feminine empowerment.

Now you may be asking yourself why I just suckered you into reading an account of a dream I once received. I'll tell you why. It's because I believe it represents something fundamental to our being women at this moment in history. I believe it paints a strange and wonderful picture of the underground currents subtending "The Paradox of Declining Female Happiness." This is the name given to the strange phenomenon of declining happiness among women, both globally and relative to men, over the past thirty-five years.

Let me explain. During the women's liberation movement in the 1960s, women fought to be given even more freedom and more rights than they'd won in earlier women's movements. The result was that women were allowed a seat at the table more than ever in the arenas of politics and culturally esteemed professions and in terms of financial assets and power. But there was a problem. Women had only been granted access into a game that had been created by and for men.

It was a game based upon values, qualities, and strengths traditionally considered to be masculine in Western cultures. ("Masculine" and "feminine" are freighted words, and it is debatable how they might even be universally defined. But for now, I think you know what I mean.) Since those traits had defined the meaning of power and worldly success for so long, women measured themselves against them.

Women began stuffing their curves into power suits, literally and metaphorically. Concerns about "measuring up" (seeming competent or being taken seriously) in professional spheres created and defined by and for men were added to preexisting concerns about being sexually desirable, being a good enough mother, and not being a "bitch." For some women, the layering of demands has created an impossible situation of never measuring up or never being able to win in all life domains at once. And in this frenzy of striving, women abandon themselves.

They abandon what it means to be fully integrated and expressed, robust, and authentic. (And this looks marvelously different for each and every instance of "woman," I'll have you know!) They, therefore, bisect even more parts of themselves in order to seem "right," and in some cases, in order to feel respected or worthy of respect at all.

When women stuff themselves into the hard-edged boxes of traditional definitions of worldly "success," they lose a part of their souls. They lose their native sense of what it even means to have a deep, feminine soul, and they lose (or maybe were never even given) a sense of the deep, deep importance of their feminine soul voice. In short, in this frenzy to "measure up," the feminine soul got stuffed down, shut up, repressed, unexpressed, and relegated once again to the collective psychic basement. It had already been there for a very, very long time. Except now, the culture had come up with a new and clever way to keep it there.

This book is about resurrecting that feminine soul, "The Deep Feminine," the great goddess, Beauty, whatever you want to call Her, one person at a time. We need Her now like a fucking blood transfusion.

THE SIGNIFICANCE OF THAT
PARTICULAR HOLY NAME

And now for the first little revelation. In Jewish hermeticism, it is believed that there is magickal power in the utterance of a holy name. Patti Smith began her first album and song, *Gloria*, with the phrase, "Jesus died for somebody's sins but not mine." The very first enunciation of the album was a magickal act. The utterance of the name, "Anandamayi Ma" at the very start of this book is like an invocation. It seems special to me that her name in particular was dropped into the center of this scene of women in business suits because many of her followers believed her to be a living embodiment of the Divine Mother Herself, the Great Mother of the World, the Queen of Heaven.

Before I conjure more poetic phrases for everything people considered her to be, let me assure you that I am not making any claims about the cosmology of a Divine Mother. I am not asserting that there is definitely a Queen of Heaven sitting up there in the clouds somewhere shedding Her vast, endless love and cosmic light down on all of earth like something from a Led Zeppelin song. Although, that would be lovely, and I'm sure that is certainly something She might do. It is difficult to assert anything about the magnitudes because they surpass our normal ways of speaking and understanding. Anandamayi Ma would often say, "I am whatever you think I am."

I believe the importance of Anandamayi Ma's presence in this dream lies in this: She was a woman who did not fit into any man-made box or structure of any kind. All her life she followed only the seraphim and outlawed volumes that spoke through her own heart, only the strange necessities of her nature, and her name continues to be known the world over. She continues to be one of the most influential spiritual luminaries ever to have lived. And she never "worked" a day in her life. If that's not success, I don't know what is. She spent all her days filled with love and radiating it out to all who met her.

The angels, burned books, and forbidden poems of your own heart and soul are speaking now too, and they won't stop speaking. I know you know this. Listen.

BAREFOOT AND PREGNANT

This tiny anecdote may help to illuminate "The Paradox of Declining Female Happiness" a bit more. When I was in middle school, a teacher's assistant was discussing the history of women's movements in the United States. When he got to the Women's Liberation of the 1960s-70s, he said, "Before that, women were really only able to be barefoot and pregnant." I looked up at him from my desk and asked honestly, "What's wrong with being barefoot and pregnant?"

Silence. Blank, blinking stare. Actually, he looked at me a bit disconcerted, like he thought I was trying to be a smartass. But I wasn't. I truly wanted to know. Pregnancy, barefooted, both feet on the earth sounded like an ultra-feminine, mystically connected, beautiful, and grounded way of being. Hell, I hoped I would one day know what it was to literally be "barefoot and pregnant."

I think this illustrates the crux of the issue. A state of being that only a body with ovaries can be in, connecting bare feet with earth, is an expression used to denote the ultimate state of disempowerment. Just take a drag of that for a moment.

It's important to acknowledge that maybe some women *have* found their fullest, highest expression within once male-dominated professional worlds. I think of someone like Ruth Bader Ginsburg, and everything she accomplished in her lifetime in the realm of gender equality. She, and many others, have fought to make it possible for all genders to make it to positions of the highest professional power and for all genders to be treated equally under the law. This is not trivial. This is hugely fucking important.

And yet, the fact remains there is a certain energy, or type of consciousness, which might be referred to as feminine, yin, or lunar (as opposed to masculine, yang, or solar). And these energies are uniquely present in all humans, regardless of gender, though some exhibit or identify more with one or the other. And it is the lunar/yin/feminine energy that is most frequently maligned, distrusted, underrepresented, and undervalued in Western culture (and in nearly all cultures). Qualities traditionally considered "feminine" are more likely to be viewed as flaws, and feminine approaches are more likely to be viewed as incorrect. We've all experienced this, and we all suffer from this, regardless of gender.

Because the feminine is so distrusted and maligned, most of us have split ourselves off from it in one way or another. It becomes enshadowed, relegated to the basements of our psyches. Now, the elan vital, the lifeforce impulse, of the human being tends to lean towards continuous integration and wholeness. Therefore, across the broad continent of our lives there can occur strange episodes of reclamation, especially of the disowned feminine.

And when these episodes occur, they can have a mysterious, occult flavor. They can be deeply confusing. Guidebooks, mentors, and containers for this process are scarce, and it doesn't seem the uncanniness of the process is fully appreciated by the framework of modern Western psychotherapy. So, there can be a lot of "what the fuck" about this process when it occurs. Let me take you right into the "what the fuck" of my experience. Later I'll explain how I understand this now, though my understanding continues to develop.

WHAT THE FUCK

In 2015, I was living in Bronx, New York, finishing grad school while interning at a men's methadone-to-abstinence residential treatment facility. The facility was connected to a multiple-tiered rehab and detox program, as well as a long-term skilled nursing facility for people with HIV and AIDS. I mention them all because I literally interned within them all.

Several unusual things happened to me that year. It all began when, during my spring break, I read *The Pregnant Virgin: A Process of Psychological Transformation* by Marion Woodman. The book details the unique, rich processes of deep psyche transformation so many of Woodman's female analysands underwent during their time working with her. These processes usually involve profound and meaningful dreams (the kind that stay with you and are never really finished with you), and sometimes radical persona or preference changes.

One woman Woodman wrote about came home in the afternoon after a day racing around at her normal frantic clip, and after she crossed the threshold and closed the door, she dropped her grocery bags, fell to her knees, and sobbed. Once she was good and done sobbing, she stood and moved around her house slowly, with deep reverence in every breath and footstep. She carried herself with great gravity, dignity, and sovereignty, as if she were an ancient priestess. The dreams that came to these women often contained important messages about what was next in their own unique process of transformation. The dreams gave the women their healing images and seemed to touch the veil of other worlds.

As if I was ingesting some initiatory potion rather than a book, *The Pregnant Virgin* seemed to spontaneously spark the same process of transformation in me. And what would unfold was unlike anything I could have imagined, and unlike anything that the book, or anyone I knew, could have prepared me for.

In order to have you join me right smack dab in the middle of the "what the fuck" of that chapter of my life, I need to back up just a couple of steps. I had moved into an apartment on the lower east side of Manhattan with Donna, one of my best friends from high school. We were barely making rent, but I felt like I was right where I wanted to be—with an amazing friend I treasured and loved deeply and in a city I'd dreamed of for so many years, The City of Dreams itself.

She was in a starry-eyed relationship at the time with Neal, who was nursing a fairly acute crack and alcohol dependency. Somehow, Neal got in on our digs without paying rent. I sensed some deep, blinkered enchantment around the two of them, and I also detected that Neal was helping himself to my painfully meager food supplies. At the time I was subsisting on one sandwich per day, and I came home one day to find that all of my food for the week had vanished. (For some, regular heroin use can make the appetite disappear at times only to roar back with a vengeance at other times.)

Suddenly I knew something, in the way that a sudden, clear knowing can sometimes go *kerplunk* right into your tummy. I knew he was too fogged by his addiction and admittedly shitty circumstances to see how he was using me, *and* my beloved friend, Donna. And Donna's clarity, Great Mystery bless her, seemed too clouded by deep, deep love. The kind she seems able to hold in her rare heart for everyone so that it beams out of her eyes as real as rain. It was as if she had already agreed to this whole addict-enabler ride as one chapter of her deep destiny or ascension path in this life (or something like that), but I had never agreed to it, or so it seemed. (Maybe some deep part of me had.)

I couldn't afford to pay rent on the place while having my stringently rationed groceries continue to disappear. I finally left in a sudden, uncharacteristic huff of righteous anger (100% directed towards Neal), which surprised even me. It caused a temporary rift in my relationship with Donna, which pained me more than any other part of the situation. However, as women are wont to do, miraculously, she and I later forgave each other and remain to this day the best of friends. She's no longer with Neal, though she (with her vast-heartedness) continues to sincerely love and wish him well.

A historical blizzard was about to descend as my housing crisis began, and fate had me move in hastily with a friend of a family friend, Darlene, who had a room for rent in the Bronx. She was an earthy, no-bullshit Puerto Rican woman who had been three times divorced and was a funeral director. The first night I moved in, she invited me to have dinner with her, and she poured me a deep, generous glass of red wine. (She used to say, "Something must be in the water... That's why I drink wine!") She was genuinely curious about my story, and about how I came to be living with her. I told her, and she looked me dead in the eyes over her full glass of wine and said, "Honey, your intuition was right on. He *was* using you. You should always listen to your gut."

I'm hopscotching around in my telling of this story, but now the stage has been set for these strange experiences that Woodman's book induced in me. I was always either in my little bedroom at Darlene's house as I read this book or on the deck with her other roommate, a young woman named Jess, who was about as close to an angel on earth as anyone I've ever met.

THE BOOKS AND THEIR SYNCHRONICITIES

After gobbling up *The Pregnant Virgin* and swimming in the murky, mysterious waters of what I started calling my own "feminine mysteries initiation," with no container, no guides, only the beautiful words of Woodman on the pages of a book, the summer semester began. New York City became hot, sweltering, aromatic—the way it's famous for being in the summer. I tried to sign up for an elective class on death and mortality, but it was already full. Looking at the remaining options for an elective, I noticed that only one really stood out to me. It was called *Global Violence Against Women*.

Now, I won't take you into the lurid underbelly of the vast, multifarious and often unsettlingly self-similar manifestations of violence against women that occur cross-culturally around the globe and throughout history, but I will tell you this: I experienced anger in that class. And then sadness. A profound, heavy, dripping, blue-black sadness that seemed to drag around and follow me everywhere, leaving little puddles.

Sometimes this sadness was so deep that it almost had a strange, mystical quality, which bewildered me. It seemed to obliterate my ego in some moments and connect me to all living beings. There were moments I wondered why I was even alive. Despite its more harrowing dimensions, I sensed a strange initiatory quality in this deep, mystical sadness.

Simultaneously, I was having profound dreams. I noticed the vividness and profundity of the dreams seemed to be linked not only to the cycles of the moon, but also to my menstrual cycle, and to the stages of soul-making I was navigating alone.

One morning I emerged from a dream with a Sonic Youth melody in my mind, and woke myself by softly whispering the words, "Slow butterfly...". I looked the song up and quickly remembered the actual name of the song is "Drunken Butterfly." Yet, I immediately knew the phrase spoke directly to this weird process of metamorphosis. It was happening, slowly but surely.

I started to crave the color red as if it was a nutrient I'd been deficient in for my entire life, and I also noticed more synchronicities that seemed to help me go deeper into this strange process of transformation. The synchronicities mainly seemed to spin off of this craving for more red in my life, but more on that later.

Moments of dissociation danced with ongoing thoughts about what it means to become fully authentic. I felt privately embattled by this, and I craved time with my journal. And, per a

Woodman recommendation, I supplemented writing with other solitary, sacred practices in order to contain and direct what seemed like a new energy flowing through me.

There was often an uncanny sense that there is some kind of magickal underworld subtending our consensus reality and an awareness that the realm of the archetypes, one might even say the gods, is closer and more present than we think, and is even present in pop culture, even in the goddamn Disney princesses. It was all an experiment in the mysterious, acausal dance between inner and outer. Within the cradle of that strange time, this book began to be written, as a product of that mysterious relationship between inner and outer, and an ongoing emblem of it.

The deep uncanniness of this episode was the part that really permanently altered my understanding of what it is to be human, what it is to be a woman, and what it means to be in a process of soul-making. It was because of the profundity, life-altering potency, and weirdness of this constellation of experiences that I thought to myself, *Young women should be prepared for this by older women! Why didn't my mother prepare me for this? Does she know about this?* And the first strokes of my clumsy pen flashed and cut into long, passionate, unwieldy word documents.

One of the synchronicities of that time involved yet another book. (Books must like to be implicated in this kind of magick!) It happened to be recommended to me by a fellow student in the *Violence Against Women* class. It was the classic,

Women Who Run with the Wolves: Myths and Stories of the Wild Woman Archetype by Dr. Clarissa Pinkola Estes. From now on, I will refer to her as CPE. This book was to be my fall semester enchantment. In it, CPE deeply explores a series of old fairy tales and myths pertaining to what she calls "the wild woman archetype." She shows how each tale might be understood as a beautiful allegory for any woman's process of psychological transformation (of the soul-making variety). They serve as maps, letting us know where we've been, where we are now, and where we might be headed.

By the time I got to the tale of Vasilisa the Beautiful, the eastern European ancient ancestress of Cinderella, I nearly flipped my lid. I noticed that many aspects of my peculiar and sometimes trying journey through New York mirrored many of the old fairy tales, which involve a female heroine bravely venturing on her own out into the woods. While in the woods, she must learn to trust her little voice of intuition. She eventually gets all the way to the house of the crone, Lady Death, the witch, Baba Yaga, the dark goddess, whatever you want to call that archetype.

After a series of strange trials, tests, and initiations, the Baba Yaga pulls one of her own fence posts from the ground, which (wouldn't you know) has a human skull lantern on top. She gives this to the young Vasilisa to carry with her all the way back home through the dark woods. Except, on the return journey, the woods don't seem quite so dark anymore. As an "initiate" of the ways of the crone, Vasilisa now not only has a teensy still small voice of intuition guiding her through the woods, but she also has a bright, fierce skull-light that will guide her home like a motherfucker.

Why did it feel so unbelievably redemptive to find the Vasilisa fairy tale at that precise moment? Because I could immediately see the major aspects of the story arc mirrored in this New York chapter of my own life. Suddenly, even though I was still "in the woods," life seemed magickal and uncanny. Somehow, it seemed I was still exactly where I was supposed to be, despite everything. It seemed there was some greater pattern influencing all of our lives, even when they are not going according to the neat little plans of our ego. In other words, I felt kissed and deeply comforted by a sudden awareness that even ordinary lives and situations are in constant contact with a realm of deep, timeless patterns and magick.

The most important parallel was what Darlene (the funeral director) validated for me the very moment I first moved in with her, when she sat me down for dinner over a full glass of ruby red wine. She told me directly, with a certainty that resonated down to the core of her being and throughout her body (which I believe we're all able to perceive), that *my intuition was correct.* Period. Her certainty gave me certainty. It was as if she was tapped into the power of gut knowing and anchored in it so fiercely that she knew for a fact that not only was her own gut knowing 1000% powerful, but so was mine. So was everyone's.

And this is what the Baba Yaga does for Vasilisa and what

Lady Death (in her many guises) so often does for the young heroine in the fairy tales. All the seemingly mundane sifting, sorting, and cleaning tasks given to Vasilisa (and other heroines) are ways for her to sort through her own internal landscape. This is how she separates out her own authentic values from any bullshit values she's imbided in her girlhood, guided all the way through by her own knowing, her own instinct. This is how the lunar part of us, the part of us that makes art and makes contact with the great mysteries, usurps the inner throne from the patriarchy within (regardless of gender).

And only then is Vasilisa granted the fierceness to see her way back through the dark woods with absolute confidence. Only then has she done the work. And only then does she bring the gifts back home.

Finding the astonishing parallels between this ancient fairy tale of mysterious folk origins and *the chapter of my own goddamn life into which it kerplunked,* gave me the sense that maybe, just maybe, the fairy tales have a life of their own on the other side of things. And maybe they somehow breathe their uncanny breath onto our side of the veil. And when they do, it seems like life is giving us little winks all over the place. We notice synchronicities, chance encounters, and a weird, almost novel-like thread connecting the unique themes of our own lives.

I had an intuition that these mysterious moments of our lives are "initiations" of some kind. The phrase "feminine mysteries initiation" kept popping into my mind, but I don't think I had ever heard the phrase anywhere, and I hadn't the foggiest clue what it meant or where to find information about it. The phrase "feminist spiritual awakening" from Sue Monk Kidd's *Dance of the Dissident Daughter* occurred to me a few times as a very close vibrational sibling.

Now for a more intimate revelation: There lived within me a distinct feeling that the process I was undergoing was *precious*. It needed to happen; it was sacred; it was an initiation. And even if I was actually becoming psychotic, I wanted to just allow that to happen... at first.

THE FEVER BREAKS

There was a point in the process that was akin to the moment a fever breaks. I had gone out that night with Jess and two of her friends. I got drunk, as I was liable to do at that time. And if foggy memory serves, the drunker I got, the more shocking my speech and behavior got. I distinctly remember that I dropped the ultra-shocking, electrifying word, "pussy," more than once. I can't quite remember the context, except my reader can rest assured I wasn't hurling it as an insult. Rather, I was probably trying to imitate the kind of raunchy, feminine sex talk that the comedian Amy Schumer is actually good at. I was rather pleased with myself in the moment. And then, as we are wont to do when alcohol turns to sugar in our blood, I woke up in my bed at Darlene's house at about three a.m. and immediately thought back on the events of the evening. "Oh, Jesus Christ," I thought, "what in the name of Jesus was I saying to Jess's friends? Why do I have to be so shocking and provocative when I drink?" Cringe, cringe, cringe.

And some soft, wise part of me responded:

Because you are an artist, and it is part of your sacred calling to be shocking, disruptive, provocative. You always were, you are now, and you always will be.

And snap. The fever broke. This knowing broke through with the clarity of the long-awaited sun after so much rain, when drenched shingle rooftops emit steam. It was the kind of knowing that comes through as an *experience* and must be accepted as personal truth.

In that moment, I brought an extremely important part of myself home for good. I stayed awake, lying in bed with this beautiful knowing, and tears streamed down my face as I watched the sky gradually lighten.

SHEDDING SOME LIGHT WHILE PRESERVING THE WEIRDNESS

Now, the temptation to sanitize my experience by neatly tucking it into a paint-by-numbers retro-understanding is great indeed. I'm a therapist, after all. Aren't I supposed to understand what these experiences are and what they mean? Well... No.

While I *have* connected some of the threads in retrospect,

we would be doing the mysteries a disservice by immediately throwing floodlights on them. We cannot just do away with the radical, irrevocable mystery at the heart of our experience as human beings.

It's also greatly tempting to suggest that the aforementioned "fever breaking" moment was the neat, happy ending of that strange chapter of my life. It wasn't, though things certainly seemed to shift in that moment. I was no longer so embattled by dissociation, nor so embroiled in private thoughts about the dangers and thrills of "authenticity."

Let me simply suggest what I've come to feel fairly confident about at this point in order to reveal, by firelight, the shapes of the animals in this strange cave of paintings.

I suspect the profound sadness was linked to having my eyes opened to the harrowing realities of women all over the planet both historically and in the moment your eyes alight on this line. It completely knocked me out, the inconceivable levels of suffering so many throughout history who represent "the feminine" have endured, simply because of who they are.

It also makes sense to me in retrospect that I went into a depressive state with no guides or containment for the process I was going through. I didn't realize that doing deep transformational work without a community, support, container, or guidance can be bad news bears.

As for the strange, mystical, connected feeling in my sadness, the great spiritual teacher Pema Chodron has shed some light there. She teaches that even the most difficult feeling states can be portals into even deeper compassion and connection. So, for example, when you are feeling something like inadequacy, you are feeling the inadequacy of all beings.

As for the uncanniness of that time, I now realize that I have a way of experiencing each episode of depression, stretching back to my teenage years, like a trip to a different layer of the underworld. It was as if an important part of me lived down there and once in a while my whole system essentially said, *Fuck this, I'd rather be down there with her.* And, as we'll see, the parts of us that live down there can be highly active with archetypal energy.

The topic of suicide is complex and we will return to it in a later chapter. However. even its treatment in this book barely scratches the surface. One could actually suggest that the impulse to become no one is, at its core, when brought into the light, a spiritual impulse. It's painful to always be identified as this one person. Human beings have an intrinsic impulse to obliterate that identity from time to time to get closer to what might be referred to as divine ground, rapture, ecstasy, or just altered consciousness. But when there are no socially acceptable, or legal, outlets for doing this, then we get "obliterated" with alcohol or have fantasies of other forms of demolition.

Finally, I'm now fairly convinced that I was a creative, vulgar, unconventionally spiritual, sexual, weird, subversive woman looking for a way to be fully expressed in the world and

33

not seeing any easy options for doing that. Most apparently available options appeared to be different ways to insinuate myself into masculine, sterile, disembodied environments where the imperative was to look like a perfect employee to someone else on paper. And when you don't see anywhere in the world where all of you feels fully welcome, the aura of sweet relief around the prospect of being no one at all seems to grow even sweeter. I believe we all invite or experience some level of anxiety, depression, emptiness, pain, craving, or listlessness when we feel we have to be constantly masked and stuffed. It doesn't feel good to not be expressed, to be constantly closed, to stuff and bury the messages of your soul. It hurts. I know you know this.

WHO AND WHAT SHE WANTS

A GIRL SHOULD BE TWO THINGS: WHO AND WHAT SHE WANTS.

-COCO CHANEL

Summoning a heartfelt yes to life and to my murky multitudes, as profound and difficult as that can be, is how I began to navigate my propensity for suicidal depression and addiction. I know it's not always so easy, because every instance of depression and/or addiction is unique, but stick with me for a moment.

For blood-honesty's sake, I must add that I'm now starting to *qualify* that yes. In other words, I believe I needed to go through a big "yes" phase in order to counterbalance some of the forces underlying my suicidal depression. But in the years since the episode this book details, I've gradually grown more towards some kind of healthy synthesis in between a radical, unqualified YES to everything on one end of the spectrum, and all out resistance to life on the other. In other words, like the great lysis of *Ulysses*, I breathe Molly Bloom's "yes, yes, yes." And on the next breath, with enormous, loving pity, I exhale Elliott Smith's lyric from Pitseleh, *No one deserves it.*

It can be harrowing to be here. But my deep prayer is that the medicine of my yes (mustered out of the abyss) offers radical permission to anyone who stumbles on this book. It's really a loving yes to the personal underworld that I'm advocating for, not necessarily to life itself and all of human history. It's an acceptance of the invitations we continually receive to the spiral dance of liberation and unfolding. I still wholeheartedly stand behind my yes to that dance, my decision to integrate buried parts of myself and to release the full force of energy bound up in that process. And I still wholeheartedly believe this was the key to my "getting better."

Ultimately, I had to own who I needed to be at a deep level (an artist), no matter how I thought that might seem to others or how scared that made me. (And I now consider an artist to be someone who lives from what Burroughs called "the mark inside," but more on that later.) At a certain point, I had to choose a soulful life, or else I would continue to be suicidal, and I knew it. It was either a life among the living dead, or an awake, soulful life, or actual death. The first option was no longer possible for me. So, the second option was do or die. Sound dramatic? At a certain point, we all must find a deeper well and imbibe its shining waters to stay alive.

Let me flesh out a little more fully where I was diagnostically then and where I am now. I believe this will shed more light on my particular underworld journey and the way I think of diagnosing from the 5th edition of the *Diagnostic and Statistical Manual of Mental Disorders* (DSM-V) generally. I was diagnosed with clinical depression when I was in high school and then Panic Disorder when I was in college. I see these diagnoses now as just different ways that the same trapped energy was expressing.

Think of DSM-V diagnoses as a forest. The borders between the different diagnoses are more porous than people typically speak about them as though they are. We may cross the border and be firmly in the "depression" neck of the woods at some point in our lives, and then we may move back out of that neighborhood at another point.

We may live in an area of overlap, or we may live "near" a neck of the woods for which we have a propensity. This applies to some diagnoses more than others. My suicidal depression had to do with cruelly nonexistent self-regard, which secretly had shame and anger underneath it, and the conviction that there was nowhere in the world where all of me was welcome. These core themes may echo in other people's depressions, or they can have a different core theme entirely.

And while we're at it (with the deep, blood-honesty type of shit), it's probably misleading to say I *completely* overcame these challenges, or that they're now behind me forever. It's more accurate to relate that I found my way to ever-increasing sovereignty and the power to know joy, pleasure, enchantment, self-trust, and deep engagement with life. It's more honest to suggest that uncovering and tending to whatever prevents us from being present each moment with an open heart is a lifelong journey. Various teachers, healers, and practices may accompany us at various intervals, but the road goes ever on once we get on board with our soul's journey. Crucially, I've found that it seems I have much more energy to create when I am dogged by neither depression nor addiction.

Now I've set my life up so that art and the creative process are front and center. I've created my own magickal psychotherapy practice where I mostly do embodied, depth-informed, transformative work with women who are depressed when they are not expressed. I have no boss. I talk openly all day about dreams, the artist's path, transpersonal psychology, and the mystery of life. I get to be myself. I don't *really* have to be a "good girl" for anyone. In other words, rather than asking for a place at the table, I've made my own table. I have the liberty to maintain a serious creative practice, which will continue to expand from here. And the road goes ever on. I am still shedding skins, starting a second, wild healing business, writing, making weird, mixed media visual art, and assiduously tilling the soil of my inner poet and author.

Most importantly, I'm fucking happy. Not cheesy, slaphappy, but deep, overall satisfaction and excitement-happy. And I still honor sadness, and all emotions actually, as holy carriers of personal truth. I'm taking good care of my body. Like e e cummings, I believe the artist's life is "the most wonderful life there is," and I have the extraordinary privilege of finding my way into it. Let's extend that further and say that the soulful life is the most wonderful life there is for every one of us. More on that, and how to make it for yourself, later.

Another key to my soul's unfolding (and the spiral dance out of shame and suicidality) was and is the power of the imagination. According to the modern philosopher and writer, Alain de Botton, suicide and the imagination are deeply linked. We only think about ending our lives when we cannot imagine another way out or another way to live. To go from "I'm going to kill myself" to "I'm going to kill this shitty chapter of my life" requires the ability to envision alternatives. Later on, we're going to deep dive into the unbelievable power of your imagination, which I think of as, in many ways, the inner mage, or the visionary inner eye that looks out onto other worlds.

In addition to this (and at risk of sounding like a mouth-piece for Millennial cliches), self-love saved me. Making the stubborn decision to love myself for no reason remains probably the most important decision I have made yet in my life. Before committing to self-love, my attachment to this world was tenuous, and I had a proclivity for (unconsciously) taking out anger on myself in various forms of self-harm. That wasn't anyone's fault in particular. My parents were and are wonderful people. It's just that, by adolescence (like so many young women), I'd become a thoroughly disenchanted, disembodied, and self-conscious person. It's complicated, but we'll get into how this might apply to you later.

People's automatic response to the concept of self-love is often, "Oh, that sounds nice." But I think of finding non-egoic self-love as nothing less than finding the GPS that will put you on your most soulful path. You won't regret it, and you'll never look back, I promise. You can start from anywhere at any time.

A sincere self-love practice, over time, heals the internal fragmentation of shame. Shame, self-hatred, and wanting to die or sink into the earth are all connected. Stubbornly *deciding* that I was going to be a woman who loved herself from here on out, no matter what, helped me embrace my inner artist and a life of expression. If I hadn't summoned the *courage* to embrace a more soulful life, I don't want to think what my life would feel like from the inside at this point (regardless of outer appearances).

It's important to acknowledge that some people are in a painful place right now and are absolutely not there for lack of courage. There are some very valid mental health (and other) diagnoses that can't be self-loved away, and you're not likely to find anyone more courageous than those who live with them. I do also realize that my current situation was created through a combination of courage, drive, and many kinds of privilege.

If you've gotten this far in this book without chucking it

at the wall, and you feel you can really only lay claim in great measure to the first two elements of that equation, I know you know privilege is not a requirement for creating a soul-led life. And it's not as though any of us has to always do it perfectly. I certainly don't. I still fall into phases of soul-offending and soul-burying until I notice my personal cues (usually deep sadness or falling back into obsessive vaping) that the orchid-child of my soul is screaming in pain as the result of some aspect of my current life . It seems I have a persnickety one, but maybe yours is persnickety too. Maybe all souls are like highly sensitive radio dials that let us know when we are on track with what we are here to do and when we are absolutely not. We'll dive deeper into how this applies to all souls later.

So, imagination and self-love pulled me out of hell. Then self-love combined with something that feels like a spark of the sublime in my body put me on my path. Edmund Burke defined the sublime as "tranquility tinged with terror." Pause with that for a moment. What feels like that in your body? Where is it in your body? For me, it's usually in the pit of my stomach or in my solar plexus area, where I get butterflies. It's that little flame of excitement, aliveness, and beauty (that often has some white hot fear dancing around it). Sometimes it's the vaguely terrifying feeling that there is no line between my heart and the whole world. It's vaguely terrifying because to the ego, this experience seems to threaten a kind of death.

Follow it. I am just weird enough to be able to entertain

the idea that part of you is tapped into transpersonal wisdom and a bigger plan than your fear and/or your ego could possibly know. That electrically alive, edgy sensation is connected to the child oracle of your soul, and her realm. I know many readers will go, "Oh nooooo! You want me to go towards the thing that has fear wrapped around it?" Yep. We are going to deep dive into that as well. Fear tends to cling to our genius, our most precious gift, our most alive adventures, our expansion, our soulful life, our naked joy, our bliss, and everything we're really here to do because that's just what fear does, "like a magnetized needle" to use the words of Steven Pressfield.

That dancing light in your belly is your ticket to expansion and to a life that's even better than the one you currently envision for yourself. Give yourself radical permission to entertain the notion that it knows more than you do. I am giving myself permission right now just by writing that. *That* is how you're going to step into a bigger life. Listen to that spark. Listen.

And know that there is no exact arrival point or destination. I'm not there yet. This is an ongoing labyrinth walk, a journey of shedding one skin and then another. What happens to a snake when it needs to shed its skin and it doesn't *listen*? I don't actually know, but I'm pretty sure it dies, okay?

As a writer and an unconventional facilitator of healing, I am called to find the lines along which intimate personal revelations promote the love, joy, and liberation of others. By taking off my personal corset, monk's robe, business suit, or whatever it is, I am giving other women permission to do the same. What a fucking gorgeous, harmonious, wild, and alive world it would be if *every* woman listened to that spark of the sublime in her body, if every woman took off her stuffy, uncomfortable business suit or corset (unless she likes that kind of thing) and allowed herself to be exactly who and what she wants. Listen, listen, listen.

CHAPTER TWO

THE WICKED WITCH
WOUND OF THE WEST

MY CULTURAL STARTING POINT

YOU HAVE NO CHOICE BUT TO MAKE A CIRCLE AND GO BACK TO

YOUR ANCESTORS AND YOUR GRANDFATHERS... THEIR VALUES

AND UNDERSTANDINGS.

-ARLETTE LOUD HAWK

In the endeavor of unearthing a frame for any kind of "feminine mysteries initiation" or feminine way of healing, it's important to acknowledge the radical contingency of my perspective and possible influences on the process I've come up with. I do not want to contribute to the White Western perspective being the default norm perspective (especially in the realm of the healing arts and especially in a book largely about feminist liberation), which is why I'm naming it rather than simply proceeding. It is, of course, only one in a manifold kaleidoscope of possible perspectives.

Racially, I am a White woman, and I have spent my life living in the West, mostly in America. I am pushing my trained knowledge of healing within the Western psychotherapy framework into a more feminine, creative, and intuitive space. There are many traditions across the world that still use and provide ways of healing that fall under the umbrella of the more feminine, creative, and intuitive, and I am not an expert in any of them. In many ways, this book is about the miracle that some basic semblance of the feminine mysteries can be dreamed back at all, even when they are totally lost.

In *Untie the Strong Woman*, Dr. Clarissa Pinkola Estes contends that, even if Holy Mother was ripped entirely out of the culture down to the last scrap of any kind of remembrance of Her, the people would still dream Her back. And so it is with feminine ways of healing. Even if they are ripped out of the culture down to the last shred, the people will still dream them back.

This book does deal, largely, with the burial of feminine mystery lineages in the West. Since this book is intimately cooriginal with my own experience, story, and psyche, and I am a denizen of Western culture, in some sense, I had no choice but to do it this way. I had to begin my own sifting and sorting through the mythopoetic material most local to me by virtue of my ancestry, upbringing, and whatever it is that determines the landscape of our dreams.

Many of my readers, I imagine, will be denizens of, or at least touched by, Western culture, regardless of ethnic or cultural background. I believe that uncovering some of the buried feminine lineages of the West *will* contribute to the liberation and healing of all, regardless of cultural or ethnic background or current location on the planet.

In terms of my ethnicity and heritage (and other factors that contribute to my perspective), I am going to challenge myself to write about this as honestly as possible, trimming out (most) pointless personal indulgences, and also anything that is purely motivated by the desire to avoid criticism. The point is to make plain where I am coming from and what may have influenced the creation of this process. This section has been revised nearly to death as the result of my deep desire to do no harm, and my awareness that I will never be entirely free of the personal foibles that cloud my lens. If you're not interested, feel free to skip ahead now to the section that starts with "Lineage."

First, my family is aware of a significant number of Irish famine refugee ancestors. This influence is significant enough that the straight line of Catholicism going back to Ireland made its way to my generation, and I was raised Catholic, attending a little Catholic school where some priests were from Ireland (including the one who baptized me), and even one of my first teachers. And since my family still has living relatives, family friends, and even a priest with whom we remain in contact in the British Isles, my parents were comfortable enough to allow me to attend college in Ireland for four years. So, Ireland has been a major character in the theater piece of my life (in ways too numerous to recount here). It's possible that something of Ireland made its way into these pages. What is certain is that my upbringing left a deep tattoo of the Virgin Mary on my psyche, and that the Marys have made their imprint on this process without apology.

Furthermore, I was also blessed to be raised with an Irish-Scottish immigrant great grandmother, who spoke with a brogue and could sing songs, tell tales, share recipes, recite poems, do traditional dances, and even speak the ancient language of the Scottish Highlands. She was trafficked into Canada at age sixteen (along with her 15-year-old sister) and escaped her captors in the middle of the night, crossing the border into the United States. She remained undocumented for her entire life. I carry the bravery that shines through her story like a talisman, and I know it's made its way into this book and process.

And recently, through an ancestry test, I became aware that (while 90-something percent of my genes come from the British Isles—Ireland, Scotland, Wales and England), my biological mother also had ancestors from Spain, Sardinia, somewhere in the region of Iran, and Angola, with those final two influences traceable to ancestors about 6-8 generations ago. That means the Angolan line of my ancestry very likely comes from an individual who was brought to the colonies as a slave, and whose genes began mixing with European genes fairly early on in the history of the United States. The manner of that "mixing" with each successive generation is also a part of my heritage. I suspect that somewhere along the line, a generation or two of individuals were just at the edge of being able to "pass" as White, and they may have deliberately chosen to start their families with White Americans in order to help their children cross the color line and avoid discrimination. I have thought about the fact that it could very well be the case I am White, in part, because my Black ancestors treasured the futures of their children. In terms of the mixing of earlier generations, however, I don't believe I need to imply deliberate choice was probably not a factor.

I have privately battled about whether or not to even include this. I've had people tell me that my family's DNA test result is probably some kind of fluke or a mistake. Maybe they are right. The only things that convince me otherwise are some profound dreams that came to me years before receiving this result, a certain very old ancestral photograph, my mother's intuition, and the fact that our West African DNA result keeps getting more specific over time as the database grows, zeroing in on the people of Angola. It's become something of a self-deprecating inside joke in my family. (We make fun of all the ways to talk about it that would be performative or that would blithely write off the differences between our experience as White people and the experiences of Black people, indigenous people, and people of color, or our responsibility as White people to hold ourselves accountable to ongoing learning, humility, antiracist policy advocacy, and reparations. We very much have White privilege and have had the White experience and we know that.)

It's hard to find a way to talk about it at all. But *leaving it out* in order to avoid appearing laughable feels like a safe choice and a lie. This is really where I am coming from. This is not an identity so much as a constant reminder, written on my genome, that the American Black-White binary is a synthetic power construct. I include all of this because a part of me believes beyond all reason that there is a deep reason why I am like this, and that remembering the constructed nature of that binary will help contribute to the liberation of all people. However, I would never want to advocate for a blithe writing off of race as something "not real." To do so would be to flirt dangerously with a "post-racial" erasure of Black identities and Black culture, and with a dismissal of the need to replace racist policies with antiracist policies when I am a privileged member of a country that is moldering with very serious human rights issues. We can remember the synthetic nature of the Black-White binary while still giving all due gravity to the fact that it continues to contribute to the needless suffering, endangerment, and horrifically, even the death of so many, and while doing everything in our power to change this shameful state of affairs.

Still, I spend a lot of time thinking about, owning, and trying to deconstruct what being "White" means and the perspective it gives me. In my own way, I began doing this as a little girl. It's as if colonial America is (and was always) a virtual reality game wherein "Whiteness" (an invention of the early colonies) was the virtual reality bequeathed to me. I know I will never be finished with this deep, reflective work nor with taking apart that colonial virtual reality stone by stone.

And here's some more blood-honesty: I'm genuinely conflicted about whether or not to call myself "queer." I've always been sexually open and explorative, capable of sexual attraction to my own gender and other genders, and all manner of vexing, fumbling, intense loves and admirations. But so far in my life, I've only wanted to have long term romantic partnerships with men. Since I've never had to choose between authenticity on the one hand and familial (or societal) acceptance on the other in the front-facing part of this particular life domain, I always felt I'd be arrogating the term "queer" if I applied it to myself. Like I hadn't earned it. Like it would amount to a trivialization of the differences between my experiences and those of others, and a flight from the discomfort of my privilege.

I believe this is all important to include because my ethnicity and sexuality betray the helpless grain of mystery and chaos underneath all constructs. And this has certainly made its way into my thinking and my creations, both in these pages and in general.

LINEAGE

Hopefully the preceding acknowledgements put into context my particular position with finding a more feminine way of healing.

There is no tradition in which I can really claim to be firmly rooted culturally or ethnically. I'm tempted to say I've got nothin' when it comes to wisdom traditions and cultural influences that may have found their way into what I've come up with here.

However, I believe pre-Christian paganism still exists and winks all over the place if you know how to look. And I've indulged in quite a bit of reading about those Western Pre-Christian traditions, always trying to find something ancient underneath my home traditions. I also received inspiration from the Catholic mysteries, the Virgin Mary, Mary Magdalene, the Black Madonna, fairy tales, underworld myths, and the wry wisdom of the women who have cared for me. What I have come up with here is rooted in a tapestry of influences, woven together by my dreams, my intuition, and my body.

Despite what sounds like an eclectic palette of inspirations, I want to avoid offering a California-style bricolage of surface-y spiritual influences. I want to offer something more religious in the deepest sense of the word—something to "bind us back" to the immediacy of embodied experience, to the soul, to radical mystery. Something to offer solace in the face of the inescapable thread of pain woven into the fabric of this world. In other words, I don't want to sell you the idea that I've come up with a unique way to make it "all better." I've come up with a magickal way to actively engage the transformative nature of life.

In the weaving of this tapestry, I am heavily indebted to many spiritual teachers, past and present, to modern philosopher

JF Martel, to feminist theologians Meggan Watterson and Sera Beak, psychedelic bard Terence McKenna, and to healers Carl Jung, CPE, Richard Schwartz, Marion Woodman, Teal Swan, Artie Wu, and Alexandra Roxo, and even to Aleister Crowley, and occult writer Peter Grey. I am also indebted to my clients, from whom I have learned so much, and who have also informed the creation of this process.

I knew there were feminine mysteries traditions that were designed to contain the process I began to undergo in 2015 and that many of them were lost in the West. I started out wholly without support in trying to discern or piece together a "feminine mysteries tradition," and in trying to find a way to be a priestess (of sorts) with no socially acceptable institution or tradition within which to work. And this book, the faithful chronicle of that journey and its results, has been written entirely from my intuition and musculature.

My sense of what "priestess" means is: Someone who is very human and humble and who does her very best, as a daily practice, to live in accordance with her relationship to the Great Mystery (or whatever you want to call it) and to plant stolen branches from the other world (or whatever you want to call that) in her communities and on the planet, in whatever way she can, constantly open to learning about better and better ways to do this. I hope it will become clearer what I mean as we continue.

Though the perspective in these pages will be hopelessly, helplessly limited to my specific cultural starting point and to my understanding of Western culture, let us also acknowledge that patriarchy is a global force, which hurts men, women, and people of all genders everywhere, and that this book is, in many ways, about beginning the process of healing from that.

My sincere hope is that there is richness and treasure for all who dip into the watery initiations of this book, and I trust there will be. Please feel free to weave the wisdom ways of your own ancestors into this process in any way that feels right. My deep prayer is that this contributes to the liberation of all, in the small way that only I can contribute to that. Please add your voice to the chorus, especially if your perspective is different from mine, and reach out to me to see if there is any way I can connect you or be of service to you. Please tell your story. Make your contribution to the book of Sophia. This is how we midwife feminine consciousness in one another.

SOUL SICKNESS OF THE WEST

The great American writer David Foster Wallace spoke about the tense unhappiness of Americans and how this makes them great targets for sales and advertising. Here's my diagnosis of the situation. We are soul starved. If my darling, distinguished reader happens to be an American, God love you. We are the inheritors of ideological systems that (in their most shadowy forms) view the earth as lifeless, exploitable matter, ripe for the using by anyone who's got a great plan for it (usually involving their own personal gain). Horribly, this attitude has often extended to women's bodies and the bodies of other oppressed people.

This is a soul sickness. The Algonquin people called it "wettiko." When this ideological sickness runs amok, it would have us all think that lands and peoples are exploitable for profit, and that by pressing a button, consuming something, or ordering something on the internet, you can fill that gaping hole you feel in your chest. The one that gnaws at you sometimes at night. The one that says you want and need to come home to soul but don't know how. We are spiritually impoverished, and it's no one's fault in particular. We've lost touch with the sacredness of the land, the holiness of each human encounter, and the temple of life.

With the constant stimulation and distraction bombardment of the hyper-busy modern world, the situation has only worsened. We are all convinced that maybe, just maybe, by consuming more, by getting drunk, by getting stoned, by binge watching Netflix, or scrolling on our iPhones, we will finally feel something like "comfort" or "happiness." These activities may help us feel that momentarily (dopamine quick fix, thy name is), and then we're right back to the gnawing soul hunger.

Roundup dandelion killer and heartburn drug commercials are perfect snapshots of the ideological sickness of the modern, American West; examples of the mind constantly asserted as the dominator of matter. The ideological structure goes something like this: "Spray science/chemicals/mind/will on any aspect of body/earth/wild that is giving you trouble or getting in your way, dominating it (mind over matter), and that'll take care of your troubles."

This is insane. Dandelions are wild, free, pretty, *and* they are a free super food and medicine. Your body complains when you eat flaming hot buffalo wild wings because there is a wisdom and a law in matter which must be revered, heard, and respected if we are to survive. Taking a drug or spraying a cancer-causing chemical to shut the wisdom of matter up will ultimately kill us.

More than this, especially in the America of Late Capitalism (or whatever this era is called), it's as if the collective male ego (and this pertains to everyone, regardless of gender) has become tumorous and over-inflamed, concerned more with propping up its own sense of rightness than it is with the truth. It's as if individuals and peoples need psychedelic and/ or religious traditions and practices that put the ego back in its rightful place, in service to the soul.

THE WITCH WOUND & THE MAGDALENE WOUND

To help my reader gain her bearings at the root of the root of the witch wound, I should relate that I think of the witch wound and the legacy of the burning times within the context of an even more ancient, buried lineage that I think of as a red lineage. I know the red lineage is connected to the ancient roots of the lost feminine tradition in the West, with Mary Magdalene as the most recent, encoded doorway left to us. Since the feminine tradition, and the feminine itself, have been literally buried in the West, the ongoing cultural repercussions include the burning times, but are certainly not limited to them.

Modern women continue to be impacted by all of this. We have inherited the void where the red lineage of the ancient feminine traditions should be, and we have inherited thousands of years of trauma directly connected to the repercussions of that burial. *All genders have inherited this.* "The witch wound" is a doorway—an invitation into a much deeper reality and process. There are good reasons why witches are surging forward in the culture currently, with their deliciousness, power, wisdom, reverence for the earth, and fun transgressive possibility. It's because their time has come.

But the red lineage I have intuited and tapped into is more arcane and is even deeper, though it's connected. It's like the red folds of the Virgin Mary's dress in *Madonna Lactans*, the deep, wide frame that holds the image of her bust and baby ("the witch wound"). I think women intuitively feel the power of red in its connection to the feminine, and intuitively respond to red as a doorway to a deep, powerful, ancient feminine mystery.

The Magdalene wound is connected to the burial of that mystery. Many of us have been raised within a religion that held that God was a man, and so was His only begotten son, our Savior, and so were all the apostles and so many of the important people mentioned in holy books. So were God's representatives on earth, the priests, and every single individual within the church hierarchy going all the way up to the pope (if you were brought up Catholic, like me).

Women were temptresses, she-devils, and whores. The only liturgically acceptable role women could play was that of the mother or the nun. Women were the gender farthest removed from the divine. Women were distractions, and it was our duty, within churches and within schools, to cover our midriffs and shoulders, and to ensure that we never, *ever* distracted the men from their all-important work with our devilish feminine wiles. Whether or not you were raised within any branch of Christianity, all of Western culture is influenced by Judeo-Christian values and the Judeo-Christian worldview, so this has probably been picked up by your radio receiver in one way or another. This deep cut, right across the part of our hearts that wants to deeply, intimately connect with the divine, is called the Magdalene wound. It is a place of deep longing within us; a place that knows and *feels* that something is missing, something sacred and deeply nourishing. Something that would honor our sexuality as in no way separate from our divinity.

So then, what about the witch wound, I hear you ask? I use the phrase throughout this book to describe the way women have been collectively wounded away from their gifts, passions, power, transgressive artfulness, wiles, instinct, beauty, darkness, light, and full expression because of a primal fear that they may actually not be safe if they were to shine in all their enigmatic glory. This is very *relevant* to the Magdalene wound, the woundedness of being raised in a spiritual tradition within which female is the gender not considered sacred. I refer to the witch wound most often throughout this book because it feels more all-encompassing to me, and it points to unique places of repression in each woman. We could just as well use the phrase "priestess wound" or even "oracle wound."

Ultimately, the witch wound is about expression. Expression from the depths, from the inner nature, not in accordance with an externally imposed performance. It is about making the feminine soul voice real and heard in the world. In this way, it relates to the throat, but it also relates to the womb, the gut, the blood, the bones, and the heart—all the embodied places from which a woman might say she "knows."

The witch wound manifests uniquely in each woman, and it usually points to the place of her greatest power. By this I mean sacred power, not the kind that seeks to be a power *over* anyone or anything. In this way, there is a sacredness to our places of deepest shame, in the way they are inspired by the light to unfurl. The following sections describe some of the ways internalized patriarchy can manifest so that you can start to get a sense of the shape it takes in you. Internalized patriarchy is to the witch wound what poor ventilation is to a termite problem. It may weave around your witch wound in unique ways. But the most important thing to keep in mind is this connection between your "shameful" or rejected parts and your greatest sacred power.

THE WRONG, WRONG, WRONG VOICE

She could see it all so clearly, so commandingly when she looked. It was when she took her brush in hand that the whole thing changed. It was in that moment's flight between the picture and her canvas that the demons set on her, who often brought her to the verge of tears and made this passage from conception to work as dreadful as any down a dark passage for a child. Such, she often felt herself struggling against terrific odds to maintain her courage to say, but this is what I see! This is what I see! And so to clasp some miserable remnant of her vision to her breast which a thousand forces did their best to pluck from her.

-VIRGINIA WOOLF, *TO THE LIGHTHOUSE*, ON THE

FEMALE PAINTER

The peak years of the European witch hunts (1560-1760) and the growth of the transatlantic slave trade and Western colonial expansion all occurred simultaneously. In *Unearthing Venus*, Cate Montana tells of her interview with John Perkins, who lived with the Shaur tribe in the Amazon rainforest for many years. He informed her that the tribe depended, for its survival, on the all-important role of its women "telling men when it is time to stop." Perkins shared the story of a Shaur shaman visiting the United States and asking, "Where are your women? Why are they not telling the men to stop?" My gut tells me there's nothing like several centuries of burning at the stake to bury feminine voices and consciousness. Let's look at how women's voices continue to be buried so we can pull this up at the roots.

Do you remember the 2016 elections? I'm sure you do. There was one infamous debate between Hillary Clinton and Donald Trump where *every* time Clinton leaned forward to say anything into her microphone, Trump would lean down into his microphone and interrupt her repeatedly with the word, "Wrong." It almost became farcical at some points.

I think many modern women have an internal part that leans down towards its microphone whenever she wants to speak up, whenever she wants to say what her soul whispers to her, whenever she wants to convey the special and irreplaceable way that she sees or speak from her deep well of inner knowing and sovereignty, and it says, "Wrong. Wrong. Wrong." Have you ever felt that way? That little voice is one form internalized patriarchy can take. And it rips women's unique visions and voices directly out of their hands and their throats over and over again.

Though no one asked for the world to be unjust, these are the waters we've all been swimming in since birth. It is impossible for us *not* to internalize undesirable forces like patriarchy along the way. Look at the images in the media. Look at the history of art and politics. What do you see? What have you been shown for your entire life? More than likely, it's been images of men as leaders and geniuses (usually White men), and women as auxiliary counterparts who are desirable and valuable only insofar as they are considered nice to look at. And if they're not? Then their existence verges on the absurd.

Think about that. Think about being forced to imbibe that water for life. We are going to deep dive later into ways to continually clear that shit from your system. I say "continually" because I would never claim that this book or any process in it is designed to make millennia of systemic racism, gender violence, and intergenerational trauma suddenly go *poof* overnight. I wish it were so simple. Recognizing it is the first step. Then seeing where it lives in you. Then taking a tailored approach to going in there and rearranging the pieces, finding *your* personal truth about all this, and re-sacralizing yourself, your body, your soul, and your space, over and over and over again.

It's like living in a toxic environment where the water is filled with chemicals and you can't help but take some of them into your body regularly. Therefore, we must periodically detoxify. Sound familiar? Ugh! That's a topic for another book.

For now, think of this book as crystal clean, sacred spring water. Whenever you join me here, we are stepping into clear water. You can think of it as Lourdes water or the shining water of a holy well.

VANISHING TO OURSELVES

YOU LEARN TO THINK OF WHAT YOU ARE IN TERMS OF WHAT THEY [MEN] WANT, AND ADDRESSING THEIR WANT BECOMES SO INGRAINED IN YOU THAT YOU LOSE SIGHT OF WHAT YOU WANT, AND SOMETIMES YOU VANISH TO YOURSELF IN THE ART OF APPEARING TO AND FOR OTHERS.

-REBECCA SOLNIT, *RECOLLECTIONS OF MY NONEXISTENCE*

Since culture and the media train women from a young age to think of themselves with reference to men (mostly, with reference to their desirability as far as men are concerned), we sort of develop two selves. There is one who is inside having your day-to-day experiences, and there is one who constantly stands outside, an imagined observer. In this way, women sometimes become the victims of their own images. This is just one more way that it can be so easy to lose our souls and our sovereignty, by becoming lost in the tangled wildwood of all the people we think others need us to be, constantly outwardly attuned, as if the perceptions of others give us our value and truth.

This has been called "the internalized male gaze": an internalization of the desires of men, as we understand them, such that a cultural male eye seems to always be cast upon us, even when we stand in the bathroom alone, naked, and getting in the shower. Except it goes even deeper than that because we can forget who we are and what we want entirely as the result of constantly appearing to and for others, learning to mold ourselves to their values, agendas, ideas, and goals. We learn to measure our value according to their apparent affirmation of it and our beauty and gifts according to their perception and assessment.

In addition to that, most of the time, our families, as microcosms of the broader culture, reinforce messages about how we need to look and behave, and what we need to do and prioritize. And as Sophia A. Nelson, author of *The Woman Code* wrote, "The power of words spoken over us, about us, or into us can last a lifetime." We each carry unique projections from our families of origin about what a woman is supposed to be and look like.

Please don't read this as some kind of indictment of my family, your family, or anyone's family in particular. We and our families come by these toxic aspects of the culture innocently. And most of the parents I've ever met would die for their kids. Still, no one really escapes childhood unscathed, and usually little girls are bombarded with comments about their appearance (be it their weight, their hair, their skin, their style) from early on.

In fact, across their lifespans, women and girls are much more likely to be complimented on their appearance than on their personality, and the reverse is true for men and little boys. Women and girls are also saturated in implicit and explicit messages about how they need to manage their lives and about the relatively low importance and value of their lives. Typically, the messages about how they need to manage their lives involve something having to do with marriage and fertility. The messages about the value of their lives come through observing or even, horribly, being involved in instances of sexual violence wherein the honor, reputation, and future of the boys involved is considered by the community to be more important than the safety, body, life, and dignity of the girls involved. I'm thinking in particular of the case of Daisy, the high school girl who was drugged, gang raped, and then left outside in the snow, very nearly freezing to death. The community considered the reputations and futures of the boys involved to be more important than Daisy's life. Sadly, this is nowhere near the only case of its kind.

DISEMBODIMENT

In ways large and small, we pick up the idea that our silence is preferred. If we could combine that silence with sexual attractiveness perfectly packaged for male consumption, all the better. BUT! Don't be a whore. And don't be so attractive in public that it's offensive, scandalous, or distracting. What a line to walk.

This section could fill up multiple additional books (and it has), and each subject I'm touching on here deserves much more thorough and considered treatment. Suffice to say the potent cocktail of regular street harassment (and other forms of harassment), the frequency and ubiquity of sexual abuse and assault, and all the ways women's bodies are commented upon, managed, insulted, deodorized, sanitized, trimmed, squeezed, plucked, stoppered up, and sterilized all should give us pause.

I once lived with a wonderful woman who was a gardener by trade, and she came home once after having to trim a beautiful, tangled, wild tree down to a very civilized and neat little nub, and she said, "It reminds me of what women think they have to do to their bodies." It's as if women participate in their own objectification at a deep, unconscious level, relating to their own bodies as tools to be wielded and as objects to be managed.

The result of being treated in public and spoken to and regarded within civic policy as though our bodies are public property and not under our own control causes women to feel unsafe in their bodies at a deep, nervous system level. And for this reason, many women are floating about three feet away from their bodies when they are walking down the street. Some stay that way for life and never come all the way back home to the brilliant symphony and genius of soma. I've called these women the "far away ones." When you meet them, you have the sense that something is missing, and something is. That wicked glimmer is gone from their eyes. Like the Little Matchstick Girl of the old fairy tale, they have stayed out in the cold too long, and they've used all their matches.

This is my weird way of expressing that women are dissociated, disembodied. I'm sure you're familiar with the "fight or flight" response. Some people don't know there is a third and fourth option for all animals with central nervous systems when they perceive danger: the freeze (or dissociation) response, and the "fawning" response. The dissociative freeze is the default response to life-threatening, imminent danger when fleeing isn't an option and fighting won't particularly help either. You can observe gazelles doing it on the savannah when they suddenly go stiff and drop to the ground as a lion lunges toward them. It's like dying before you actually die.

Think about this. Women feel unsafe in their bodies in an ongoing, chronic way that they can't flee. And fighting is neither a relevant option when applied to a pervasive psychic atmosphere nor in situations where we may actually be physically overpowered or held down. These small instances, on some deep nervous system level, come across as pale echoes of the more extreme scenario of actually having physical control, and possibly actually your life, taken from you. So, on a central nervous system level, many women are constantly dying before they actually die. When we are chronically in a disembodied freeze response, we become alienated from ourselves, unaware of our own true needs, inclinations, and desires.

The least known response of all, the fawning response, is one that likely rings some bells for you. It's when we respond to a perceived threat or danger by suddenly putting on big, starry, Disney princess eyes and by beginning to fawn, placate, kiss, coo, please, adore, and serve the perceived threat. Sometimes, when neither fighting nor fleeing will work, we might survive if we whip out those Bambi eyes and dote on or even seduce our captor (or the source of danger) just a little bit. This response, too, can be very automatic and unconscious. It can manifest as relaxing into sex we don't *really* want (when we're afraid of what might happen if we refuse it). I believe another manifestation of the "fawning" response is the "good girl" mask. *Oh, that's what you need? Oh, yes, of course, right away!* Smiley face, smiley face.

Our ancient nervous systems can't differentiate between a mean boss type of threat and a big, hungry cat type of threat.

65

And if we are living under the gun of constant stress, we may be in the fawning response, or the freezing response, for a good deal of our waking lives. We may have even identified with these responses to some degree, believing that is just who we are, or this is just how life feels.

Actually, it was only recently discovered that the classic fight/flight/freeze response more aptly describes the male nervous system response to danger. The female nervous system, apparently, has a more pronounced "tend and befriend" response in the face of life-threatening danger.

DISOWNED ANGER

Women and little girls are typically socialized out of their anger. Anger is a normal, healthy reaction to having our boundaries crossed, or sometimes to situations that feel unworkable. When we are socialized out of our anger, then we become these flimsy little daisies who are ready and willing to let anyone steamroll us at any time. *Okay, sure!* Having the right to anger taken away is an important component of oppressing any group.

And when we repress and compartmentalize anger, it doesn't just disappear. Hell no. It stays with us, and it just squirts out in other ways, taking the form of panic attacks, anxiety, depression, and maybe even cancer and other forms of physical illness. It takes a shit ton of energetic and mental bandwidth to compartmentalize anger. In other words, yes, it is fatiguing. And it taxes your mental bandwidth in such a way that you are actually more likely to drop offline in the middle of a conversation or meeting and to lose something that was said or that you were going to say. (Being socialized to be constantly concerned about how you look *also* taxes your daily mental bandwidth, by the way.)

Women's energies and passions have been pathologized since the birth of the modern clinic, often called "hysteria." I would wager a guess that many "hysterical" women were actually angry women, and rightfully so. A woman could be diagnosed with "hysteria" simply for liking books a lot. Women would sometimes have their uterus removed (hysterectomy) as a "cure" for "hysteria." Or they would be told they needed to engage in sexual acts with their doctor to be cured. Paradoxically, these doctors may have actually been onto something with a sexual cure for "hysteria" if the "hysteria" symptoms had anything to do with the woman splitting off the carnal aspects of her nature. In other words, maybe these ladies really did need to get laid, sans the rape-y aspect.

Before the heyday of "hysteria," instead of pathologized, women's dynamic energies and passions were often condemned. Condemned, pathologized. It all sounds like different ways to take the energies, passions, truths, voices, and souls of women and keep them firmly underground, muzzled, and masked.

FEAR OF TAKING UP SPACE OR OF GETTING TOO "BIG" IN OTHER WAYS

Shame or fear about taking up space is another way internalized patriarchy can manifest in women. This can come across in our posture. It can even manifest in the way we drive or occupy public space in the form of the road, the sidewalk, the bar, the airplane, or the subway. This stems from a diminished feeling of ownership of, or entitlement to, public space. We may even have shame or fear about the way we occupy space in our organization or chosen profession. It can even manifest as a fear of speaking up in meetings, classes, or other gatherings.

In general, women collectively fear becoming too powerful, too successful, too big, too visible, too talented, too *anything* that busts out of their good girl box. We shy away from owning all of our gifts and all dimensions of our womanhood for fear that those who hold stakes in things remaining as they are may punish us. We also fear that other women may punish us as the result of their own patriarchal wounds.

It's true: The witch wound can and does also manifest in our relationships with other women. There can be a fear that other women are going to feel there's no room for us to shine if our shine is too similar to theirs and that they will therefore reject us. There can be an *expectation* that other women are wounded in this way and that it will get acted out on us. And this only serves to add to our fear of stepping into our power.

There are other ways the feminine wound can manifest, such as the feeling that no matter what we do, no one will ever respect or take us seriously. And that we cannot freely enjoy our sacred connection to the natural world, our beauty, and our sexual power, and at the same time feel safe. Volumes could be devoted to each of these sections alone, but hopefully this brief overview has helped you begin to outline the shape of the witch wound as it lives in you.

CHAPTER THREE

LEGACY OF THE BURNING TIMES IN THE MODERN CLINIC AND IN MODERN WOMEN'S LIVES

EXTINGUISHING THE CUNNING FOLK AT THE BIRTH OF THE CLINIC

THE MENTAL HEALTH SPACE IS READY FOR DISRUPTION.

THAT'S HOW I SEE IT.

-MASTIN KIPP

In order to ground therapy or any other form of healing for women in the feminine principle, it's not only important to look at the millennia-old reasons why women continue to feel unsafe in their bodies, voices, passions, transgressions, and sexuality. We must also consider the birth of the Western psychotherapy profession itself in order to wrest it from these old systems that terrorize, oppress, silence, and sterilize the feminine in all of us. We need to see how the feminine has been excised from our ways of healing. Things often reveal their greatest secrets at their roots.

Depth psychologist and researcher, Oksana Yakushko, has done some marvelous work looking at the connections between the burning times, the Enlightenment, and the birth of modern universities and the medical professions as we know them today. In early modern Europe, somewhere between 40,000 and 100,000 women were executed as witches. But if you go back to Hipatia and other early female "heretics," philosophers, intellectuals, saints, and transgressives, and also consider extrajudicial killings, it may not be possible to ever know the true number.

Sometimes the women killed as witches in early modern Europe and America were the wise women, healers, village herbalists, and midwives (sometimes called "the cunning folk"), the carriers of folk traditions, and even sometimes (I suspect) of old, pre-Christian ways of knowing, healing, and relating to the land. They were keepers of women's health practices, and perhaps even representatives of the sacred, visionary medicine plants. And if you think about women's folk healing, passed from one generation down to the next, what kind of healing do you think of? That's right. It's not hard to imagine that the village healers sometimes practiced midwifery, fertility care, and women's health (i.e., early Planned Parenthood).

These women began to be exterminated and continued to be exterminated for century after century after long, horrible century. It's important to mention that sometimes the procedure for prosecuting a witch involved seizing all of her land and assets, which sometimes, sadly, appears to have been reason enough for neighbors to condemn wealthy widows. I suspect, also, that interpersonal feuds factored in frequently and probably also petty envies. Beauty, for example, is often interpreted as a scandal, and women have long worked out their own patriarchal wounds on one another. (One witch execution record describes the condemned as "the prettiest girl in town.")

It's important to note that, in some parts of the world, witchcraft-related killings are very much a modern reality, and the intra- and extrajudicial killing of women for their power, passion, sexiness, cultural transgressions, unusualness, and gifts has taken place and still takes place all over the world on an inconceivable scale. The ancestral trauma aspect of the witch wound absolutely applies cross-culturally and trans-ethnically.

Though some details I am about to share are disturbing, they illustrate the deep misogyny at work in these historical episodes that tried to extinguish women's wisdom ways and the spirits and passions of women. Witch's "scolds," used during the burning times, were literal muzzles that women were made to wear when they were too "bossy" or outspoken. I believe it is also important to note that condemned witches, just like their "hysterical" sisters of later centuries, were also sterilized, along with any women not considered to be "savory" types. And, disturbingly, this practice of forced sterilization continues with immigrant women and women of color in the U.S. prison system. Also, many of the questioning and torture methods used on accused witches were sexual in nature, and inquisitors would often look for "the devil's mark" in the labia and perineum area of the accused woman's body. Publicly.

When the witch craze began to death rattle, the West entered a historical period now known as The Enlightenment. It was out of Enlightenment thinking and developments that modern universities were born, and only men who were members of the most privileged classes could attend. It was out of these early modern universities that the modern Western medical professions were born. And the weird arm growing out of the side of those professions is this fascinating little discipline called modern Western psychotherapy. Sit tight because we're about to enter some uncharted seas.

If the modern Western medical traditions, and by extension, modern psychotherapy, were born out of this final extinction of the last vestiges of the feminine wisdom ways known to the West, then what does that say about the ability of the discipline of modern Western psychotherapy to hold the complexity of what it is to be a woman and to approach psyche-soul healing in an earthy, feminine way? Don't get me wrong, cunning folx. I have an ongoing love of the modern Western psychotherapeutic tradition in spite of myself. It is so deeply needed, and it is a complex art form so often misunderstood and underappreciated. It's just that it may be time to shed a deep, penetrating light into this aspect of the heritage of the tradition and see if we can possibly balance it out with some of the lost wisdom ways. Perhaps this is something that modern practitioners can each do in their own way, blending embodied intuition with old wisdom ways into which the practitioner may be initiated.

As much as I love and respect it, I intuit a huge, gaping cavity of "missing" in Western psychotherapy and so many of its modern manifestations. Although this statement alone does not entirely encompass the state of affairs, it leaves the feminine psyche, both of the clinician and of the client, something of an uncharted territory. Think of this book as a compendium of confessions that I am making on behalf of all women, past and present, who have been killed for using their voices.

I hope I can impress upon my lovely reader that my little disruption of the classic Western mental health tradition is not rooted in a distrust of science or reason. It *is* my intention, however, to suggest that the famous adage, "The sleep of reason produces monsters" can be fruitfully interpreted as a suggestion that pure reason by itself can be a kind of sleep, and that other ways of knowing are needed in order to balance it out. Terence McKenna said it best when, during a discussion of nuclear power, he suggested, "We've reached into the heart of matter without reverence." The "other ways of knowing" could be referred to simply as imaginative knowing produced by the clairvoyant eye that looks on the inner world, a knowing that is rooted in the heart and womb, or a more lunar kind of consciousness.

There are two important reclamations suggested by this chapter and by a more feminine way of healing generally: Reclamation of lost interiority and reclamation of a "feeling of healing." I'll sometimes refer to the second as an "aroma of ritual" or an "enchanted circle." Both reversals are intended to wrest the profession from the grip of a reductivist, behaviorist vision and of sterile medicalization.

LOSS OF THE "BRIGHT KNOWLEDGE": FROM REDUCTIVE BEHAVIORISM TO A RECLAMATION OF INTERIORITY

MANY PEOPLE IN OUR CULTURE ONLY FOCUS ON MAKING CHANGES IN THE OUTER WORLD. WELL, OF COURSE WE NEED TO COME UP WITH PLANS FOR OUR LIFE, BUT WE NEED TO BALANCE OUT OUR RATIONAL PLANNING WITH EXPLORING OUR INNER WORLD AND LEARNING HOW TO CULTIVATE A RICH, PEACEFUL, AND POWERFUL INNER SPACE. WE NEED TO MOVE FROM OUTER VISIONING TO THE POWER OF WORKING WITH OUR INNER VISIONS. WE NEED TO WAKE UP OUT OF THE COLLECTIVE TRANCE THAT TEACHES US TO ONLY FOCUS ON THE MATERIAL REALM. IT IS TIME TO EXPLORE HOW TO OPEN OURSELVES TO NEW DIMENSIONS OF LIFE.

-SANDRA INGERMAN

From the monasteries of 13th century Tibet to the temples of Asclepius in ancient Greece and beyond, an astounding number of healing modalities found cross-culturally and throughout history used some form of visualization or guided imagery. Additionally, countless world cultures have used practices for slowing down and journeying inward, altering our normal way of perceiving and affecting transformational change at a deep level. Even *Interior Castle*, the humble spiritual classic of 16th century mystic, Teresa of Avila, sets forth a unique and thoughtful map of the internal territory the soul must traverse on its ascension course.

Then, behaviorist John Watson called all of it "bunk." Let's briefly touch on the drab little moment that behaviorism had in the history of modern psychology. The aptly named school of thought had its heyday in the 1950s. In my opinion, it was an attempt to cover the strange, mystical art form of psychology with the fig leaf of science by reducing human beings to outwardly observable and measurable behaviors. The unquantifiable internal landscape of imagination was, in many ways, dusted off as a ghost by behaviorism—something that, for all intents and purposes, did not even exist.

Don't get me wrong. Behavioral interventions certainly do work. People respond to reward and punishment. But to reduce human beings to a set of outwardly observable and measurable behaviors and to call anything even vaguely alluding to the interior life "bunk" seems dehumanizing. Our inner landscapes are so vast when we tap into them, and so filled with treasure and untold wisdom. Your interior world is your visionary world. You'll see.

Despite the behaviorists' attempts at discrediting them, deep imagination and visualization techniques have since gained more credibility with studies demonstrating their effectiveness and impact on the nervous system and body.

The first time I attended a workshop where I was certified in the Clinical Applications of Deep Imagination, the power of the initial session I was guided through nearly blew my face off. Without planning or having any preconceived notion of what "people" or guides I would meet once I journeyed inward, I received a clear picture of my Scottish great grandmother who I hadn't seen in decades. She sat in a cottage in a tangled, charming woodland (that I could see, feel, hear, and smell). And she conveyed a message, with her presence alone, about the importance of combining groundedness (think: stews filled with root vegetables) with levity (think: laughter) as one of her great secrets of strength.

I emerged from the journey with tears streaming down my face, and I wasn't the only one. I noticed that there was a new brightness to the eyes of the workshop participants whenever they would emerge from a Deep Imagination interior space. There was not a soul in the room who did not leave that workshop utterly surprised at the power of the imagination and the internal world. I thought it was bullshit airy-fairy dust, too, until I tried it. For lack of a better way to say it, it really is as if the inner eye of the imagination looks out on another world as real as this one.

Additionally, our cultural training in the modern West really would have us believe that, no matter what our condition, problem, or ailment is, there is some external, physical solution to it. People seem to have a hard time wrapping their heads around the usefulness of seeing negative outer circumstances as a signal that there is inner work to be done. And just as much difficulty with the idea that, by doing the inner work, those outer circumstances (or at the very least, the experience of them), will change. But, that is the reality reversal I ask my clients to make and that I'm asking you to make in these pages. You'll find it is actually a gentle, compassionate, yet powerful way to approach life's frustrations: to view them as meditation bells or clues to personal growth areas. (Obviously, I'm not claiming this will cure the human condition, and I'm also not claiming injustice and cruelty are the result of someone needing to do their inner work, at least not the person on the receiving end.)

Deep Imagination practices are not the only form of inward journeying currently being embraced by Western psychotherapy communities. The Psychedelic Renaissance is powerfully underway at the time of this writing. Many research institutions like MAPS are looking for ways to demonstrate the power of entheogenic experiences for meeting psychotherapeutic goals expediently and powerfully, and to legalize some of these substances for clinical use under the supervision of a therapist and a psychiatrist.

Of course, indigenous cultures around the world have been using plant medicines as ways to go on shamanic journeys and to affect deep, radical internal healing processes for millennia. Ayahuasca, for example, has been likened to five years of therapy in one night. It is always important to acknowledge the ancient traditions connected to the use of visionary plants in any ongoing considerations of how they might be woven into healing processes facilitated by someone who is not a denizen of those cultures. Not only to acknowledge them, but also to do enough research into those traditions to understand whether or not the kind of use we are considering would be harmful, disrespectful, exploitative, or appropriative. (Amazingly, however, some visionary plants seem to have *no* ancient indigenous tradition behind them and to actually be modern discoveries. Salvia divinorum—*the diviner's mint*, or *eye of the shepherdess*—is one example.)

It's also important to acknowledge the impact on natural ecosystems that the harvest of these plants can have and do our best not to contribute to the enterprises that are doing ecological harm. And we should acknowledge the fact that countless people of color are in prison for life on drug charges (for possessing or selling marijuana, for example, which is now legal in many places, or other psychedelic drugs) while other more privileged people catch the wave of The Psychedelic Renaissance and start profitable psychedelic businesses.

Still, journeying can be done without the use of any psychotropic substance. The work of modern shaman, Sandra Ingerman, provides a good example of the connection between inner, guided vision journeying and shamanism as it appears across world cultures. She, like the pre-Christian people in the countries considered Celtic and so many other peoples, believes that when we look with our inner eye, we are a seer, we have "the bright knowledge," and that we are accessing information from another world. Also, a magickal journey can be had with regular old chamomile.

THE DEEP WISDOM, HELL AND JOY OF THE BODY

We would be remiss if we did not mention interoception (the felt, inner sense of the body) in our discussion of reclaiming interiority. When we drop into the body, it is filled with nonverbal information, signals and clues as to what we've been holding onto, what has been shoved into the unconscious, and therefore, what needs tending next on our healing journey. Our bodies are constantly telling us our truth if we dare to listen.

Sometimes the body is so chronically clenched, or is holding so much pain, that we would prefer to stay up in our heads or as far away from soma as possible. I do not mean to trivialize chronic pain conditions or suggest that "If only sufferers would drop into their pain and learn from it..." No. Though each case of chronic pain in any form (and the story of its genesis) is so unique, it's still worthwhile to state very broadly that when these conditions can be (for the most part) managed, the wisdom of soma can still be accessed. *Sometimes we have to bravely bring our awareness to the hell that our body has been holding in order to, one way or another, bring it to another place.* And it is only by reacquainting ourselves with our brave, steadfast bodies that we open ourselves to the full joy of the body, and to all of its wisdom.

FROM THE CLINIC TO THE ENCHANTED CIRCLE

What comes to mind when you conjure the modern clinic in your imagination? Maybe linoleum floors, fluorescent lights, insurance paperwork, stressed out, overworked people, and the smell of antiseptic cleaning agents? Don't get me wrong. Modern, antiseptic cleaning agents are great. I'm writing this during COVID for Christ's sake. The point is, I would wager a guess that your imaginary model of the modern clinic, like mine, does not really have a *feeling* of healing.

Let me help you get a better sense of what I mean. I once went to get a massage from a student at a massage school at a special rate. As I entered the waiting area, I noticed the lights were lowered. Soft, Solfeggio music played in the background, and a faint, pleasing aroma of essential oils hung in the air. I heard faint footsteps and hushed voices. There was reverence in the air. I thought to myself, *This place has more of a feeling of healing than any doctor's office or health clinic I have ever been to in my life.*

82

Sterile, antiseptic clinics have their place, but they should not be the only places of "healing." A feeling of healing puts our nervous systems into "rest and digest" mode, which is something we should do regularly, daily, to restore our bodies and minds, and it is certainly the state we should be in if we are doing any kind of deep healing or preventive work. We need to regularly enter spaces that have this feeling of healing, even a feeling of the sacred, in order to cultivate deep wellness.

I encourage my clients to create a feeling of healing around them before and during our sessions, using whatever implements best suit them. I do the same. I actually imagine (and subtly perceive) myself to be cultivating a specially curated energetic field when I am getting ready to see clients in the morning. Often essential oils, incense, candles, and meditation help to complete the effect. Whatever works. (I recognize that some readers may be curious what the fuck I'm getting at with this 'subtle perception of energy' crap. I don't know. I can't think of a better way to describe my experience.)

The concept of an enchanted circle or "zone," replete with the aroma of ritual is not as trite as it might sound. Magickal thinking may be inherent to the way we function as human beings, and if you add "the aroma of ritual" to any healing practice, I believe deeper and more genuine effects and transformations are promoted. In other words, we may have a deep, irrevocable need to step into spaces that feel sacred or enchanted as part of what keeps us well. This concept also makes the healer more similar to the artist, because the artist creates an enchanted circle or a zone within which the participant is altered or transformed and is the final ingredient.

And what happens in healing spaces should be truly, deeply transformational. When I am working with clients, I perceive myself to be engaging in full mind-body-spirit-soul medicine because healing mentally and emotionally *absolutely* impacts your physical health. I believe we are literally preventing physical disease when we clear emotional gunk, stuck energy, and trauma trapped inside the body. I find that creating a feeling of healing and of the sacred in the container around me aids in this process. In short, we are creating a sacred alchemical cauldron.

What's special about what happens in a cauldron as opposed to a "clinic"? Foucault wrote in *The Birth of the Clinic* about "the clinical gaze," describing the clinician as a sinister figure who looks upon the patient almost as a scientist in a lab looks upon a specimen. Before I have you shuddering, let me assure you that there is another, softer "gaze" that the clinician can bring into the enchanted circle of the healing relationship. This softer (yet sometimes strikingly penetrating) gaze is rooted in the body, in the hips, not in surface-level expertise or in any knowledge gained in a book. It is rooted in the non-dual relational field cultivated between therapist and client. It is rooted in *both* therapist and client trusting what is arising in that relational field and in the subtle body in each moment.

FINDING THE FEMININE WOUND IN THE MENTAL HEALTH PROFESSIONS

I THOUGHT I HAD TO GIVE UP MY INNER WILD WOMAN TO FIND WHAT IT MEANS TO LIVE A SACRED, SPIRITUAL LIFE.

-ALEXANDRA ROXO

There is power in a modern woman's confessions of what it's like to feel wooden and muzzled. Perhaps I am entirely alone in my experience of the feminine wound in the mental health professions, but it is truly my experience. Like Virginia Woolf's female painter, it is what I see.

The path towards becoming a therapist was always so much more than a simple career trajectory to me. It was a path of Seva yoga, or a spiritual practice of "selfless service," which I undertook (kind of) for lack of a better, readily available option for living a sacred, spiritual life. Along the way, I *did* come to feel I had to surrender my sexuality, my story, my voice, and my vision as an artist. This is how the witch wound can manifest in by-the-book Western clinical practice. It can also manifest in the mental health professions in our impulse to hide our affiliation with the sacred plant medicines for fear of actual federal punishment.

Many mental health agencies feel like places of the feminine wound, and modern female mental health practitioners, both within agencies and outside of them in the "wild" of private practice often feel like they are expected to be a gigantic boob, miraculously effluent with a never-ending supply of milk. They are expected to hold so much, so much of the time.

Collective angst about the systemic failure to make healthcare affordable and accessible to all is frequently projected onto mental health professionals. We are in the lowest paid of the highly educated professions. (Note: This field is occupied largely by women.) Insurance companies make us bend over backward to get paid, *maybe* in three months, *if at all.*

During one completely burnt-out afternoon when I worked at an agency, I paused for a moment in my car in the afternoon sunlight. It was one of those days of behemoth demands and toxic stress levels. I seemed to always be wired on caffeine and trying to do at least three things at once as fast as I possibly could. And the same deep voice that spoke to me that night in the Bronx whispered,

This is how this culture treats its priestesses.

Was this voice referring to my clients? Hell to the fuck no. Was it referring to any person in particular, like a boss, program director or CEO? No. It's more complicated than that. It was referring to the systems I had to work within and the patriarchal culture that birthed those systems. We often don't realize how deeply saturated we are in all of it. "Services" are considered reimbursable by insurance and larger systems to the extent they are medicalized, and through measurable, outwardly observable timestamp type of data. This means the more time and work the worker bees can put in, the better. If you can have fewer people doing more work, better still. Stretch them.

The decision of whether to work in a mental health agency is a deeply personal one. So is the decision of whether to accept insurance (for therapists in private practice). I do not mean to imply I have found the "right" way or the only way. Some of the people I have met who work in mental health agencies or who accept all behavioral health insurance plans are about as close to saints as anyone I've ever known in my life. They are doing such important work, often within radically compromised and infuriating systems. So, I do not mean to imply that my vocational unfolding applies to all.

But leaving agency work was certainly an important step in my own unfolding. Then getting off of insurance panels once I was in private practice. And now, creating radical healing and educational spaces that operate way outside of any of the aforementioned systems.

At this point, I'd like to keep a small therapy practice, and I will do so as a woman who is alive to her vulgarity and weirdness, whose story and explosive poems are publicly available, and who loves her clients. This may cause more by-the-book therapists to bristle, but I believe our profession is shifting in this direction. I also believe I am of the utmost service when I walk my talk, resurrecting buried parts of myself, taking the corset and the witch's scold off. This is one way to subvert the traditional power dynamic between therapist and patient. By being a goddamn human, creative, imperfect, and filled with tenderness.

THE FEMININE: OUTSIDE, BURIED, ENSHADOWED

[T]HE FEMININE IS SO DIFFICULT... TO TALK ABOUT... BECAUSE
SO FEW PEOPLE HAVE EXPERIENCED IT.
-MARION WOODMAN

Jung called Her "anima" (his own internal feminine, and that of any man). In fact, he based his entire idea of individuation, the goal of good psychoanalysis, around the integration of anima. Jean Shinoda Bolen called the same thing Goddess Consciousness. I have started to refer to Her (as she lives in me, in speck form) as my Moonchild, my soul, or lunar consciousness—this part of me that is like a radio dial with a needle of orchid-sensitivity, alerting me promptly when I am off track or I am offending what is truly sacred to me.

When looking for an archetypal Feminine, or a universal concept of the feminine that applies cross-culturally, we are more likely to find multiple femininities. Other than associations with childbirth, breastfeeding, and child rearing (and therefore, heavier associations with the body, matter, and earth), there is not really a universal concept of what it means to be "feminine" that we can find across cultures and historical eras. The only strong thread that can be found is that the feminine, across cultures, is *what is enshadowed*. Well, what is enshadowed needs to be integrated, as part of any alchemical healing process.

When I write The Feminine, (with a big or little 'f') I am referring to an arcanum—a vast, primordial mystery. Far too vast and too primordial to ever be fully known, by me or by anyone, just like The Masculine. And it is not what the culture tells us the feminine is.

The feminine lives mostly in the realm of the unconscious, in individuals, and in the culture. Florence Scovel Shinn wrote that the unconscious is the soul. And Marion Woodman wrote that the soul is feminine in each of us. So, there is an inherent connection between the feminine and the watery unconscious. I will often refer to the collective feminine as the great goddess. There are many different aspects of the feminine that a person of any gender may be reclaiming from the shadows at a given time. This is the time to bring those aspects back up to the topside world. We need them now desperately. We are literally dying for Her.

Despite the mystery enshrouding the true arcanum of the feminine (or the great goddess), I believe we have all experienced Her, and we know Her in our cells. We know how to recognize Her frequency.

The first time I saw Her, She took the form of the immaculate Virgin Mary statue that stood on the outside of the little Catholic church where I attended mass each week as a child. Her softly weather-chewed face, and the faint tracks of moss and lichen, and occasional insects that climbed Her form seemed like natural extensions of Her essence. She was outside in the elements, in the wild, where you could smell the cypress and juniper trees growing around Her. But She also, for some reason, was not allowed to be inside.

One May Day when I was little (which was once the pre-Christian festival of Beltane), my mother stole some dew-moistened roses from our neighbor's front yard early in the morning and placed them at Her feet. Our Lady. This wild act of affection would stick in my memory for years, though at the time, I would not have been able to conceive of the reasons why. I believe now it was because I could sense the true devotion of my mother in those stolen branches, practiced within a tradition given to her by her mother, and her mother before her. I'd never seen her steal anything for Jesus before. The gesture was romantic, spontaneous, secret, and alive, unlike so much of the religious practice into which I'd been initiated. A secret of women I could carry with me like contraband.

THE MARYS AND THE VIRGIN-WHORE SPLIT IN THE WESTERN PSYCHE

THE GODDESS IS THE UNSPEAKABLE WISDOM THAT GROWS INTO THE VERY CELLS OF THE BODY. SHE LIVES WITH THIS SACRAMENTAL TRUTH AT HER CENTER: THE BEAUTY AND THE HORROR OF THE WHOLE OF LIFE ARE BLAZING IN HER LOVE. SHE IS DANCING IN THE FLAMES.
-MARION WOODMAN

There has been a fundamental, deep, and lasting split in the Western psyche when it comes to the feminine. One of the most important episodes in the long story of burying the feminine in the West was the *literal* burying of the Gospels of Mary

Magdalene. In these gospels, Mary is accorded essentially the same level of spiritual esteem as Christ, and Christ considers her his equal. *His equal!* She was called The Apostle of the Apostles. This fact, as well as the transmission of uniquely feminine wisdom and divinity that comes through her gospels, were completely buried. Literally placed underground in clay vessels and forgotten for the better part of the past two millennia.

Here's the next major episode: After the Black Death, the realm of nature and the body were seen as chthonic, chaotic, and dangerous. They needed to be owned, controlled, measured, and rigorously understood in order to create man's ultimate control over the terrifying, primordial chaos and darkness of the natural world. The cult of the Black Virgin ended after the Black Death, and then the burning times began.

The burning times occurred coevally with a proliferation and deepening of the cult of the Virgin Mary and of the Immaculate Conception. In these historical episodes we can discern a splitting of the feminine into the disembodied, ethereal, light-skinned, "good" virgin on the one hand, and into the dark, terrifying, carnal, wildly sexual, demonized feminine on the other hand. The Virgin/Whore split in the Western psyche deepened and solidified. This is the split we have all inherited, the split that the collective unconscious is trying to heal in the dreams of so many women and people of all genders.

With this split, the closest shot in hell the feminine has of ever being divine is through virginity. Think about it: We only have genitals because we are going to die. If we were eternal, immortal beings, there would be no reason for genitals and no (biological) reason for sex. This association of virginity with the divine realms is projected mostly onto women. As is the idea that lust and carnal desires are inextricably caught in the chaotic, dangerous, magical, and unpredictable realm of the feminine.

The feminine is seen as the mistress and overseer of death and childbirth. The feminine has also been seen as the temptress and distractor of men from their normal, industrious activities, always beckoning them into a sensual, chaotic, magical, and "darker" realm. In order for women to be accepted in this kind of world order and not demonized, they must cleave to the "virgin" side of the split, shoving their wilder, darker, more erotic sides into the unconscious. This split exists both individually and collectively in the West.

The vast shame projected onto the female body, its mysteries, and its strange consonance with the great, mysterious creative matrix is alive and well today. Consider the collective implicit (and explicit) imperative to keep breastfeeding hidden, to never discuss our monthly cycles or menopause, and to keep birth hidden. It's interesting how we also keep death hidden. All the mysteries of the body. Women also feel they should not discuss the normalcy of unwanted pregnancies, of miscarriages, of masturbation, of postpartum or perinatal issues, and of the difficulty and loneliness of motherhood.

So much of the female experience is enshrouded in silence, solitude, and shame. Until recently, the ubiquity of sexual harassment and rape on the street, in places of employment, and within family settings was largely not talked about. And so many of these universal (yet silenced) aspects of the female experience point to the very mysteries of life and death themselves.

For a good example of the way the Virgin-Whore split plays out in modern times, watch the *Framing Britney Spears* documentary. This split was projected onto her when she went from being the charismatic, virginal American sweetheart to a blossoming young woman exploring and enjoying her sexuality. The vulturous, relentless message of the media was that she could not be both. She could not be sultry *and* be the darling, sweet girl we all knew and loved, both at the same time.

Notice the novelty of the idea of a sacred, sexual woman in the West. The idea that a woman could be a hot, sexy, steamy, sacred priestess seems utterly alien to us. And yet (as we shall see), the red goddess (Innana/Ishtar) did indeed have priestesses, and sacred sexuality *was* their work. It was how they expressed the divine love of the great goddess for all.

THE FEMININE PLEASURE TABOO

Modern women are still, largely, socialized to think of others first. Make sure everyone else is happy and comfortable and has what they need, and *then* take care of yourself with whatever's left. One of the most surefire ways to get back in touch with your wildish, instinctual nature is to start focusing on your own pleasure, and actually prioritizing your pleasure. You cannot serve, enlighten, or brighten anyone else unless you first know and honor your own pleasure.

Thought leader Regena Thomashauer, affectionately known as Mama Gena, encourages women to see pleasure as a vital nutrient, like leafy greens. And she believes most modern women are suffering from no pleasure in the diet.

Pleasure does not have to mean masturbation, although it *can* mean that. It means absolutely any little thing at all that will make you light up and squirm with delight, happiness, or excitement. That could be eating a piece of Belgian chocolate, playing with puppies in the park, going for ice cream, learning French, treating yourself to the high self-worth hair or outfit you've been wanting, or reading Shakespeare out loud.

Women and little girls are not taught the importance of this. On the surface, this contributes to the frazzled, overworked state of so many women. But at a deeper level, it contributes to women not fully inhabiting their bodies. Sensuality, pleasure practice, and embodiment are inextricably connected. Pleasure practice is an invitation to stay dropped into (and sensitive to) the subtleties of the body and its many ways of sensing and knowing.

THE FEMININE POWER TABOO

PASSIONATE, FREE-THINKING WOMEN RAISE PASSIONATE, FREE-THINKING CHILDREN, AND PASSIONATE, FREE-THINKING CHILDREN ARE VERY DIFFICULT TO MANIPULATE AND ALMOST IMPOSSIBLE TO CONTROL.

-MARIANNE WILLIAMSON, AMERICAN AUTHOR, SPIRITUAL LEADER, AND POLITICAL ACTIVIST

Not only are so many fundamental aspects of the female experience enshrouded in silence, but feminine power has also been made taboo and is seen as dangerous and problematic. There are two things we might mean when we say "feminine power." On the one hand, we might be referring to the inherent sexual power of women. On the other hand, we might be referring to women pursuing, or attaining, worldly power.

The inherent sexual power of women lies in the fact that their bodies are hypnotic to men and women alike, regardless of sexual orientation. Social media algorithms and the history of art bear this out. People like to look at images of pretty women. There are even deeper dimensions to this, and as I flesh them out in this paragraph, I will be writing with reference to the classic, hetero, man-woman sexual dynamic in order to make my point, understanding that this does not characterize the full spectrum of human sexuality. Stretching back to the dawn of our species, the male part of the sexual dyad has tended to be the one with a more pronounced, extraverted sex drive. And he is biologically driven to "spread his seed" far and wide, if he can. On the other hand, the female is biologically driven to *select* a good partner. Pregnancy is a higher stakes game and a bigger investment for her, and she only has so many "runs." This is why men try to flatter, please, and impress women. They want to be the one she *selects*. Also, a woman has what a man wants. It's between her legs. Now, if you possess a body that people inherently value and desire and what men want is between your legs, then you possess primordial sexual power. The power to start or end wars, to turn the tide of history, or to make or break million-dollar deals is in the flutter of one beautiful eyelash.

That kind of power feels scary and uncontainable to those under its influence, so throughout history it has been contained, controlled, and sterilized in every way imaginable. Making sex work illegal, for example, is one way to place this primordial power in the hands of the state, to the detriment of women everywhere. (Studies show that incidences of rape and sexual assault are lower in countries where prostitution is legal. That topic is a whole other box of frogs, but let the bare fact sink in.)

As for the taboo around feminine *worldly* power: It is still socially and physically dangerous to be a woman who is too powerful or "too big for her britches." My beloved mother began to receive death threats when she ran for public office after Trump's election in 2016, to give one very intimate example.

The word "power" is tricky because it certainly has some cultural grime adhering to it. Please understand that I am not advocating for feminine power in the sense of power *over*. I am advocating for women becoming conscious of the kind of power they inherently have or want and for women being allowed to safely have or pursue that kind of power. Natural gifts, strengths, and abilities are a form of power. Intuition, creativity, and even empathy are powers. *Potency* could be a good way to think of it. I am advocating for women finding their areas of natural potency and exalting them as superpowers. Ultimately, the witch wound is about power (or potency) and expression (the ability to freely own and express natural potencies).

INTERGENERATIONAL TRAUMA AND THE WITCH WOUND

I THINK EVERY STRONG WOMAN IN HISTORY HAS HAD TO WALK DOWN A SIMILAR PATH, AND I THINK IT'S THE STRENGTH THAT CAUSES THE CONFUSION AND THE FEAR. WHY IS SHE STRONG? WHERE DOES SHE GET IT FROM? WHERE IS SHE TAKING IT? WHERE IS SHE GOING TO USE IT?

-PRINCESS DIANA

The fear modern women continue to feel when stepping into their full power and sovereignty has its roots in the past. The burning times alone would do it. But before, during, and after that episode of Western history, women had always been, and continued to be, punished in all manner of ways for stepping out of line.

After the dawn of the agricultural age (about 10,000 years ago), the idea of "property" came to be for the first time in our history as a species. Women were first the property of their fathers and then of their husbands. One's wealth and estate had to be protected, as did one's genetic legacy, which meant that the behavior and virginity of the daughter and wife were of the utmost importance. Women were expected to adhere to these very specific roles, and even before and after the burning times stepping outside of those lines might be punishable by death, extrajudicial or otherwise.

How might those millennia of trauma and horror impact modern women? There has been lots of research in recent decades into epigenetics, but besides that, there is the real, demonstrable phenomenon of ancestral, or intergenerational, trauma.

We absorb the psychosphere of our original homes like little sponges, as far back as fetal life. Indeed, the farther back we go in the lifespan, the more susceptible we are to the influence of our surroundings. This means fetuses, babies, and small children soak up the energy and emotions of their primary caregiver. The foundations of our neural architecture are laid during the early stages of life. The impact of the first two years can last a lifetime.

The same can be said of the primary caregiver, and their primary caregiver, and their primary caregiver. The earliness of that potent influence makes plain the connectedness of the neural architecture of the offspring to that of the primary caregiver. And given that the primary caregiver was connected to their own primary caregiver in the same way, it's easy to imagine how trauma gets carried through the generations. Layer on the ensuing interactions with the family (or community) of origin throughout childhood and later years, and it is easy to see how intimately and deeply the family psychology maps onto the individual. The same is true for every generation of the family.

A modern woman does not need to feel a tangible connection to the burning times through the generations of her family to be assured that she is impacted by this, because different shades of the same exact sort of persecution have been, and continue to be, perpetrated against women all over the world. Women are tragically killed (often by those closest to them) all the time, worldwide, usually for stepping out of their prescribed role, and often for nothing at all. Just for having a body that someone else feels is their right to use or to project their own deep shame onto. Or for being trans or part of an ethnic minority group (a reality that also extends, horribly, beyond the United States of America). And the cases of BIPOC women being killed by police or dying in police custody in the United States rarely garner national attention.

To this very day, women continue to be punished in ways large and small by their families, places of employment, and perhaps sometimes, by their own friends for being too powerful, too gorgeous, too wild, too unusual, too brilliant, too passionate, too bossy, too anything. (Yes, women can sometimes be the harshest patriarchs.)

Even when the punishment is nothing more than a snarky comment or suggestion that you "tone it down," this faint echo of ancient, and horrible themes can trigger off a powerful response even in modern women. It's as if their nervous systems register that they might literally not be safe if they do not heed the warning, conform, and tone it down.

I believe women feel this unsafety any time they are thinking of speaking up, of saying something that is true for them on a soul level, of doing anything that seems too "occult" or magickal, or personally empowered, or of blending sacredness with their sexuality in an open, shameless way.

In this way, the priestesses, oracles, and witches of our psyches continue to be burned. As do the shamans, artists, seers, medicine women, truth speakers, saints, heretics, radicals, and holy whores.

It is not something to get twisted up in a ball about. It is not your fault at all. It's just that it makes spades of ancient sense why we might feel afraid in every cell of our bodies to stand in our power. We are up against a lot, and we can still overcome. **This is why the part of you connected to your fiercest power is likely the part you've buried.**

The first time I was about to read one of my poems publicly, I felt a distinct sense of unsafety coursing through my body. Then, at the moment I began the public reading, I felt like a vessel for some otherworldly power that could play me like an instrument. Huge fear, huge potency. We all experience this and shrink, to some degree, from our full expression. Forgive yourself. Don't expect yourself to overcome thousands of years of trauma in a snap. And know that you can still push into your gifts and your power, despite the fear.

WRITING PROMPTS FOR YOUR OCEANIC
LISTENING PRACTICE

-To Begin to Discern the Shape of Your Witch Wound:

When have you wanted to express something, or publicly wield some form of expression, but felt afraid to do so?

-To Get a Taste of What's on the Other Side of This Process:

Write for three full pages about what your life would look like if you completely approved of all of your desires, especially the desires of your deepest self (or your soul) as you currently understand it. Let these desires be the first signposts, the first vibrational indicators, of what is on the other side of this process for you. A little taste of the land you're going to.

CHAPTER FOUR

LOST FEMININE
MYSTERIES

————•◦•————

MOTHER, WHOSE WITCHES ALWAYS, ALWAYS,
GOT BAKED INTO GINGERBREAD, I WONDER
WHETHER YOU SAW THEM, WHETHER YOU SAID
WORDS TO RID ME OF THOSE THREE LADIES
NODDING BY NIGHT AROUND MY BED,
MOUTHLESS, EYELESS, WITH STITCHED BALD HEAD.
-SYLVIA PLATH, "THE DISQUIETING MUSES"

Africa was once known in the West as "the dark continent" because so little was known about it. To Western psychology, lunar consciousness remains something of a dark continent, as do uniquely feminine processes of deep transformation.

The feminine mysteries as practiced in ancient Rome were totally lost by the time Christianity was adopted as the state religion of the Roman empire. For that reason, not much is known about them now. However, there are *some* mystery traditions about which we know a thing or two, as enshrouded in… well, mystery, as they continue to be. Let's take a quick look in order to get a sense of what a mystery initiation in the ancient world was all about. And be aware that this exploration is by no means exhaustive. It focuses on lost psychedelic and feminine mystery initiations in the West, which were thoroughly lost by the time the witches were burned and the modern Western clinic was born. Indigenous cultures all over the world possess a wealth of deep transformation traditions, ancient lunar practices, and mystery initiations. Consider this an invitation to go explore what I cannot fully do justice to in these pages.

INTO THE MYSTERY HALL WITH US

Did you know that the principal spiritual consolation of the West before Christianity was a place called Eleusis where mystery initiations took place every year around the time of the harvest? Men, women, slaves, prostitutes, and aristocrats alike could all attend, and those who had partaken in the mystery were not allowed to ever speak of what they had undergone to non-initiates. The reason for this was likely twofold. First, the mystery was so sacred as to be unutterable. And second, it appears likely that the initiates underwent some kind of entheogenic experience on the Eleusinian plains, pointing to an experience that would be very difficult to put into words. Though initiates were not to speak of what they saw, they commonly intimated that some kind of "vision" took place during the initiation. However, the initiation hall is shaped nothing like a theater. It appears more like an open space where many individuals might gather, sit, or lie down. And the preserved artifacts include numerous vessels and cups for holding and distributing some kind of very special potion.

Many modern scholars are convinced, for reasons too deep and variegated to get into here, that the initiates were drinking some kind of ergotized beer containing LSA compounds, the precursor of what we know today as LSD. And in the ancient world, everyone who was anyone had to be initiated at Eleusis. And this went on every single year in Greece for over 2000 years. Imagine that. The primary spiritual home of the West, for a period of time as long as Christianity has been around, was a place where everyone got high on the ancient equivalent of LSD. The greatest minds of the ancient world went there and wrote about it in vague, cryptically gushing terms. The consensus seems to be that the "vision" is difficult to put into words and that it unites all who have ever undergone it in a sibling-like bond for life. Also, that the "vision" is utterly life-altering, connects the initiate to a sense of "eternal life," and for many, was the most jaw-droppingly beautiful and important experience they had ever had. If that is not a description of a psychedelic experience, then I don't know what is.

It also seems fairly clear that the experience initiates had at Eleusis was deeply interwound with the cyclical underworld-resurrection myth of Persephone and Demeter. In terms of gathering pieces for a reconstructed "feminine mysteries initiation," what we have here is a container within which initiates underwent an important internal journey that paralleled a myth of descent into the underworld and resurrection.

MAENAD MAGIC

We would be remiss if we did not spend a brief, glittering moment with the maenads in the endeavor of trying to trace a thread from modern, feminine processes of transformation to more ancient mysteries. In ancient Greece, the maenads were the female devotees of Dionysus, the beautiful, suffering god, and the god of madness, wine, and ecstasy. (By the way, it is thought that in the ancient world "wine" was not what we know it to be today. Rather, "wine" referred to any potion or beverage made from a combination of plants known to be mood- or mind-altering in one way or another. The particular entheogenic effect of the wine blend was referred to as its "flower.")

The maenads were all women, from the young to the very old. And on certain days of the year, they would make the journey into the hills together, sometimes with the young and strong carrying the very old, as the accounts go. They wore animal skins, and they collected special plants and fungi on the way up. Once there, it is thought they partook in some kind of entheogenic blend, which put them into a visionary state. They played special music and engaged in wild, ecstatic dancing throughout the night. When describing the maenads, classical tragedian Euripides writes:

The entire mountain and its wild animals were, like them,

In one Bacchic ecstasy.

As these women moved, they made all things dance.

This quote seems to point to a boundary-dissolving essence distilled within the maenadic rites and within the femtheogenic consciousness these women embodied. Bound up in this boundary-dissolution is an interconnectedness, especially, with the landscape. And this seems to point to one of the fundamental mysteries of matter: That all things are entangled and cooriginal in this world of movement and form.

These women were the bridge between Neolithic, shamanic traditions (wherein the women were the shamans) and the witches of Europe. In fact, many accounts of the maenads from the times when the tradition would soon fall into disrepute sound uncannily similar to the more recent paranoid Christian descriptions of the witches. They were often described as "wild" or "possessed" and sometimes even as flesh-rending.

In fact, these women *did* perceive themselves to be possessed by Dionysus, their bridegroom, within the maenadic rites. And contrary to the bent of some later descriptions, these women were not retreating to the woodlands and hills in order to release the patriarchal pressure valve and all the rage and hurt associated with it. Rather, they were reviving and relishing in a pre-patriarchal observance that was meant to turn everything upside down: roles, gender, and even the idea of "sanity."

Women have always needed to express their wildness, their passions, their gifts, and their sacredness, even when they were hunted down for doing so. The maenads did it in their mountain rites, the witches did it with their transgressive souls and cunning wisdom, and the early Beat women did it with their wild subversions, experimental drug use, and creative courage. They were often punished for these activities, demonized by the press, sent away by their families, and sometimes even bullied or rejected by the literary men in their circles. Each of these women, in her own way, turned roles, gender, and even the idea of "sanity" on its head.

Note well that both lost mysteries involved entheogens. In other words, they involved the internal, visionary world, and some form of shamanic inner journeying or ecstasy. The inner, visionary world is exactly what was mocked by the behaviorists, who represented the pinnacle of the long process of turning Western psyche-soul healing traditions into a totally stripped down, acceptable "science." True to what we know about the lost mysteries, the process in this book deeply honors and hinges on the inner, visionary world, and on paralogic and flipping concepts on their heads.

Also, I am very humbly calling into question some of the conventional ways of understanding "sanity" within a Western mental health framework. The maenads, Joan of Arc, the Beat and hippy women, and the witches are my paragons in that radical endeavor. My own lived experience, as shared here, hopefully adds depth, dimension, mystery, and *hope* to some classic mental health concepts.

IN THE ABSENCE OF HER PRIESTESSES AND HER MYSTERIES, SHE MEETS US IN DREAMS

WITH THE ARCHETYPE OF THE ANIMA WE ENTER THE REALM OF THE GODS, OR RATHER, THE REALM THAT METAPHYSICS HAS RESERVED FOR ITSELF. EVERYTHING THE ANIMA TOUCHES BECOMES NUMINOUS—UNCONDITIONAL, DANGEROUS, TABOO, MAGICAL.

-PATRICIA 'IOLANA, *IN SEARCH OF GODDESS CONSCIOUSNESS*

The great goddess continues to carry out Her taboo, dangerous, paradoxical work and Her mysteries. It's just that, when all Her priestesses and mystery schools have been banished from the daylight world, She does this in the glittering darkness of the dream realm, our night visions. She can't be shut out forever. It is in Her nature to surge forward like weeds and wild medicine plants shooting up through the asphalt. She is unconquerable spirit and supernatural resilience.

That's why, despite the feminine mystery schools of the West being all but entirely buried, there is still hope for finding Her ways of knowing, healing, and self-transformation through dreams and other encounters with Her realm in the unconscious.

This is one reason why Western psychotherapy, oddly, is actually a perfect forum for dreaming Her back (specifically, within its depth traditions). Her characteristic ways of communicating are paradoxical.

In one sense, it seems mystery may be inextricably wrapped into the very arcanum of the feminine. In another, perhaps the feminine only seems so mysterious because She for the most part (in most people) has not been made conscious. (Here I am referring to the feminine soul, the individual doorway to Sophia, or the speck of the great goddess that lives in each of us, however you want to think of it.) Even so, when we make Her more conscious within ourselves, She remains an arcanum, a magnitude the depth and scope of which no individual human could ever come close to fully apprehending.

Feminist writer Camille Paglia once wrote, "To be woman is to be occult." The etymological root of that word, *occult,* refers to what is in the dark, what is hidden. Think about the essence of biological femaleness. It involves having a womb. Something that is fundamentally hidden away, unseen, but is still the magical cauldron of new life, consonant with the great Creative Matrix Herself. This is what is so endlessly tantalizing about the striptease. One layer is removed, and then another, and then another, until the woman stands before you naked. And even after she becomes totally naked, you *still* don't see the essence of her womanhood, because the essence of her womanhood is occult.

This book is a psychopomp (an underworld guide) and a striptease. And life itself is a striptease. We slowly remove one layer after another until we stand naked before the world and our creatrix. We shed skins. We are threshed from our husks. We become more and more whatever it is we always were. That is what I am doing within the pages of this book, and it is what I am welcoming you to do as well.

Interestingly, the ancient Queen of Heaven, Inanna (thought by occult researcher Peter Grey to be The Red Goddess), removed one piece of clothing after another during her own underworld journey until she stood naked before her underworld counterpart, who was, strangely, throughout this entire process, giving birth. This is what we are doing. We are midwifing a more authentic, transformed version of you—a version of you that makes the feminine soul, as She lives inside you, your queen. We are following a sacred call, and we are bringing back to the entire process all the mystery and sacredness that it deserves.

RECLAIMING PRIESTESSHOOD

There are and have been countless priestesses who had to carry out their ministries in secret because there was no institution or religious home for them in the West for so many millennia. They have carried out their holy order as teachers, mothers, grandmothers, writers, social workers, nurses, therapists, artists, musicians, and in too many roles to name. Without an institution within which to be honored, our priestesses are wild, unnamed, and unknown. And we need them now. We need them to stand up, come out of the closet, and begin unabashedly doing their work as mystics on this planet. The fate of the life web depends on it.

This is intimately linked to my own process of getting naked in this book, so let me remove one more garment here. As an artist (who works mostly with words) and a clinician, I straddle very tricky lines in the postmodern West. In order to remain faithful to the soul of art as I perceive it with the sensitive radio dial of my soul, I have to either *not* be a practicing clinician, or I have to be a very racy, unusual one. When the artist creates, she steps into a transmoral space of no rules—she has to. She cannot predict what will happen in that space, nor who it may disturb, offend, unsettle, or upset.

One might say it is part of the sacred role of the artist to disrupt and unsettle, because she must tear a hole in the Symbolic order we all inhabit in common parlance. She must tear a hole in the agreed-upon sky, revealing the dancing Real behind it. Often, the Real is not popular or easy. That doesn't mean the artist sets out to be challenging to others. But she can't be motivated by *not* being challenging. She often brings forth the archetypal textures that are balancing medicines for the times. And she can't help but reveal some of the deepest caverns of her own being as she does this. She must be a priestess of the Real and a spiritual porn star. This runs directly counter to the imperative that modern Western clinicians keep their public personas scrubbed clean of anything that could ever disrupt any clinical relationship in any way. It's not that I plan to directly disrupt any relationship or offend any specific person. It's that I have no idea what will come through when I create, and I have to remain faithful to the otherworld sparks that I conceive in the creative process.

In other times and places, the artist and the healer were the same person. The shaman, the witch. The one who wears a certain mantel, possesses the mysterious power to heal, and engages in strange workings that don't belong in the bustle of ordinary concerns. I have been struggling to find my way without a home tradition. I know I am not alone.

Not only has the West lost its (public) priestesses, but it's lost all traditions linked to sacred initiations into womanhood. The gorgeousness and richness of the maenadic rites and other pre-Christian women's mysteries in the West are long gone, except for some traces that might still be sniffed out by the most adept armchair sleuths or the most prophetic dreamers. Now, the nearest thing to a widely accepted initiation into full, acceptable womanhood is when a man puts a ring on your finger (effectively *selecting* you).

A DIAMOND IS FOREVER

Let's highlight the mismatch between the *shape* of what's missing on the one hand, and what we currently *have* on the other. This will be in the spirit of continuing to flesh out the problem, the hurt place where something is missing on an individual and collective level. (Soon enough, we'll attend to the business of filling that void.)

I'm sure when you hear the slogan, "A diamond is forever," no one needs to explain to you what is being marketed. It was the slogan for the biggest marketing campaign of the twentieth century.

Consider this: There are no initiations into womanhood in Western culture other than a ring, marriage, and children. (I will refer to this initiation sometimes as ring-marriage-babies going forward.) It is not my intention to disparage these profound passages in a woman's life. I respect them, and I understand the unspeakable spiritual importance of each of them.

But none of them are about a woman being one-unto-herself. The shadow of this is that people (consciously or unconsciously) do not consider women to be complete on their own. I know this may, on the surface, appear to refer mostly to a void in White Western culture, but I'm referring to a pervasive psychic atmosphere that affects women, regardless of ethnic or cultural background. I am not making definitive statements about cultures that are not considered "the West" because I am not an expert in any of them, though I strongly suspect women of cultures not considered "the West" will be able to relate to this.

Once a woman reaches a certain age, one of the first things she gets asked at family gatherings is who her guy is and what's going on with her marital-and-motherhood status. This can be pretty profoundly disempowering for women because the traditional way it is supposed to go in the West is that, ultimately, a man selects you for these things. I know it doesn't have to go that way (and the deeper, more primal truth is that the woman selects). But the traditional Western paradigm is set up so that the man is the one who becomes so moved by this woman's exceptional desirability that he must claim her for his own. Then he must go out of his way to buy a ring and plan a romantic way to "pop the question." And if that hasn't happened to a woman yet, at a certain age, well then perhaps something is wrong with her.

I know this is not the mental equation that most modern, liberal people literally walk themselves through in a simple *If* _____, *then*_____ syllogism. Yet the pervasiveness of questions about a woman's marital-and-motherhood status weaves a web of messaging around young women that seems to say, loud and clear, "You are defined by whether or not you have been selected by a man." There are specific and nuanced cultural considerations that come into this question of when a woman "should" be married and how families speak about this, and I am not an expert on all of them. However, it does seem to be the case that in the vast majority of traditional marriage paradigms, women are expected to get married and perform certain roles, and they very rarely have a ton of say in the matter.

Ring-marriage-babies is an initiation that does not honor the woman as ever being or becoming one-unto-herself, a human being who is complete and enough, at any point in her life. Besides, it's based on a 250-year old Romantic era notion of marriage, jauntily placed into the shape of the hole in women's lives where Virgin initiations would be. And it's not a great fit.

RITUALS & WRITING PROMPTS FOR YOUR OCEANIC LISTENING PRACTICE

-To Lighten the Load:

If you get still and honest with yourself, you might find that a significant proportion of the thoughts that spin through your head on a given day have something to do with what you *should* be doing. Maybe also what you should be thinking, achieving, or being. These *should* thoughts probably spare neither your professional nor your personal life. All of that *should*-ing can be such a burdensome yoke that you may not even be fully aware you are constantly wearing.

Take a moment. Check in with yourself. How have you been should-ing all over yourself these days? Spoiler alert: The odds are good a lot of that is some "good girl" crap that you are going to do yourself the favor of re-examining. How much of that is other people's messaging about what you are supposed to be and value? Vow to never let anyone tell you ever again who you are or what you are supposed to be. Only you get to decide that.

-To Find the Garden Where the Butterfly of Authentic Happiness Flutters:

What are others expecting of me? Are you thinking about that right now? The odds are good that just triggered something for you. Whoops! You may even put the book down, so let me glamorize you back into the charmed circle.

We are going to flip this on its head. The expectations you perceive others to have of you are ruining your life. What are *your* values? Not anyone else's. Yours. Arrange your life around those. Almost every self-help story begins with, "My life looked great on paper. I had achieved everything I set out to achieve, and I still felt empty and completely fucking miserable." That's because you set out to achieve what it seems like *other* people value and want. Stop that!

We're going to turn on your instinct and explore your authentic values more deeply later on, but for now just get a sense of them. Write the first things that come to you.

-To Reassign Anger to Its Rightful Role:

When women and little girls are socialized out of their anger, it becomes the domain of men. Funny enough, it's also associated with power in the media in myriad ways. But guess what? Anger is a natural, helpless reaction to someone crossing your boundaries. (It can also be a natural reaction to situations that feel totally unworkable.) Anger lets you know when you are not okay with something. *You.* Not someone else. No one has exactly the same boundaries as other people.

What is your relationship with anger? When anger is disowned, it can squirt out in unconscious ways, and I don't want that for you or anyone. When was the last time you felt really angry? What personal boundaries might that indicate for you?

-To Get Reacquainted with the Wisdom and Power of the Body:

How would you characterize your relationship to your body? Before you get into the *appearance* of your body (and its adherence to, or distance from, socially sanctioned ideas of feminine beauty), I want you to focus on your actual relationship to *being in a body*. Do a quick body scan, allowing your awareness to travel from the top of your head slowly all the way down to your toes and see what you notice. Is there any discomfort or noteworthy sensation anywhere? Tune into that. Allow any information to emerge about what that sensation is communicating to you. Your body won't lie.

Many women find, doing exercises like this, that they have not been inhabiting their bodies at all. There may be some pain or discomfort that you routinely tune out. Come into your body. It only has good messages for you, as scared as you may feel to access that level of truth.

Most women are dissociated from their bodies, to some degree, as the result of feeling chronically unsafe, or as the result of vast reservoirs of sadness or rage they'd prefer to keep out of conscious awareness. Disembodiment can also be the result of making the body "the enemy" in some way, often because it won't conform to some set of aesthetic standards. Conversely, studies indicate that the more a woman identifies with being physically "hot" or attractive, the less likely she is to be able to tune into her own heartbeat. This could be as the result of feeling not entirely safe, of participating in her own body objectification to some degree, or a combination.

Do you feel tightness in your chest, your throat, or any other area of your body when you really tune in? Most people do. You might especially feel it when something triggers or upsets you. I think of those spots as emotional and energetic tangles linked to your "stuff," i.e., your emotional baggage. EMDR and other forms of deep therapeutic or healing work can help to untangle a lot of that gunk.

Women especially might be stuck in their throats. You can hear it in the voice. You can observe it in the quality of the breath. Tightness in the throat often points to a fear of the body or a refusal to fully inhabit the body. Sometimes this is because the body actually does not feel like a safe place to be, as the result of actual, unresolved trauma, or because the body and heart are holding painful emotions.

How do you sit? How do you hold yourself? How do you walk? Do you feel like the tin man in need of some juice, or do your hips roll like music? Be honest. Take inventory.

-To Reclaim Pleasure:

How would you characterize your relationship with sensual pleasure? Do you feel tuned into the myriad ways it can be experienced? Some women have never had an orgasm, and, darling, I don't want that for you. That's like never having one psychedelic experience (not even with some gentle, entry-level blue lotus tea), never dancing in the rain, or never saying the phrase "Fuckity fuckity fuck a duck" even once in your whole damn life. You are worth learning how to have orgasms. This is your "one wild and precious life." And get yourself some reading-Shakespeare-out-loud pleasure while you're at it (if that's your thing). Find out what your pleasure "things" are. List them, if it pleases you!

-To Start to Find Your Soul Letters:

Do you often feel tired, like you want to take a nap, or your energy is just low in general? Keep reading. Have you been having interesting, profound, or strange dreams lately? Again, keep reading.

Do you have low-level, rolling anxiety, or soul sadness? Do you feel a gaping hole in your chest or an emptiness inside? Is it so overwhelming you will impulse buy, drink, smoke, get high, ladle hours of television into your psychic maw, have reckless sex, binge, purge, or even cut yourself in order to escape it? Again, my darlings, keep reading. And take inventory of these behaviors if they are a thing you do.

Do you sometimes wonder what the damn point of life is? I don't blame you. This is such a fierce journey and a place of such deep mystery. The world sometimes seems too cruel for any kind of good meaning to ever be mapped onto it at all. Keep reading. No judgment.

Now read back through what you wrote down for each of the writing prompts of this chapter and circle some of the themes that stand out. Think of these themes, signs, experiences, and symptoms as letters from your soul waiting to be opened. The thing about soul letters is that you would be well-advised to open them. Because if you don't, they tend to increase in volume, pace, and intensity of delivery.

The process I will guide you through is about opening them. Think of them as morse code signals coming up from the psychic basement where your feminine soul has likely been buried. Ultimately, the process is all about integration, reclamation, and resurrection. You might also call this soul retrieval or shadow work. Whatever you call it, you are bringing exiled parts of yourself back into the circle of your love, complete with all their buried treasure and their vast energy. These parts often hold the key to our greatest attributes, our most precious uniqueness, and all the vitality we need to answer the longings of our souls. Ultimately the goal is to resurrect the speck of Sophia that our souls represent with deep love and deep listening.

So how did I go about creating a radical feminine mystery process?

CHAPTER FIVE

METAMORPHOSIS: DREAMING BACK A FEMININE ECOLOGY OF PSYCHE/SOUL

I WANT TO DRAMATIZE THE CONFLICTS OF WOMAN. CONFLICTS BETWEEN MATERNAL LOVE AND CREATION. BETWEEN ROMANTICISM AND REALISM. BETWEEN EXPANSION AND SACRIFICE. THE CONFLICTS OF WOMAN IN PRESENT-DAY SOCIETY. THE THEME OF DEVELOPMENT OF WOMAN ON HER OWN TERMS, NOT AS AN IMITATION OF MAN... [T]HE EFFORT OF WOMAN TO FIND HER OWN PSYCHOLOGY AND HER OWN SIGNIFICANCE, IN CONTRADICTION TO MAN-MADE PSYCHOLOGY AND INTERPRETATION. WOMAN FINDING HER OWN LANGUAGE, AND ARTICULATING HER OWN FEELINGS, DISCOVERING HER OWN

PERCEPTIONS. WOMAN'S ROLE IN THE RECONSTRUCTION OF
THE WORLD.
-*THE DIARY OF ANAÏS NIN*, VOLUME IV, 1944-1947

A group of American Indian men in traditional dress took me
down a trail away from a colonial settlement, winding off
into the remote American landscape, on our way to elsewhere. I
was always several steps behind them. Looking down, I noticed
I wore a doctor's white lab coat, the classic dress of an initiate
into the ways of the Western clinic. We reached a place on the
trail where I knew I could go no farther. I had not been properly
initiated. I understood and accepted this with humility and
stopped in my tracks, alone on a winding dirt trail, enveloped by
dry, whispering grass.

Looking down even farther, at my feet, I noticed a pile of
red and yellow snakes writhing all around them. I had nearly
stepped on them. I picked one up, a yellow one, and balled it
up so that I could fit it into my lab coat pocket. I walked back
to a little township and went back to my ordinary business as a
clinician. I soon forgot that the snake was even there. Finally, I
noticed her weight and gasped. I'd forgotten! The weight was
cold, like death. Was she dead?

I pulled her out, almost afraid to know her status for sure.
Cold-blooded, as all snakes are, she was still alive. *Thank God*, I
seemed to think to myself, *Thank God she's still alive*, as I allowed
her the freedom to coil up my arm and around my shoulders.
I woke up.

It is not my intention to unsettle my reader too deeply by leaving the threshold between dreaming and waking sometimes unmarked. Rather it is my hope that this drunken dream-weaving lifts another veil: the one that seems to provide a clear and clean demarcation between the strange, helpless meaning of dreams, and the bland realism of the waking world. It is an enchantment designed to evoke lunar consciousness, the second sight of the poet. It is another wicked invitation into the watery initiation realms where feminine consciousness may be allowed to erupt in your waking life. It is educational in the deepest sense: It is meant to draw out what you already know.

WOUNDED HEALER

This dream, like all dreams, has many layers, and I won't be able to exhaust its meaning here. This dream, like all dreams, will never be finished with me. What I immediately knew upon awakening was that the white lab coat represented my full initiation (as a licensed psychotherapist) into the ways of the Western clinic. What I also immediately knew was that this snake represented something quite *other*. It represented wilder, more ancient, and intuitive ways of knowing and healing.

In classical Greek mythology, there are two deities that represent the two sides of healing: Apollo, who represents the clean, removed, brightly lit, masculine, and more clinical side of healing. And Asclepius, who holds a snake, and represents darker, more feminine and intuitive ways of healing: the ways of the wounded healer.

This dream represented my psyche's attempt to push beyond my training in Western psychotherapy into a more embodied, intuitive, and deeply personal way of healing others; a way that would be more in touch with ancient healing traditions across the world without trying to claim any of them as my own. A way that would blur the line more and more between artist and healer. Because ultimately, both bring to light what is enshadowed; both work with the magnitudes; both are like shamans in that way.

This snake came to represent my inner medicine woman: the instinctive side of healing which pairs with training to turn it into an art form. I even brought this concept into my way of communicating with colleagues in consultation groups. I would say, *This client is displaying X, and I know I should try Y, but my inner medicine woman tells me, categorically, that Z comes first. It is not yet time for Y.*

I don't believe I have come to the end of knowing what this snake represents or how to integrate it into my art and healing practices. Like a snake, I will continue to shed skins, and so will my life and practice. Like Inanna, one piece of clothing, and then another, will be removed. Like butterflies, we are all made for this process of soul-making, for tending each phase of the mysteries of life.

For now, I understand this snake as the embodied instinct that guides and directs me in every moment with my clients. It is the confident knowing that comes from my hips and womb (not from my brain or any specific credential), and passes through my heart on its way to my mouth. It is the poetic instinct as it lives, moment by moment, in the act of healing. It is the magick that is activated when I meet with my clients soul-to-soul, rather than mind-to-mind only. It turns the healing process into a larger magick which outstrips both of us and must be allowed. It turns it into living poetry and deep engagement with life in the present moment.

The process that I use in healing and bringing more love, joy, and creativity into the lives of others (and my understanding of it) will continue to be refined as long as I live. I will never allow it to stagnate. It is as alive as all wild things are.

What I intuit now is that the snake of Asclepius, the wounded healer, plays an important role in more feminine psychologies and ways of healing. The wounded healer does not adhere perfectly to the sterile, cold, removed Apollonian rules of the clinic. The wounded healer is imperfect, deeply human, vulnerable, and not afraid to show that she, too, is bleeding. She does not pretend to be "complete," "resolved," or "superior" in any way. Rather, she lives the truth that we are all made for the ongoing process of soul-making. She does not use expertise as a disguise. Rather, she brings the vulnerability of her naked humanity, with genuinely kind eyes, into each session. She makes mistakes and admits it. She prizes real human intimacies and understands that their rarity increases by the day. She lives anastasis: the reaching of the abandoned to the abandoned. She has an intuitive sense of this larger magick that is invoked when she lets go into the field created between her own heart and soul and that of her client. She trusts and allows this. My gut tells me that this may sometimes entail the healer telling her own story and lifting the veils over her heart and soul as part of her craft.

ALCHEMY

THERE'S A QUALITY OF LEGEND ABOUT FREAKS. LIKE A PERSON IN A FAIRY TALE WHO STOPS YOU AND DEMANDS THAT YOU ANSWER A RIDDLE. MOST PEOPLE GO THROUGH LIFE DREADING THEY'LL HAVE A TRAUMATIC EXPERIENCE. FREAKS WERE BORN WITH THEIR TRAUMA. THEY'VE ALREADY PASSED THEIR TEST IN LIFE. THEY'RE ARISTOCRATS.

— DIANE ARBUS

When I traveled alone to India in my early 20s, I saw someone leading a calf up a hill towards a Hanuman monkey temple. The calf appeared to have some kind of amoebic deformity on its side, the size of a large human hand. Its owner had painted the deformity bright Pepto pink, and had even tied ribbons and bells around it, to show its great holiness.

It is my hope that these images from the dream world and the waking world provide useful *and* beautiful fulcrums for fleshing out a more feminine way of healing, bringing only the Shinola I had to separate from the shit as I pieced this together through intuition and dreams. To encapsulate it in the most concise way that I can, feminine ways of healing are more about alchemy than excision. What do I mean by that? Let me give you an example.

New clients have come into my office and basically told me they would like for me to surgically remove their shame. It doesn't work that way. Whatever people want for me to remove or take away when they come in to see me is the exact thing that I will probably tell them to go into, with compassion. That is their teacher, their ally, the thing that holds more treasure than a pirate ship pulling into the harbor. In the New Testament, it is written that the stone the builders have rejected will be the cornerstone.

When you go into and stay with the shame, the pain, the emotional block, the part of yourself that you've rejected or disowned, and you bring breath, awareness, and tending to it, something magickal happens. The stuff that you thought was your shit can actually be transmuted into your treasure. When we bring those parts into the circle of our awareness and love, they can morph from a low side expression, back to a neutral expression, and then, through your awareness and conscious choice, into their exalted expression. And all of that stuff you wanted to tuck away forever in shame tends to be the *very best stuff* about you: your greatest gifts. The most badass things. The brilliance. The artistic talent. The transgressive impulses (which the world needs now like oxygen), the passion, the insight, the originality.

Rage can be alchemized, shame can be alchemized, deep emotional pain can be alchemized, parts of yourself that you consider "bad" or unwanted can be alchemized. Even trauma can be alchemized into resilience and growth.

In classic alchemy, shit, or lead, is turned into gold. Through feminine, alchemical processes of healing, we can choose to turn everything we hate about ourselves and everything we consider to be our "shit" into the sources of our greatest and most authentic vitality, over and over again. It can be composted for the garden of our creative projects. It can be transfigured into angel dust for building a business, or starting a revolution with surging vitality.

Like the calf in India, the thing about you that makes you a "freak" or that you consider to be a deformity may be the holiest thing about you. It's, at the very least, probably the most dissident thing about you. It makes you an aristocrat.

THEMES OF DESCENT, EMBODIMENT, AND INSTINCT

ANYONE WHO HAS GONE INTO THE FLAMES AND BEEN TOUCHED BY THE GODDESS KNOWS THE MANY DEATHS THE EGO HAD TO UNDERGO IN ORDER TO EXPERIENCE THE UNIQUENESS IN ONESELF AND OTHERS. LEARNING TO LOVE IS A LIFELONG TASK. ONLY IN AN ETERNAL MOMENT CAN WE EXPERIENCE OUR TRUE IDENTITY. AS WE BEGIN TO UNDERSTAND WHO WE ARE, WE CAN BEGIN TO UNDERSTAND THE ESSENCE OF OTHERS, AN ESSENCE THAT IS UNIQUELY LOVABLE.

-MARION WOODMAN, *DANCING IN THE FLAMES*

If we are finding the parts of ourselves that are most buried, most disowned, most enshrouded in shame, and turning them into gold, then we have to go to where those parts of ourselves live. We have to go to the underworld. We have to go down. I sometimes refer to this downward path as the "left-hand path," a phrase alternately used in Western esotericism, and also in Tantra. I don't particularly mean it in either sense, not least because I barely know a drop of the ocean that Tantra represents.

Another designation could be "the red path" (as opposed to "the white path" of pure ascension and transcendence). This downward traveling can mean simply bringing the awareness down into the body or into the heart and finding the raw material there, without need of words or concepts.

It can also mean going down into the underworld of the psyche, a word whose root essentially means butterfly, or *breath, life, soul.* The underworld of the psyche contains everything that has been relegated to the unconscious because of rejection or shame, whether external or internal. It also contains all the stories that run on autopilot and direct our lives from behind the scenes. We must go down there if we truly want to deeply heal. Superficial approaches that do not reach down to the roots will produce superficial results. Underworld approaches touch down on the deepest pulse of the ongoing evolution of the soul. This is where we find and kiss our Sleeping Beauty awake.

It may even be said there is no distinction between body and soul, according to a more feminine ecology of psyche. The feminine mystic William Blake wrote, "Man has no Body distinct from his soul; for that called Body is a portion of a Soul discerned by the five senses, the chief inlets of Soul in this age."

Life seems to take us on underworld journeys whether we desire them or not. You can choose to actively engage the transformative nature of life, or you can wait until life throws you into some scorching hot fires of transformation on its own. You can learn about these archetypal patterns and apply them to your own hard times. And this red path of descent is not about going to hell and hanging out there just because that's where all the interesting people are.

This is about resurrection, about finding the deep veins of gold in the underworld and bringing some of it back. Resurrection was always the domain of the red goddess, Inanna. Incidentally, it was also the domain of Mary Magdalene, whose presiding over the resurrection of Christ points to her connection to this ancient red priestess lineage. And—surprise, surprise—Mary Magdalene's nickname was "Red." Her mistaken designation as a whore was actually a beautiful synchronicity in this way. The red lineage is the lineage of the holy whore, of sacred sexuality and sensual alchemy. The essence of the holy whore is unconditional love for all, especially those (or those parts of ourselves) that we consider dirtiest, most shameful, and most contemptible. And we engage that energy in this process.

When we descend into the body and fully inhabit it, there we also find our instinct, an important component of any feminine psychology or way of healing.

FEMTHEOGENIC CONSCIOUSNESS

As women, we must learn to speak the language women
speak when there is no one there to correct us.

-Hélène Cixous

By creating a new, wild healing space and by honoring the intimate revelations of this book despite still being a psychotherapist in private practice, I am leaving the "father's house" of Western psychotherapeutic traditions. And in so doing, I am removing a mask. I didn't realize how suffocating it was (to me in particular) until I started to take it off. Western psychotherapy *can* feel like a paltry expressive forum to the feminine psyche, which wants to dance, be human, and speak poetry, the language of the soul or the "night-self," as Anais Nin described it.

Though "femtheogenic" is taken from "entheogenic," a word that describes the experience we have on psychedelic drugs, I contend no drugs are necessary to access this kind of consciousness. We all had it when we were small children and we spoke deep wisdom that seemed to come straight from heaven. However, psychedelic journeying *has* been one way that I've dreamed back a feminine ecology of psyche. The typical progression of a psychedelic journey involves dropping into the body and the present moment, confronting fear and resistance, and then (ideally) melting through that to find the love that we always already are.

Femtheogenic consciousness sees (immediately and always) the primacy and power of love. It wants to rip the high-necked Victorian dresses off of anything and everything that wants to cover over love, tuck it away, or sterilize its subversive power.

Femtheogenic consciousness is the consciousness that arises within a woman when she is speaking from the medicine woman in her gut and when she speaks the deep truth that has always been in her blood. In the pre-Christian world in the British Isles, women were considered to speak with the ethical and spiritual authority of the otherworld. We might also call it lunar consciousness, this way of seeing and knowing from the depths, rather than on the basis of external standards or customs.

This way of speaking and knowing sees the interconnectedness of all things. From the perspective of femtheogenic consciousness, *of course* your soul work is good for the world. It is good for the world in intricate, subtle, and profound ways you will never fully grasp. Also, the lines between artist and healer do not need to be so separate. *Of course* the healer is being an artist, and vice versa, carrying on with the good work of disruption. And *of course* this is all sacred. When my little femtheogenic soul voice spoke on that day of bone-deep agency exhaustion, I had an altar in my tiny Tenderloin apartment that featured the Virgin Mary, Lady Death, Mary Magdalene, Inanna, and Ishtar, and I placed a small sign over it that read, *Really, I am an artist, and I work for Her.* A reminder of what I always already know. Femtheogenic consciousness is the place where we always already know.

Femtheogenic consciousness has a natural holism about it. It does not see things as so separate. The higher your Adverse Childhood Experiences (ACE) score is, the more likely you are to experience addiction, smoking, and cancer in your adult life. When we unpack and work through the emotional baggage, I believe that a good femtheogenic healer is *literally* doing powerful preventive medicine on the mental, emotional, physical, energetic, and spiritual levels. I have seen this in my office. Femtheogenic consciousness sees the mind, body, soul, spirit, and energy system as intimately interconnected. How could they not be? It sees the ultimate health problem as a state of fragmentation, between or within any of these dimensions of the human being. "Holistic" sort of goes without saying in this realm, and so does "somatic." No particular certificate is needed. Just the right way of seeing, and deep listening.

DANGEROUS LOVE AND THE QUEENDOM OF HEAVEN

Love is the first and the last in this process because, ultimately, this process is about learning to welcome even what you might call your "demons" into the circle of your love. This is a love that embraces all, that has always already conquered all. The centrality of love in the way I do *all* of my work, including therapy, makes me a little radical, and I realize that. Love has always been radical and dangerous because it is disruptive to systems of power.

The kind of love I am referring to is a mystic love, a Christ consciousness love, which considers nothing to be separate from itself. You can consider it a love that you always already are; a part of you that is always already at the summit of the spiritual mountain.

The mystic, Marguerite Porete, who wrote *The Mirror of Simple Souls,* was hip to the kind of thing I am talking about here. She was burned at the stake in 1310 as a "relapsed heretic and Free Spirit." She lived and died for what she perceived to be the truth: that the soul is already one with God, and God is love. We all already are love, we always were, and we always will be.

I am interested in the applications of this kind of love in modern therapy or other healing relationships. This matches up nicely with Ram Dass's idea that there are, fundamentally, three levels of awareness. Most people live their lives on what he calls "level one," in competition, looking out for their own best interests, and feeling separate.

He calls the therapy mindset "level two awareness." Moving from level one to level two can be hugely beneficial for people, he contends. I don't disagree. In its purest form, the move from level one to level two is about making the choice to look for the heartache underneath all unappealing behavior. It is about gaining insight into that and remaining curious about that. This is beautiful and wonderful. The vast majority of people, Ram Dass states, live most of their lives in level one and level two.

Level three, however, is the mystic state, the state we sense and enter in the presence of a holy person, the state we are in when we fall madly in love, or the state we may sometimes enter during spiritual practice or on certain classes of entheogenic drugs.

My highest angels push me to explore how level three awareness can be brought into therapy or other healing relationships. For the most part, I am referring to an attitude that both healer and client can cultivate with regards to the client's exiled parts, no matter how "unappealing" they may seem on the surface. I am also referring to ways that level three awareness might be entered, or experienced, by the healing dyad, if only because the client is entering a space of unconditionally accepting regard. Does that mean I'm interested in therapists and clients falling madly in love with one another? No. It means I believe there is a way that a pool of mystic love can be cultivated, and at times, experienced, in the healing relationship, and that this might be one of the greatest sources of healing. I see the potential of this concept even if we are devoted skeptics and we merely play with these ideas.

If you are furrowing your brow and wondering whether I'm loopy (at best) and potentially dangerous (at worst), pause for a moment and consider some of the most profound experiences of love you have ever had. Moments when it seemed like your heart was going to burst. It could be a random thing that happened once during your spiritual practice, or maybe it happened when you knew you were in love with someone, or when your child was born.

To help you find your own experience of this, I will share a bit of my own and that of others. I have had experiences of being overwhelmed by a deep, all-permeating love that was only between my heart and "the all that is," or whatever you want to call it, and it was so powerful it nearly ripped me in two. It is often unpredictable what will overwhelm us or what will bring these experiences on. The simple idea that love is always there is enough, even if we're not in the state of being actively pierced or overwhelmed by it.

Other writers, healers, and psychedelic people have discussed a state of suddenly knowing that there is a living web of radiant love connecting all beings and everything in this world. In certain states they may actually *see* it, or they might suddenly just *know* it, or they might feel it in their hearts.

When we get onto the same "channel" as this love, we can be utterly overwhelmed and transformed forever. It feels like suddenly stumbling on a bottomless well of love within your own heart that was already, always connected to the living love of all beings. And it feels somehow that everyone you've ever known, everyone who's ever demonstrated love to you, is implicated in it, though it is not specific to any one person. It feels more like each of these individuals who have loved you were pointing you to this greater mystery of love, offering hints of it, and adding to the storehouse of love impressions in your heart. And the overwhelming sense is that you do not need any one specific person to help you access this. It is living and eternal and available to you at any time. The best any other person can do for you is to put you in contact with it, offer an example of it, or dose you with a reflection of it. But no other person or institution has the power to endow you with it or take it away. It is always yours and always available.

You might say there is a portal to heaven in your heart, or that the queendom of heaven is already within you.

It is not my intention to discount the importance of human relationships or to imply that you don't need other people in order to experience love. There are many manifestations and experiences of love and they are all important. Relationships are a sacred and hugely important practice. You have access to this mystic love, so share it. You are sharing it every time you make the simple decision to be kind to a stranger, for example.

When we integrate what is buried, what is enshadowed, we bring these underworld parts back into the circle of our love. Though it is radical for a licensed clinician to talk about or summon mystic love in the context of healing relationships, I am and have always been a radical. And I take seriously Angela Davis's idea that "radical simply means grasping things at the root." In order to grasp our reason for needing healing at the root, we must find these buried parts, and we must approach the entire heroine's journey with an attitude of love. Not just cutesy Valentine's card love, but with (at the very least) a nod to the love that put Saint Teresa in that somehow simultaneously ecstatic, orgasmic, and agonized pose in the famous sculpture, "Teresa in Ecstasy."

So, we are integrating what is enshadowed, bringing it back up to consciousness, like Persephone coming back up from the underworld to herald the springtime so that the earth can turn green again. Integration work is important for bringing all of you to the world in the authentic service your heart calls you to perform. This is especially important for women who are currently redefining what this even looks like.

We all need to bring the feminine back up from underground if we are to create a safer, more harmonious, loving, and sustainable world. We all need to awaken the great goddess and actualize Her in ourselves and in our lives. This will deepen your resonance with all that sustains your lust for life, and all that helps you practice openness as opposed to protective, melancholic closure. It starts with one woman, one person, waking Her up as She lives inside them, and living according to Her sacred decree.

BODY, MOON, AND SOUL CYCLES

THE PSYCHES AND SOULS OF WOMEN ALSO HAVE THEIR OWN CYCLES AND SEASONS OF DOING AND SOLITUDE, RUNNING AND STAYING, BEING INVOLVED AND BEING REMOVED, QUESTING AND RESTING, CREATING AND INCUBATING, BEING OF THE WORLD AND RETURNING TO THE SOUL-PLACE.

-DR. CLARISSA PINKOLA ESTES, *WOMEN WHO RUN WITH THE WOLVES: MYTHS AND STORIES OF THE WILD WOMAN ARCHETYPE*

I would be a monkey's uncle if I tried to describe the strange experiences I had in 2015 without including the intimate interwovenness of the entire process with my body and moon cycles. This is part of what was *so* psychedelic and *so* difficult for me to wrap my head around.

No one had taught me about this in grad school. Heavens, no. My mother (and no woman) ever told me about this. It struck me as unbelievably mysterious and sacred that my process of natural transformation, occurring through profound dreams, synchronicities, and ongoing reclamation, was inextricably braided into the rhythm of my menstrual cycle, and the rhythm of the moon. What in the name of Gemini cripes was going on here?

Once again, femtheogenic consciousness sees things in a much more interconnected way. In the words of Alan Watts, "You and I are all as much continuous with the physical universe as a wave is continuous with the ocean." And in the words of Terence McKenna, "Nature is self-similar across scales." From this perspective, it makes sense that a transformation process of psyche would be inextricably connected to earthly body and heavenly bodies too. But... I wasn't learning this shit in school. Was I losing my mind? That was the question I was honestly asking myself.

It became clear that I was having my most profound dreams around the time of my menstruation, when I felt more introspective, and would want to cocoon and journal more. And I was having moments of reclamation and noticing magick *out there* in the world when I was in the middle of my cycle, around ovulation time. It's probably worth mentioning that I had just gotten off of birth control pills after being on them for nearly ten years. So I was experiencing my natural hormonal cycle for the first time since I was fifteen and noticing the remarkable way it would sync up almost perfectly with the moon.

Many of the dreams I was having involved pregnancy and childbirth metaphors: Images for bringing to life the new, the incubating. The process *was* very much like a pregnancy, finding my creative potency and midwifing the next chapter of myself and my unfolding. It was a sacred process that I continued to return to and nurture in the kept darkness of my journal and my dream world, allowing it to unfurl on its own time, and really allowing it to reveal itself to me. This is the way of the feminine psyche when it comes to processes of deep transformation. We nurture it slowly and carefully like a pregnancy, and then, on our own time, we push, we breathe, maybe we howl, and in a certain sense we break open, allowing the butterfly of new life to emerge.

And this process happened rhythmically, happening in tandem with my menstrual cycle. I would open and close like a sun-sensitive flower, feeling more attractive and creative during my ovulation time (which fell on the full moon when I first got off the pill), and wanting to incubate and "return to the soul place" during my menstruation and the new moon.

In the years since I first had this *Pregnant Virgin*-ignited experience, I have heard other people with ovaries discuss their changes in energy, mood, sensitivity, and even psychic ability during different times in their moon cycle. Energy healer Donna Eden has stated that before menopause, she was at her very most psychic when she was on her period, and everyone in the town knew it, so she'd be completely booked up for readings at that time! Spiritual teacher Teal Swan has stated that menstrual cycles are like miniature seasons, but different for each woman. Menstruation is definitely my wintertime, the follicular phase is the spring, ovulation is the summertime, and the hormone-shift just before menstruation feels like the fall. What is it for you?

If you are in a body that does not menstruate, then how do the phases of the moon seem to impact your body-soul-psyche? Be aware of this as you go through this process of transformation and any future processes. The moon has been typically associated with the realm of the unconscious, dreams, emotions, intuition, and the feminine. Following the cycles of the moon can ground us into the present moment and into what is. During the full moon, we can look at what's been illuminated, what we want to do with it, and what can be released or transformed. And the new moon is typically more of an incubation time, a time of profound dreams and of intention-setting and manifestation-oriented spell crafting. Getting in touch with moon time takes us away from the Monday through Friday nine-to-five rinse and repeat cycle and into one that is rooted in deep time. When we live by instinct, we naturally fall into moon rhythm, and even seasonal rhythms.

While menstruation *can* function as a sort of truth serum, PMDD is also important to acknowledge. It is something that modern clinicians are not trained to necessarily rule out or look for in menstruating clients, unlike other diagnoses that cross medical and mental health lines (like diabetes or hyperthyroidism). Special considerations should be brought to bear for readers diagnosed with PMDD, though I contend that tracking the impact of moon cycles should still be helpful and illuminating for them.

WAYS TO KNOW THE ALCHEMY HAS BEGUN

Conversations with my clients confirm that it really is true that when someone enters a profound growth phase, they may feel **energized**, they may have **profound dreams**, and they may start to notice **synchronicities** and chance encounters. To break this down a bit, people sometimes feel that there is a new kind of energy, which seems to flow through them. They may experience it as a new *color* of energy (if they are visually inclined), or perhaps simply as a heightened energy and vitality.

This may be attributable to the release of the vital energy that was being used to keep them blocked and stuck, allowing them to feel more vigor and excitement. It is important to guide and direct the energy through spiritual or contemplative practices, like journaling, before it reorganizes itself into a new state of balance. The release happens throughout the *working* phase of the healing journey. This is the release of the healthy, balanced energies of the part that had been buried, neglected, or disowned. It can almost feel like something brand new surging through, but it is an energy that has always been native to the person, just stuck under the hood.

It is important to clarify, however, that new energy doesn't necessarily always mean feeling *energized* right away. On the contrary, someone might feel sluggish as things are shifting around internally. There may be a sense of slight unraveling as their internal ecology gets reorganized. It is *very* important to have containment, guidance, and support during this time.

Since an archetype is being constellated during this release process (more on archetypes later), it is typical for people to have profound dreams that offer representations of the archetype or reference points for the journey that the person is on. Also, when an archetype is active within us, we notice it in the outside world through chance encounters and other synchronicities that seem to point the way on our journey, in a process that blends inner and outer.

This slight blurring of the boundaries between inner and outer may unsettle some, which is why this process is not for everyone. This process may be sparked in you by simply reading this book. If you sense it has, I highly encourage you to find a container of some kind, ideally through working one-on-one with a therapist or healer who you trust. But this alone is not enough. You need sisterhood. You need community.

This *can* be a delicate state to be in. The container *and* the sense of self need to be strong. I believe this is the process Jung was going through while writing *The Red Book*, when he almost became psychotic. This is not anything to be fucking around with, once again, dear readers. He later stated it was his strong ego that prevented this. Think of the ego as a little rowboat on the vast, billowing sea of the unconscious. That little rowboat needs to be sturdy and seaworthy, especially when there is a surging swell or even a storm brewing.

There is a wild, creative energy bound up in this process because when we shed one skin, we welcome the unknown, which is the fertile ground of creativity. We are leaving one place behind and stepping into the dark land between what was and what will be. This dark, unknown place is the initiation ground, and, like rich, black soil, it is a place of unbelievable creative fecundity.

In order to feel comfortable in this liminal space between who you were and who you are becoming, you've got to trust yourself. You've got to become acquainted with a part of you that can see in the dark. Remember Vasilisa's little doll? The lunar part of you, the feminine, knows how to swim this dark landscape of the unknown. When we cross the threshold into Her realm, we may even fall in love with the unknown instead of fearing it. This is the realm of pleasure, creativity, mystery, and magick.

When you activate this process in your life, you are reactivating the magick and wonder that was always there beneath the surface. How often do you stop in the middle of a busy workday to notice the way the sunlight is filtering through the bright spring leaves of a tree? In these moments of pause and letting go of superficial, temporary identities, we can be present again with the mystery and profound freedom of being alive. That mystery is once again, undeniably, there. It never went anywhere. We just had blinders on. When you enter a deep transformational process, you are taking your blinders off.

Be prepared to notice your connection to the mysteriousness of life more often, and to the profound freedom of life. You could literally leave all your shit where it is right now and start walking barefooted to another country. You could start a new life as a whole new person when you get there. *Isn't that amazing?* Perhaps you'll take your sojourn within this book's pages as an invitation to become a little less afraid of just how free you are. There is nothing you *have to do* except eat, sleep, breathe, drink water, pee, and poop. Take your blinders off. Stop taking everything so seriously.

You will probably also notice more synchronicities, and more moments of reflection and simple wonder. In this process, you are engaging in intentional creating where your *life* is the artwork. Turning the magick back on in your life not only makes *your* life more enchanting—it also re-enchants the world so you can feel the magick and life force pulsing underneath chance events and within rainforests and other places of sacred power. When you perceive enchantment in the world again, the world *matters* more. A whole lot more. The destruction of sacred places on the earth becomes so much more unconscionable when you have chosen to re-sacralize them within your own experience. Partly, this involves rejecting the worldview that the earth's resources are nothing but dead, exploitable matter. There is a light in matter, and matter has its own law, which must be revered if we are to survive as a species.

RITUALS & WRITING PROMPTS FOR YOUR OCEANIC LISTENING PRACTICE:

-To Ignite the Alchemical Magick in Your Own Life:

Make a commitment to log dreams, synchronicities, and the effects of the moon as they occur to you during this healing and integration period. This will help you glean more insight into this living moment of your unfolding. This will also help you notice dreams, synchronicities, and the effects of the moon more, and you will be amazed how intimately connected each of these things are to your ongoing integration process. (And don't worry about making your dream practice too elaborate at this point. We'll deepen this practice later on. Just jot down the main details you remember.)

-To Fall Into Rhythm with Deep Time:

How would you describe your menstrual seasons, if you are currently in a body that menstruates? How do lunar cycles impact you? Commit to honoring the side of the cycle that feels more introspective and the side of the cycle that feels friskier and more energized to you.

-To Invite Your Ancestors (and Other Wisdom Ways) Into the Process:

It's important to be honest about the cultures we may be deriving our healing ways from. What ways of knowing or healing did your family or ancestors practice? If you're not sure, it might be interesting to find out. All paths ultimately lead to the organic development of a one-of-a-kind wisdom.

-To Foray Into a Feminine Mystic Mindset:

How would you characterize your relationship to femtheogenic consciousness and to mystic love? When have you experienced it?

-To Get Some Clues About the Parts You'll Be Integrating:

Is there anything about yourself that you consider ugly, shameful, weird, or undesirable? How might you start to play with finding approval for those parts of yourself?

PART II

CASTING THE CIRCLE AND BLACKENING

CHAPTER SIX

CASTING A CHARMED CIRCLE

THE FOUR STAGES OF THE GREAT WORK

According to classic alchemy, there are four stages of alchemical transformation, sometimes referred to as the *Magnum Opus*, or the Great Work. The stages are given color labels: Blackening (*nigredo*), Whitening (*albedo*), Yellowing (*citrinitas*), and Reddening (*rubedo*). These are paralleled in the feminine mysteries stages of (1) creating a container, strengthening resolve, and getting comfortable with the darkness of the process, (2) allowing the material to emerge and be ventilated, (3) finding resolve while exalting or refining the material, and (4) resurrecting/reintegrating.

This entire chapter is all about that first stage: creating a container. This is because, when we enter a feminine mysteries initiation, we are entering liminal space. Liminal space is the betwixt and between, a place of great creative fecundity, where magick and alchemy happen under the guidance of someone with the right knowledge.

Places and times where the veil between the worlds seem thin are liminal. Halloween is a liminal time. The seashore or an old growth woodland can be liminal places. Guidance and containment are important simply because it is a very vulnerable thing to have entered a betwixt and between place in a process of personal transformation. We are sort of spiritually skinless when we are in these spaces—we've been threshed from one husk, and we've yet to grow or step into another. Additionally, huge energetic fields and emotionally charged material may be activated within us. (More on this later.)

When we activate a spiritually powerful process or a deeply transformative process without appropriate containment and guidance, we may enter liminoid space. Think of taking acid for the first time at a house party, losing your friends, and having a really weird time. That is liminoid space, and probably the very friendliest version of it. This is not something to play with. Once again, seek trusted guidance. Please, por favor, for the love of Sam.

So in order to keep the initiation ground liminal and not liminoid, there are some things we need to get in order. We need to ensure containment and appropriate guidance. We need to strengthen the sense of self, get clear on our intention, and keep the heat on, but at the right temperature. This is really a lot like placing yourself in a cauldron of transformation. Let me address each of those in turn.

CREATE A CONTAINER

Before proceeding, please ensure you have a spiritual (or contemplative) practice of some kind, that you have basic self-care in order, and that you have community or support in some form. You need to check off all three before diving deeper. No skimping or cheating allowed. I know you may think you are the one exception who ever lived, but I'm telling you: You're not. I was not. Let me break each of those three necessities down for you.

First, self-care. Are you able to get sufficient sleep on most nights (around eight hours)? Are you able to drink lots of water and eat about three reasonably nutritious meals per day? Do you have your relationship with any mood- or mind-altering substances pretty well under control? If you answered no to any of those questions, I would encourage you to make that your focus for now. And make no bones about it: Your journey towards being able to eventually answer yes to each of those questions is every bit as important, profound, archetypal, and heroic as the journey outlined in this book. It's just that those are journeys this book is not designed to address, and you deserve the very best of the kind of support that *was* designed to address your current struggles.

Next, spiritual practice. Do you have a practice for getting centered, connecting with Spirit or Source or whatever you want to call it, or just for letting everything go and calming your mind for a moment each day? If not, I highly recommend that you select a practice to work with the entire time you are reading this book. It could be a spiritual practice you've been doing for a long time that you'd like to continue. It could be something from the past that you'd like to revive. It could be something new you've been wanting to try. It could be simple prayer and/or ten minutes of meditation each morning or evening.

If you'd like to experiment with a new practice from another culture, please be respectful. Do some research, and even speak to some elders of the community if you can, and find out what they have to say about the practice. Now, please make sure you are taking refuge in your practice for some small moment of sacred retreat daily. It doesn't need to be elaborate. Simple is great.

Finally, please, please, please make sure you are not lonely. Better yet, make sure you can find and join a support group, Sangha, or coven that speaks to you. Make sure you have a short list of at least three people you could call if you were having a hard time. Friends are some of life's best magick. Best of all, find a deep transformational coach or a trauma-informed therapist who is hip to these alchemical, depth-informed concepts to give you one-on-one support as you make your way through the kind of transformational journey into which this book will invite you.

STRENGTHEN YOUR SENSE OF SELF

Before we proceed, how healthy do you consider your ego to be? If you have a fairly healthy, yet flexible, confident yet humble sense of self, and you have all the other things in order, then we are copacetic. Please continue. Conversely, do you have an unstable, seriously deflated, overly inflated or brittle sense of self? Be honest. If so, then consider the development of a healthy sense of self to be the next leg of your journey, and one that must be undertaken before proceeding with the process in this book. And again, if that's where you are, honor it. That process is also a heroine's journey.

Now, ego is a tricky word, especially in this context, and I will not get all the way into it here. You might be wondering, *Why in the hell does this lady want me to strengthen my sense of self if my sense of self is about to undergo a radical transformation?* Great question, smarty pants!

A lot of spiritual rhetoric is about having an experience of ego dissolution or about eradicating the ego altogether. I will not disparage experiences of ego dissolution and the various means by which those experiences can be attained. However, I do not believe the ultimate goal of any spiritual quest is to smash the ego. Your ego, when it is healthy and in its rightful place, is a helpful little amigo. It helps you know how to sign checks and whose mouth to put food into. It helps you navigate this three-dimensional reality where you need an avatar in order to get along at all. I might be wrong. There might be some spiritual luminary who could say otherwise.

What I do think I know for sure is that, if ego eradication is the goal, it's a very tricky business. Often, ego eradication becomes its own sneaky little ego trip. Full, permanent eradication of the ego starts to seem like an absurd proposition. Maybe it can be done, but that's not the process offered here. Rather than a linear process with a final eschaton, this is more of a picaresque, cyclical process, which honors all the little deaths and rebirths that ask to happen in the span of one lifetime. A strong sense of self will carry you through many life/death/life cycles without blowing all your circuitry.

Strengthening your sense of self involves looking at who you were as a kid, and who you've been all along. It involves finding all of those threads that have always been there that you love, and that you know are your authentic energies and ways of being. It involves looking at that little, dear, sweet, wild person and allowing her to grow into an adult and loving her forever.

That's you, love! Stop getting down on yourself, that's all I'm saying. Have some sense of core identity or energy that has always been there and that you love. You're not going to radically transform out of that. And the more grounded you are in that, the less your little ego rowboat needs current statuses and titles to bolster it. The less disastrous it will be if (or when) those current titles and accoutrements disappear. You are so much more than any relationship or job. You always were and always will be.

When you affirm your strong sense of self, it shouldn't be, "I'm a goddamn *manager* where I work!" It should be more like, "I'm the kind of person who is able to go after a goal with fierce devotion," or, "I'm the kind of person who takes big risks in the name of love, and I love that about myself." See? It's not dependent on your current job or status in life. All of that could change overnight.

The ego must be patched up and seaworthy before we initiate an archetypal transformation process because it needs to be able to stay afloat on the sea swells of that process. We don't want to go into this with an overinflated ego either (which is usually a compensation for a deeper sense of smallness, invisibility, or shame). We want an ego that can surrender and allow divine energies to flow through without identifying with them.

The journal prompts at the end of this chapter are meant to support you in strengthening your sense of the divine, energetic thread, the unique soul signature, that you brought onto the planet with you when you were born.

GET CLEAR ON YOUR TRUE INTENTIONS

Sometimes when we're engaged in hardcore spiritual practice, taking entheogens or going through other processes of radical transformation, we can enter liminoid space when a shadow intention hitches a ride on our spiritual seeking journey.

I'll give you an example. Someone is hellbent on becoming "enlightened." They've spent some time around some spiritual teachers who seem to emanate an unearthly bliss and who truly seem to inhabit another plane. They want to be one of them. So they set off, ardently, on their quest.

But they don't realize that underneath all of that hardcore seeking and questing towards enlightenment was a deep sense of body shame and shame about the more earthly aspects of human existence due to some unresolved childhood trauma. The shadow, or unconscious, intention behind all the hardcore seeking was really to escape being human. It was a stance of resistance to the seeker's own humanity.

We are multidimensional beings with a physical body and nervous system and with a mysterious, heavenly system too. If we are in resistance to any part of that system, it is going to have a reaction. The physical body and nervous system may rebel, sending the seeker into a strange liminoid space, which (from the outside) can resemble a borderline psychotic state, but it is experienced from the inside as a place of feeling hopelessly, disturbingly unmoored.

So, get clear on your intention. Why do you want to undergo a process of deep transformation? Why, really? Who and what are you doing it for? Are you in any way trying to escape yourself or your humanity? Journal about this and be *very* honest. If you *are* trying to escape yourself or your humanity, get one-on-one support with that before diving into this kind of deep transformation process.

I'm going to get a little bit in your face and tell you I believe there is nothing more spiritual or holy than being totally human. Have you ever seen His Holiness The Dalai Lama making jokes publicly about farting on airplanes? Well, I have. If you have access to the internet, look it up! He's not ashamed! He's a full-blown, bona fide human being. *And* he is His Holiness. Both/and. Not either/or.

What makes human beings and the human experience divine is our profound task of loving all the way down and all the way through our shit and other people's shit. Look at the history of our species. The shades of horror it offers seem infinite. Look at our current situation. The suffering of human beings (and other species) at the hands of human beings (in ways both direct and indirect) is inconceivable, even in the moment you read this line. And yet, we all enact our divine capacity to love, despite all this, and while fucking up, making mistakes, and being all-too-human on every level. Not even the angels do that. If you're trying to escape the shit, or your shit, you're reneging on taking the human curriculum.

To quote Oscar Wilde, "We're all in the gutter, but some of us are looking at the stars." We bridge heaven and earth and contain every shade, from the most extreme at one end to the most extreme at the other.

COMBINE GROUNDEDNESS WITH LEVITY

Sit down and visualize yourself sending roots from the bottoms of your feet, from your root chakra, or both, all the way down to the core of the earth, anchoring in as if into ore. I know the core of the earth is actually liquid hot "mag-ma," okay, but just humor me here. Imagine you can get anchored in it. And imagine that long energetic cord has a lot of give, so you can move around all over the surface of the earth and stay firmly anchored. Do this daily as you go through this practice. You can do a deeper grounding visualization and practice, or you can take five seconds to visualize it.

Eating grounding foods like root vegetables and stews is also helpful. Take baths, if you can. Put your actual feet on the actual earth. Talk to people you know who are no-bullshit and who read Lapham's Quarterly.

And be willing to laugh at yourself, and to laugh in general! If you *do* care about eventual "enlightenment," something tells me it has a lot to do with lightening the fuck up.

KEEP THE HEAT ON, BUT AT THE RIGHT TEMPERATURE

There's a certain new, magickal energy that surges through when we enter an initiation or a moment of profound transformation. You want to keep that energy flowing, but at the right volume and pace. You don't want to overwhelm yourself, and you don't want to be unfaithful to it or let it peter out either.

Let's attend to getting too hot first. You'll know you're too hot if you feel sort of hypomanic (buzzy or a little dissociated or detached with racing thoughts), or you feel sort of depressed. Or you'll feel flooded with new plans and ideas and unable to focus on practical ways that you might ground them into the real world and your real life while ensuring your basic needs continue to be met. This should not happen if you have found proper containment and guidance, so in case I haven't said it enough, get that shit locked, please and thank you! All containment measures outlined in this chapter are meant to ensure you don't get too hot.

You could supplement with additional practices for bringing the energy down and focusing it. This could be meditation, or it could be any good form of self-soothing that works for you to bring your level of stimulation down and back within your personal window of tolerance. Anything based on bringing you into your body and helping you feel grounded and anchored is really key here. Finding your personal healing image (or images) and placing them on your altar can also offer a sense of containing, directing and guiding the new energy that is flowing through. These are big energies, and we need a digestible image or representation of them. Also, put this book down and think about other things from time to time.

In order to keep the heat on, keep tracking your dreams, synchronicities, and the cycles of the moon. And keep following along with the process outlined in this book. Even if you don't, you may find that you've entered a liminal, transformative phase of your life anyway. If so, I trust you will continue to receive (through dreams and synchronicities) the practices and healing images that will guide you in this moment of soul-making. Keep noticing that, and the heat is still on. Once you're solid in all of these areas, you've created a cauldron and assembled your ingredients, and you are ready to proceed.

CAST AN ENCHANTED CIRCLE

You, your status, and the laws that govern your typical reality are changed once you enter an enchanted circle. The healing space should be an enchanted circle, and so should art. So should sex. In this way, the healing space and relationship are an ongoing, living artwork.

Many of the rituals and journaling practices suggested here require nothing more than a pen, a journal, and your own human heart. That, and the right guidance, is all you really need to do magick. Having said that, never underestimate the power of a little ritual fanfare. Light a candle or incense when moving on to the ritual and journaling segments of this book from now on. Create an actual *feeling* of healing. This would impress upon your unconscious that you are entering a ritual space and an enchanted circle, amplifying the effect of the work you do within that space.

Your feeling of healing may be unique to you. For most people, it involves gentle lighting, invigorating or soothing natural scents (like lighting incense, using an essential oil diffuser, or lighting a candle that gives off a subtle aroma that puts you into a relaxed or reflective state of mind). It may also involve very soft music, Solfeggio tones, or simply the sounds of the rain or the wind in the trees of a sacred grove.

Please only consider your enchanted circle complete once you've attended to the containment measures outlined in this chapter. And incorporate all the same circle-casting measures when you rhythmically sit down for a session with your therapist, mentor, or healer. Ensure that you will not be disturbed during your healing time and that the time is set aside and protected. For some, a walk in nature or in the park may be the ticket. Your healing feeling may occur while sitting at the base of a tree. Imagine you have actually sprinkled salt around yourself in a circle and called in the four directions, if you like!

If you'd like to go further, write all five of your sense faculties in your journal with space underneath each one, and then list things that give you a feeling of sacredness and safety for each sense. Integrate components of that list into your healing time and into reading this book, as you feel called. The language of the central nervous system is raw sensory data. When we bring components of this list into our healing spaces, we are communicating messages of safety and sacredness directly into our nervous system, creating an ideal environment for deep healing work.

Because once you dip into these concepts, a deep part of you is taking little sips and recognizing the archetypal material. Your soul may offer profound or repetitive dreams. You may begin to notice synchronicities related to those dreams. You may enter a new stage of your unfolding. You may step into the next chapter of a more soulful life. Books can be catalytic, even magickal, objects in this way. And now that you've been informed, let us take another slow and reverent step towards the underworld.

RITUALS & WRITING PROMPTS FOR YOUR OCEANIC LISTENING PRACTICE:

-To Get Clear on Your Intention:

You'll have days where you question this "living a more soulful life" business and it's all going to feel too hard and scary. Prepare for that in advance by setting a very strong, clear intention and identifying your deepest reasons why.

A simple, supply-free ritual would be to state out loud, "I intend to devote my spiritual practices and this process to the highest good of all beings, welcoming in only energies, at the right volume and pace, that are in alignment with this intention. And so it is." Or write it out and post it above your altar, or anywhere visible.

Set a strong intention (or say a prayer, if you prefer) in alignment with your heart's truest desire, and the most powerful things you could do for yourself, in this moment of your life. These days, the only prayer I say is, "Help me surrender to what love wants to do through me. Grant me the courage to be led by soul." You might go deeper and fill three whole journal pages with a daring, glorious written picture of what your life would look like if you were completely soul-led, abandoning yourself to the desires of your deepest self (not the desires you've picked up from Instagram, from the Joneses, from your parents, or from society), if you haven't already. You could fold these pages up and place them on your altar, pinned down by another sacred object, as a sort of letter to the divine. I have been amazed to find these old, folded, forgotten pages on my altar while cleaning or moving, and to find that every single thing on the list had come true.

Remember to get clear about what you are doing and why. For example, "I am integrating my inner artist in order to live my fullest life, which I know will be in alignment with the most authentic service I can offer to others, which is in alignment with the highest good of all." I am going to challenge you to keep asking yourself why until you hit an inner wellspring, a holy, essential why that makes you cry. You're going to have to really dig deep. It may require for you to ask yourself why up to seven times. (As in, "Why do you care about service to others?" "Because it makes life meaningful." "Why do you want a meaningful life?" etc., seven times.) Type up the why that made you cry and post it somewhere where you'll see it every day. Or make art about it or find a visual representation and place it on your altar.

-To Strengthen Your Sense of Self:
List ten things about you that have *always* been the case and will continue to be the case even if you lose your current job, or even

if your current business venture or marriage or whatever fails. You may want to ask for help from people who've known you for ten years or more. People who knew you when you were little are ideal. If you're having trouble coming up with more than one or two, then I urge you to seek support with working on *that* issue, first and foremost, before you dive into the type of deep transformational work that this book describes.

To take this even further, imagine the most beautiful things people could say about you at your funeral that you believe are actually true on some level. Write them down. What about the compliments you know you deserve, but which you've maybe never received? Write those down, too.

If you want to go all the way, you can record yourself reading those out loud three times, and listen to that recording every single morning for this entire process. You truly are a dear, unrepeatable, precious, radically original transmission. Allow yourself to feel and know that once in a while.

-To Catch a Glimpse of the Future:

Imagine you're able to look into a crystal ball and see the deepest, brightest possibilities for your near and distant future. What do you see? What flashes before your inner eye? Journal about this future version of you. Then answer these questions: Do you feel like you can still be yourself *and* be this new, powerful version? What is your image of what it means to be a more powerful and more empowered version of you? If there are any parts of that image you don't want, you don't have to have that!

-To Ensure Seaworthiness:

Take inventory of how well you are caring for yourself and your body these days. Where might you make little improvements? Please ensure that things are feeling pretty stable in your life and that you can practice basic self-care (three meals per day and roughly eight hours of sleep per night) before you dive deeper into this book. If things aren't feeling too stable or you aren't able to practice very basic self-care, focus on that before proceeding.

CHAPTER SEVEN

BUILDING AN INITIATION INTO VIRGIN WOMANHOOD

YOUR MAN CAN NEVER TOUCH YOU

WHERE THE MOON TOUCHES YOU.

(EXCERPT FROM A POEM IN ONE OF MY JOURNALS)

Here's a story that illustrates exactly how big of a dork I am. It starts with my decision to exit a three-year relationship with a man who I had hoped would become my husband and the father of my hypothetical-one-day children. A challenge which, at the time, felt completely fucking Augean. But I felt I had no choice. It was not an emotionally healthy relationship, and he was not willing to work on it with me.

At the time, lots of people I knew were getting married, including two out of my four brothers (one of them just a year older than me and the other one four years younger). I lived alone in a dinky studio apartment in the Tenderloin. It's a difficult place for a single woman to live alone. I had to call on my ability to dissociate at will, seeming to float a few feet over my body like a night bird while walking home at ungodly hours on some evenings. (At the time, I worked at a mental health agency that required I sometimes make myself available for 24/7 crisis calls. The calls sometimes required for me to get out of bed and physically go to the site of the crisis at any hour of the night. And the nearest monthly garaging was a few blocks away from my building.) Besides, it seemed like my century-old apartment was haunted with the ghosts of 1920s prostitutes and gangsters, or maybe the pioneers whose graves had been disturbed when the place was built, or the Ohlone Indians who once made the pre-colonial San Francisco Bay Area the most populous region in North America after what is now Mexico City.

I decided to use the privacy of my little, mysteriously gusty apartment to conduct a simple, quick ritual. It was not just any ritual. It was one that could easily be written off as a Millennial being grotesquely self-absorbed and narcissistic. But I don't see it that way. I'll explain why in a moment. I married myself.

I pulled a crimson red scarf over my head, like Mary Magdalene's veil or like a priestess of Inanna. It had been gifted to me by my grandmother, Jean Margaret Mahoney, many years before. And I lit a melted, chunky, red dragon's blood candle from a local witch shop and sat before the mirror and... This is where it gets pretty dorky, darling reader. I actually played a song from the *Game of Thrones* soundtrack, the one called "I am Hers, She is Mine," that plays during the The Young Wolf's secret nighttime wedding to his lovely bride. And, just like that scene from *Game of Thrones*, I repeated the words, *I am hers, she is mine.* Casting my gaze down at the candle and back up at my face in the mirror with each repetition until the song ended.

By the end of the song, it was as if a magickal working had actually taken place. I thought I looked a little different. Looking in the mirror at the end of the ritual, I saw a strong woman. A woman with whom I wouldn't mind spending my life. A woman who I would choose any day of the week, who I am committed to, and who I will never leave until I die.

I want you to try this. That's your assignment. Do it now. (If you don't have the ritual supplies, simply close your eyes now and imagine yourself performing the magickal working behind the snowy curtains of your own heart. Add your own flare, if you feel called.)

THANK YOU, ROMANTIC ERA

Our modern conceptualization of marriage in the West is only about 250 years old. It was birthed in the Romantic era, when it was considered a radical, progressive idea that two people should marry for love. Not only that, but the full Romantic era ideology about how this is all supposed to go involves some pretty whimsical beliefs to which reality rarely conforms. For example, there is a "special someone" out there who God put on earth just for you, and when you meet them "a special something" happens. It could be a fleeting glance on a train (the classic, Romantic era-inspired image), in an elevator (the more modern equivalent), or at a get together with friends. When you meet this person "you just know."

And not only that, but as your soul mate, they should desire you and only you forever. And sex should be an ongoing expression of your deep, inviolable love for one another. Within this paradigm, infidelity is high treason and is the most disastrous thing that could ever happen. Consider this alongside the modern phenomenon of fifty percent of marriages ending in divorce.

Allow me to soften this a little by admitting that the ideal long-term sexual situation for human adults is genuinely fraught. We are all different. Most adults in whom a sexual impulse lives and who want a long-term partnership, will almost invariably at some point (or various points) struggle to maintain fidelity to their partner, simply because they are a sexual and emotionally complex human being.

I wonder if there is a way we could view this as less of a moral disaster. The reason this is fraught, however, is that polyamory and open relationships are not for everyone. So I would never want to prescribe them as the universal solution. For some people, forays into polyamory and opening their relationship to other partners may cause emotional turmoil, chaos, and pain. It appears the most humane approach is to view this as a case-by-case type of deal. And relationships evolve. It seems like a matter of what is right for a given couple at a given time.

Before the Romantic era, in most parts of the world, marriage was about property. It was about the co-management of an estate and about procreation. Love did not really need to enter the equation. Love, romance, and great sex were reserved for extramarital dalliances on the side, usually the socially acceptable province of men only. So, the Romantic era notion that one should marry for love was quite revolutionary and beautiful, my Piscean heart admits.

But what an audacious idea: That one person could complete you, be your best friend, your best lover, and your co-conspirator in all of life's ventures. That you could live together in genuine, authentic happiness and deep sexual fulfillment, and without any major issues or unhappiness. *It does genuinely happen* just often enough to deepen the allure of what is already a very alluring idea.

It fascinates me that more and more people are questioning the singular validity of our current, Romantic era conceptualization of marriage, and that alternative lifestyles and life partnerships are being considered and discussed on a collective level like never before. Also note, this is all taking place at the end of the Age of Pisces. The Romantic era concept of marriage strikes me as highly Piscean: This idea that you have your one true beloved who you must live with and hold on to until death, denying any other urges or curiosities that would lead you astray from the marital bed, even suffering for the marriage if needed.

I do respect this endeavor, and I don't want to disparage it. It's just that it seems love and mating in the Age of Aquarius will involve individuals becoming one-unto-themselves and having multiple life partners (simultaneously or consecutively) or just one or none. In any case, there will be a rainbow of choices, and they will choose consciously, not out of cultural or familial necessity or press ganging.

Speaking of choosing consciously, what do you want? I mean, *really*. If it's between you and your own soul, what do you desire for your life in this domain of romance, marriage, sex, and parenthood? It may take you some time to really dig deep and come up with your truest answer to this question. I had to use deep meditation and visualization to figure out what it is for me. Set all familial and cultural messages aside entirely, unless upholding your culture is one of your primary values. Get clear on what you value (in the realm of sex, love, life partnership, and romance) and how you can live in alignment with that. *What you authentically value*, not what someone else values. It's the best way to invite happiness to flutter through the garden of your life.

Whatever your answer is, it couldn't hurt to marry yourself first, could it? I'm a licensed mental health professional. I'm telling you it won't hurt. The worst thing that might happen is that you feel a little silly afterwards. It's good for you to be a little uncomfortable and feel a little silly from time to time. It keeps you humble. Let this ritual of commitment to yourself be your real initiation into womanhood. Dress it up however you want. Get down on one knee. Offer yourself a sparkling garnet ring. Take yourself to your favorite hiking spot or restaurant or down to the sea floor in your scuba gear. Will you? Yes, yes, yes.

ROMANTIC ERA MARRIAGES AND WOMEN'S SELF-IMAGE

The idea of marriage bequeathed to us by the Romantic era is lovely. But, like everything, it casts some shadows. One is that it perpetuates the idea that a woman's final arrival in life is a man. All genders are given the message that finding a marital partner is one of the holy grails of life. But this idea is especially problematic for women, and *especially* modern women.

Ever since the 1960s Women's Liberation era, women have been getting more and more educated and have been climbing the ranks to higher and higher stations in the professional world. And along with those shifts, the average age of women getting married and becoming mothers has steadily increased. In some families (such as in mine), Grandma got married and had her first baby at around age twenty. Mom got married at twenty-four and had her first baby at twenty-eight. But many Millennial women, especially in places with a high cost of living (like San

Francisco) do not have their first baby until age thirty-seven or thirty-eight. Those are drastic shifts taking place in just three generations.

And yet, the cultural idea of when women are "supposed to" get married and have children remains basically the same. And that idea comes from a time before women were getting PhDs, running businesses, or becoming Vice President. It comes from a time of profound woundedness of the feminine, frankly. Attaining to these high educational and professional stations takes many years of intensive labor and unswerving devotion. You're lucky if you find the right life partner through happenstance as you're climbing those mighty professional mountains.

But sometimes you don't. And *if you even want that*, searching for it then becomes its own significant side project. And if you want to do it all before the end of your naturally most fertile years, you are going to have to be a little bit of a warrior. This is something that no one ever told me.

It seems to be one of a number of aspects of the female experience that are enshrouded in silence, and that we must stumble on in solitary surprise. However, the void where loving guidance and preparation should be can be accounted for (in my case at least) by the fact that my mother and grandmother simply did not know. Neither of them had attempted to attain post graduate degrees *and* found and run thriving businesses *and* write books before getting married or becoming mothers.

They were both blessed to have wonderful men get down on one knee before graduation day (in my grandmother's case) and *on* graduation day (in my mother's case).

My grandmother completed her bachelor's degree and walked on graduation day already married with a baby in her belly under her gown. Legend has it, she was up and about two days after giving birth in a darling little designer dress that showed off her waist while she vacuumed. She worked sometimes as a travel agent but mostly didn't work and didn't need to.

My mother got engaged on her graduation night after completing her master's degree. And a few years later, she was pregnant with the first of her five children. From then on, she switched from full-time mothering to part-time working and back to full-time working again when we were teenagers. She began professionally self-actualizing in earnest after her children were mostly grown.

I believe I am not alone here. In many cases, Millennial women who attempt to professionally self-actualize before prioritizing a life partnership and starting a family are the first in their families to ever do so. And in these cases, applying classic standards about when a woman is "supposed to" be married and having babies could almost be classified as cruel.

So, the world is not only still processing what it looks like when a woman is both fully empowered *and* fully expressed from her depths (not trying to fit into a man-suit). The world is also still figuring out that traditional marriage-and-mothering timelines often place extreme pressure on women who highly value their ability to actualize their unique vocation.

A MORE NURTURING ATTITUDE TOWARDS LOVE, SEX, MARRIAGE, AND ROMANCE

PEOPLE ARE IN OUR LIVES FOR A REASON, A SEASON, OR A LIFETIME.

-SOPHIA NELSON, *THE WOMAN CODE*

My dream is for women to have a much healthier, more deeply nourishing and fabulous attitude about marriage and relationships. It looks like this: If someone asks you *again* who your "guy" is (or tells you they're surprised you're not married yet, or says you shouldn't feel bad for not being married yet, or they indicate in any way that you must've gotten something wrong somewhere along the way if you're "still single"), I pray you look them in the eye and say something radical and true from your heart, from the depths of your pussy. Even if it totally electrifies them or splits their ribs open with God. It could be something like this, "There have been many great loves in my life and, mercifully, the government hasn't gotten in on all of them. Have you ever been to a sex party?"

Love, in any one of its vexing forms, is a grace, a perfectly gratuitous instance of Beauty, like a butterfly's wing. It liberates. The ways it challenges us to liberate ourselves and others are always unique. It should always be considered a "success" that we are able to love at all, whatever kind of frame that love came in.

So even your past breakups and romantic detours were successes. You loved hard. You lived. That's a success.

You can take this nourishing stance even further by imagining you are bringing all of your favorite, remarkable people with you (in spirit) into family gatherings or any situation where you believe you may have to face any of this. The great Maya Angelou actually advised this in a famous lecture, specifically regarding any challenging situation, like a job interview. Bring the ancestors. Families and groups need people who deviate from their expectations. Those people are the artists, the ones who keep things colorful and vital, the ones who push the family consciousness forward.

Now imagine that Maya Angelou is a part of your family. Can you imagine greeting the great Maya Angelou at a family gathering, and one sentence in, asking her, "So, who's your guy these days?" I don't think you can imagine that. I don't think anyone can. No one wonders about that because she was so great and so robust, so complete. Does it ever cross your mind who her partner was? It is utterly not important or essential to her completion or to the fact of her character and greatness.

In some ways, the heroine's journey is about coming to realize that you yourself are the grail. It's about coming to realize that you contain within you all you'll ever need to find your way through any dark woods, to be on your exalted path, to experience love within your own heart, and to know the next step forward, and then the next. It is about coming to realize that you contain the holy of holies.

This does not mean the heroine sits on her ass and suddenly realizes she is a treasure beyond measure. No, no. She must also journey, and her journey is fierce. (Remember that journeys can be external *or* internal. Sometimes the heroine goes so far in that she's far out.) If you value yourself highly, you will realize your love is the holy city. It is the communion with the divine at the central tabernacle of your being. You only open that tabernacle (as far as romantic love goes) to someone who shows themselves worthy. I've had to learn this the hard way, and I don't want that for you. According to *The Woman Code*, you should know someone for at least an entire year before becoming romantically involved! That may not be your jam, but still worth considering.

As far as mystic love or agape love goes (on the other hand), no one really needs to demonstrate themselves worthy of that. You emanate that far and wide every time you are kind, loving, or compassionate. Please, please, be a "holy whore" when it comes to that kind of love, while honoring your own boundaries, of course.

BECOMING VIRGIN:

You must all, somewhere deep in your hearts, believe that you have a special beauty that is like no other and that is so valuable that you must not abandon it. Indeed, you must learn to cherish it.

— Sophia Loren, *Women & Beauty*

It would be wise for us to establish Virginity before working with the magnitudes. Sound paradoxical? Listen, we're not talking about never-had-sex-before virginity, you marvelous miscreant! We are talking about the ancient, archetypal capital-V Virginity. Virgin with a capital-V means "she who is one unto herself." Think of the Vestal Virgins who guarded the holy, eternal fire at the temples of Vesta. They were priestesses. They did not need a human partner to "complete" them. The station of Priestess is already robustly complete. It is a full circle, not a semicircle. And that is what we become as Virgin women: A full circle. Perhaps a circle with a rift in it, to be more accurate. No one has no need of other people. It might be the human condition to have an irrevocable hurt place of sympathy, an empty space of holy longing that sweetens the tide of intimacy.

We can contain our holy longing and also be Virgin in the virgin rainforest sense. We can be a wild place of power that is completely untouched, governed by its own laws, and unspoiled by the agendas, exploitations, and monopolies of pooplords. Visitors are welcome in virgin rainforests. But they must respect the primal power of the place and revere the delicate web of sense and balance it manufactures and sustains in its own precious way. They must never dream of meddling with the way that the forest maintains this delicate web. Take the pipelines out, end the rampant disrespect and destruction, dethrone the despots, and the forest becomes virgin again. She knows how to heal herself.

Marrying yourself is one step in the project of becoming Virgin. The rainforest must be given back to herself, recognizing

Heal Your Witch Wound

she needs those power plants and factory farms like she needs an asshole on her elbow. The next part of the project involves allowing the self-healing processes of the forest to be allowed to unfold.

SPIRITUAL DIMENSIONS OF SELF-LOVE

Here is where I'm going to explain why marrying yourself and committing to loving yourself should not be written off as some kind of Millennial snowflake narcissism. Your relationship with yourself is the single most important relationship in your life. You are the wonderful person who has helped you stay alive long enough to be reading these words. You are the person with whom you came into the world, and with whom you will depart. You are the person who has been through every last moment of each of the struggles and adversities of your life. One breath at a time. It was all you.

Loving yourself is not about self-aggrandizement or "being all about yourself." It is not about prideful arrogance either. It is about caring for yourself as a loving parent would. It can refer to a gentle attitude or stance towards the self, and it can also refer to ongoing gentle action towards the self (the way a parent consistently loves and nurtures their child). We can wrap self-appreciation and self-compassion into this as well. Committing yourself to self-love is not about prioritizing yourself so much that you neglect, hurt, or renege on your responsibilities to others. I don't believe a loving parent would guide their child to do that. Through true self-love, you are learning to be a loving parent to yourself.

Self-love is not self-cherishing, a term from the Buddhist tradition—a viewpoint that reinforces the ego. Self-love may actually do the opposite—it may challenge the ego, believe it or not. True self-love wants what's best for the soul. The self-love that wants what's best for the soul is like a through-line to the energy of Holy Mother within. This *is* the little doll that Vasilisa's mother gave her, like an extension of herself. Self-love is a vitally important aspect of becoming intuitive. Self-love is how you tap transpersonal loving wisdom itself, as it applies to your own life. When you direct and guide your life from that place, you will never lose your way.

Furthermore, the pathological schemas, thoughts, and beliefs, which undergird anxiety and depression (and may be present alongside many other mental health concerns) frequently involve uniquely tailored ways of negative, cruel, or maladaptive self-relating. If you want to be significantly anxious or depressed, keep being mean to yourself. Don't listen to me.

The expression, "Your own cup has to be full first," has become such common knowledge that it verges on annoying when repeated. Here's a better thought exercise. Imagine some of the most loving and compassionate beings who have ever walked the face of the planet. Think of some who are living today or who lived recently so you can conjure images you may have seen of them. I think of Anandamayi Ma, Amma the Hugging Saint,

Thich Nhat Hanh, and His Holiness the Dalai Lama. What do you think their internal environment is like? Do you think they are filled with self-reproach, absorbed in hating themselves, or busy tossing insults around inside their private mental theater, saying things like, *You're a piece of shit; You're ugly; You're an idiot?*

I seriously doubt it. One does not exude that level of palpable compassion and love when one is filled with the jagged barbed wire of relentless self-reproach. People tend to talk to others the way they talk to themselves. The meanest, most critical person you know? The inside of their head is probably an awful place to live. The most resplendently compassionate and loving people you've ever seen? Their inner world is probably a garden of love and compassion that they tend daily. They are overflowing with it. Imagine yourself overflowing with it.

Now, I know self-love sounds like a lovely, abstract idea. How do you get some of that for yourself? This is one of those things, like forgiveness or self-worth, you have to *decide* to cultivate. And then work on it. When it comes to self-love, I want you to take all negative connotations away from the word "work" because this is going to feel good. But it is going to be a practice. A simple and beautiful one.

This is a practice I picked up from the spiritual teacher and YouTuber, Teal Swan. Here's what you do. You pick a day on the calendar. It could be today, tomorrow, or any day you like. And you decide that, starting on that day and for 365 days onward, you are going to ask yourself a tiny little question before every single decision you make, no matter how tiny or seemingly insignificant. It could be a totally minor choice between types of produce at the grocery store. The question is, "What would someone who loved herself do?"

When you begin this practice, something amazing will happen, usually about two or three weeks in: You will start to feel like you are in good company with yourself. You will start to feel like you've reactivated your own divine GPS, and it's going to take you somewhere good as long as you keep listening to it. You will start to feel like you're going to be all right after all, no matter what happens with this relationship, or that potential crisis. You will realize you cannot, you will not, ever go back to your old ways.

If you ever forget or fall off the bandwagon, no cause for concern. Just gently bring yourself back. A loving, gentle parent doesn't require perfection, do they? Stuff may come up for you around this idea, like, *Oh my God, I can't do that. I'm gonna get in trouble doing that!* With who? It could be something else. This is one of those segments of your journey where one-on-one support from a mentor, therapist, or other healer is really valuable in case anything is getting in the way of your being able to practice this.

Most of us are not practiced at loving ourselves and can hardly even visualize what it would look like to love ourselves. That's okay because asking yourself this little question over and over again, day after day, causes you to imagine yourself into whatever the correct answer is *for you*. You don't need to identify as someone who loves herself now. You're doing what *someone* who loved herself would do. And after you've practiced this for about one year, it will become your natural way of being. You will have literally wired it in neurologically. Of course, you may backslide from time to time, but you can always bring yourself back. That's what someone who loved herself would do. The practice grounds self-love into everyday life, into the body. It forces a gentle pattern change, which is all healing really is.

Ram Dass advocated for practicing self-acceptance, or self-allowance, before working up to self-love. This is a valuable idea, too. You may start by experimenting with *allowing* yourself. Whatever it is about yourself that you get really down on, you're *allowed* to be that. Anyone who says you're not can go remove the hair from across their ass. Hmm, *what would someone who allowed herself do?* A deliciously dangerous question!

Ultimately, I want you to fall head over heels in love with the wild, brave part of you who shows you all the ways you're not free, the part of you that shows you the way to life and loving again. That part of you *wants* to be here, both feet on the earth. That part of you is sort of like your personal Empress, your personal Queen of Life. We'll return to her later.

LOVE: THE GREATEST MYSTERY OF ALL

THE MYSTERY OF LOVE IS GREATER THAN THE

MYSTERY OF DEATH.

-OSCAR WILDE

Now we're going to ground this in the mystical. Love is universal, like consciousness or water. Love is love. Fill yourself with it (with genuine, real, deep love and friendship towards yourself), and you will exude love. Real love, unforced love. *Real* love for yourself is qualitatively and radically different from narcissism, irresponsibly self-serving behavior, self-absorption, or letting other people down when they're counting on you. If you can summon and cultivate that, you will be filled with love itself. That makes it so much easier for kindness and real love for others to spill out of you. And that is qualitatively different from artificial, forced niceness. It's the real thing.

Asking yourself, *What would someone who loved herself do*, every day for a year is one indispensable practice for grounding loving behavior towards yourself into your neural pathways. But how can you really *feel* love in your heart and cultivate that, pressing the love button all day or whenever you want? Good question. Let's explore that.

We are going to extend the radical spiritual heresy of some of the greatest female mystics to this whole self-love thing. Those ladies who straddled the heretic-saint-mystic lines back in the days when they would burn people at the stake for all

189

types of shit. The common heretical thread among them is this idea that you don't need any institution or (virtually always male) representative of any institution to act as an intermediary between yourself and the divine. Now I want you to add the word "partner" to that list. You don't need a partner in order to experience the love of the divine in your heart.

Ram Dass spoke about this too. If you've ever fallen in love, I'm sure you can pinpoint a moment, or maybe several, when you felt a love so vast it almost terrified you and threatened to rip you apart or explode you into a million little pink stars to hang in the night sky forever. Do you remember that? Ever felt a love that completely bowled you over, knocked you out, split you right down your center? I'm sure you have. And you associate the person who triggered this explosion of love in your heart and across your being with that very love, as if they were the only source of it. And you must see them again, and again, and again. You can't get enough of them. You want them all to yourself, the miraculous source of this life-altering earthquake of love you once felt. You probably continue to feel it with this person in various forms. The tiniest little thing, almost imperceptible, might trigger a powerful surge of deep empathy centered squarely on the person you love.

And it's not that this person doesn't have anything to do with that love. They do. We all have everything to do with love. We are mistaken, however, when we believe they are the singular source of the love-surge experience. The culture and popular media would have us believe that they are. That in order to know the mystical, psychedelic, blissful state of being "in love," we must find some special person and fall in love with them.

I call bullshit. You can be in love right now. You can live in love. Nothing feels better. I confess I don't do it perfectly, or all the time, and I could ramp my practice up for sure. But let's talk practices for ramping this up, and for cultivating the love of the divine in your heart at any time. This is the most important technology we have.

Sit quietly and bring your awareness to your breath. After a few breaths, drop your awareness down into your heart and just hold it there for a minute or so. Sometimes there is a natural sweetness that sits in the heart space and you may feel subtle hints of it when you bring your awareness there, or you may not, and that's okay too. You may feel some sadness, or anything else that your heart has been holding. With your awareness in your heart space, I want you to bring to mind images (whether they are actual memories or photographs you've seen) that represent moments you were perfectly, deeply, completely loved. Or they could represent love itself, or they could be certain, special images of your loved ones. Choose the ones that have love electricity for you. The ones that are most likely to cause some kind of sensation in your heart at any point in the day if you think of them.

And now I want you to place those images at the center of your heart and allow yourself to feel every deep feeling of love associated with them, with no bars held. Not only that, but consciously intend to savor and strengthen the feeling. Most people aren't aware that they have the power to *choose* to savor and strengthen any feeling they want. Savor it. Keep adding breath, focus, and energy to it. Intend for it to strengthen. It will.

And that's it. You can milk that for as long as you want. I suppose I have to make a sort of epistemological leap here by telling you I believe all love is love, and all love is divine. So when a thought of a family member or anyone else triggers that deep feeling of love in your heart, it is the love of the divine. It *is* the divine, or God if you prefer, or the Great Mystery. Whatever you want to call it, it is always available to you, and it lives in your heart. You do not need an intermediary of any kind. You have direct access. Calling your love for your father or your child the love of the divine does not depersonalize it. It is highly personal. But the love in your heart is you, and it is so much more than you. It is an inlet that connects to a vast ocean. It is all the same water.

There may come a time when you are practicing this and you are moved to tears, or you are suddenly surprised or bowled over by a powerful wave of love that exceeds anything you were even trying to feel or cultivate. It may happen during regular meditation, when you are not even trying. And in those moments, you may realize that the love of your family, your ancestors, loved ones living and deceased, and people you've never met, continues to live, eternally, and is being directed towards you at all times, though you may not always feel it. And when that big wave of the love of all those people comes towards you all at once, you realize it cannot be other than the love of the divine. Each of those people was just a different face or character being worn by the divine for a time, and behind everything was always this singular, vast, overpowering love. It won't happen every single time, so don't feel like you fucked up if this overwhelming tidal wave of love doesn't wash over you the first time you sit down to meditate. But if you keep practicing, it will. If you keep living, it will.

The profound importance I place on cultivating love within the heart certainly puts me way outside of the "normal" mental health professional box, which is okay, because I'm moving beyond that box now anyway. (Even if that means I just continue to be a racy, weird therapist.) It's the skin I am currently shedding. We don't teach people about this in school. Rather, we teach them through culture and the media that we can only get love through outside sources. And people wonder why they feel so empty, so filled with craving, and so beset by itches that will never stop itching.

By connecting women to the mystic love in their own hearts, I am doing something considered radical within the last 2000 years. In the beautiful work of Meggan Watterson, I learned that legend has it that Mary Magdalene was "lifted up seven times each day by the angels." I believe we are lifted up by the angels every time we go into our hearts. We could all take a leaf from the book of Thecla who walked straight into the river and baptized herself after Saint Paul told her she "wasn't ready." Take this power back for yourself. You already have it. The holy of holies is right here in your own heart. It always was, and it always will be. You don't have to wait. You are ready.

Once you've cultivated this love, it's yours to share and spread. We are cultivating mystic, femtheogenic love, for ourselves and for the world. *Loving* the world in this way doesn't have to mean that every part of the world earns your stamp of approval. It means you *care for it*. You *give a fuck* what happens to all the precious living beings here.

"Happily ever after" happens when you meet your divinity and get on the exalted path of a loving relationship to yourself, and therefore, a loving relationship to all who are blessed to be around you. Happily ever after happens when you allow this wild love, this love that requires no institution, no religion, no intermediary, no other person, to fill you to overflowing on the inside. It's the greatest revenge against institutions of oppression, against anything and everything that ever sought to trample on, dim, or destroy the human heart, soul, and spirit.

It's a choice that appears dangerous to most institutions and dominator cultures because it flies in the face of the rhythms and mottos that hold their structures in place. It's why people who have found a way to live in wild love forever are often persecuted, exiled, stamped out, or even executed. This is a threat to the powers that be. But don't be afraid. The world is changing. And the truly fearful thing is to come to the end of your life never having lived, never having enacted your divine capacities as a human being.

MEET YOUR INNER MASCULINE

In the process of becoming Virgin, it helps to meet your inner masculine and integrate his energy in service to this deep, soulful part of you that really wants to express. (Remember that we're all a blend of both energies, whatever you want to call them.) He may have already appeared in your dreams. He often does when you begin a process like this or begin some new, big project. He often seems bright or filled with light or love, somehow, and he seems totally, utterly devoted to you. Or he may show up as a man in your dreams for whom you have a curious longing. This is your own internal masculine energy, and it is energy that wants to live in service to your dreams, your creative projects, and your more soulful life. This is the energy that will send your manuscript to fifty different publishers, that will push you onto the stage to read your poems out loud, or that would have you share your artwork publicly.

A fun thing you could do is call to mind the last time you met a man and either had a flash-in-the-pan instantly "in love" experience (if you're into men romantically) or otherwise felt magnetically drawn to him, hypnotized by him, or strongly compelled by him in some other way. What was it about him? What were the qualities (actual or imagined) that really got your goat?

Now, how can you integrate those qualities into yourself and into your own life? For example, I was once ultra-attracted to a man who had lots of tattoos. It was like he had this electric sexual power over me, but he was also being a total butt. I thought, *Well, I guess maybe that's what my inner man looks like. Let me book a tattoo appointment for myself...* This may seem superficial, but I don't think so. I always considered my tattoos to be a hyper-romantic teenage marriage to my dissent. It can be anything at all. The type of work he does. The way he speaks, the way he moves, whatever you imagine his foreign travels to entail. Distil whatever that alluring masculine essence is for you and integrate it. In your own way.

This might bring some stuff up for you if you have been wounded or traumatized by people who represent the masculine in your life, or if your own inner masculine is wounded. (Hint: It usually is, in just about everyone, regardless of gender.) If this is bringing stuff up, please seek the support of a healer or therapist.

Something to know about your inner masculine: We all have various internal "parts" and the masculine parts can be healthy or unhealthy, expressing on the high side or on the low side. Sometimes our inner masculine takes on a hyperactive squire kind of energy, hooking into all the overcaffeinated messages of capitalism, wanting to enlist all of his drive and dynamism behind ensuring we "hunt well" and hit all the marks within this cultural framework. But in all of that surface-y dynamism and stampeding, something more delicate can get trampled, something I call the feminine soul. The healthy internal configuration is for the inner masculine to bend the knee and pledge his sword to her, following her royal decree way before adhering to the frenzy of external, patriarchal standards, values, and dictates. We'll get deeper into this internal ecology of dynamic forces and "parts" in the next chapter.

RITUALS & WRITING PROMPTS FOR YOUR OCEANIC LISTENING PRACTICE:

- Do the self-marriage ritual outlined in this chapter if you haven't already.
- Commit to a continual self-love practice.
- Commit to a daily pleasure practice while you're at it.
- Use the practice detailed in this chapter for cultivating a feeling of divine love in your heart.
- Integrate and start getting to know your inner masculine (by journaling about ways he's appeared in dreams, or about men who've had a hold on you over the years, then about ways you could distil the essence of that "menergy" in your life). Reference the final section of this chapter for this practice.

CHAPTER EIGHT

A PLAN FOR FEAR AND OTHER BAD LEADERS

THERE IS NO COMING TO CONSCIOUSNESS WITHOUT PAIN.
PEOPLE WILL DO ANYTHING, NO MATTER HOW ABSURD, IN
ORDER TO AVOID FACING THEIR OWN SOUL. ONE DOES NOT
BECOME ENLIGHTENED BY IMAGINING FIGURES OF LIGHT BUT BY
MAKING THE DARKNESS CONSCIOUS.

-C. G. JUNG

Inevitably, whenever we begin to move in the direction of a more soulful life, take responsibility for our talents, or try to come out of any closet, fear comes a knockin'. Fear also tends to make a special appearance whenever we are moving towards greater authenticity, making moves to step into the life of our dreams, or bringing a creative project to life. Fear and resistance will point directly towards those moves our souls are dying to make, like little compass needles. Fear is usually telling us something like this:

This is the life you know. This is the persona you're comfortable with. You know how to navigate this life. This persona has helped you survive up to this point. Change it, and will you really be safe? Will you survive?

Resistance shares a front lawn with fear, and usually says shit like this:

It's not really a good idea. People will laugh at you. You'll fail, and it will be disastrous on multiple levels. There's no point. Your ideas suck. You're not worth it. Who do you think you are, anyway?

Believe it or not, *lots* of people let these internal forces completely rule their lives. They might not even be aware that they're doing it. You can't blame them. It really can feel uniquely challenging and scary to live more soulfully. Sometimes, it might even feel like you're losing your mind or you're blowing up your life. Good Lord, who wants that? Living a soul-led life is not always an easy-peasy crystal staircase.

In some ways, it truly *is* easier to let fear rule your life. But, paradoxically, it's also harder. A lot harder. Why? Because that gnawing emptiness at the core of your being isn't going anywhere. You can find other ways to deal with it, ways to numb yourself, to run away from yourself, or to drown yourself in conventionally accepted forms of zombification (like binge watching Netflix while you gorge yourself on Cheetos, for example). You can take the edge off, or you can *listen* to the edge and remember that the best form of self-soothing is always to make the bold, unusual, glorious choice to follow your bliss.

Marion Woodman shares a wonderful analogy for psychoanalysis in *Sitting by the Well*, a series of interviews with Tami Simon. She observes that a good, yearlong episode of analysis can feel like a slow trek through a very thick jungle. Each step requires for you to whack down a branch or two or several. And each branch has little messages and symbols inscribed upon it. You survey each one with care, taking stock of recurring themes. Gradually, unique threads of connection, insight, and meaning on your journey of soul-making become clear.

At a certain point, though, you get tired. It all feels like so much hard work. You wonder when you'll be done. You can sense some kind of clearing ahead. When you finally arrive, you see it is actually a river. And on the other side of the river, what you see is horrible: It's just more of the same horrendously thick overgrowth. You fall to your knees, ready to completely give up. Just then, you notice that someone is standing there on the other side of the river. And you realize that another part of you has been moving towards you this entire time.

This part I call soul, or the part of you that can easily navigate the underworld realms, the realm of the gods. You haven't yet reached whatever inner citadel you have longed to encounter, but you have finally reached a point where you can link arms with your soul. And you can trust that there is a way forward, and that it won't be quite so difficult from this point on.

Hopefully Woodman's beautiful metaphor reassures you that choosing a soulful, authentic life will not, and should not, feel like constant upheaval and pure difficulty. Not at all. It may bring some sense of upheaval and difficulty in the beginning, but it doesn't have to. It depends on you: where you are in your life now, how alienated you are from yourself, and how much of this work you may have already done. Just, whatever you do, do not allow fear or resistance to convince you that choosing a soulful life will mean that you will be constantly working like a dog doing arcane, inner work for no reward. Don't let fear or resistance tell you that soulful living is the primrose path to poverty, hardship, and disrepute.

When I was going through my quarter life crisis, I had the wonderful fortune to have lunch with a professional composer, and he told me, "Whatever you would do for free is the thing you are going to make the most money doing." It doesn't matter if making lots of money is important to you or not. I am sharing this to inject you with an alternate viewpoint that will set those little fear-based messages reeling. And the viewpoint the composer shared with me only seems more and more true as I continue to encounter people with the ovaries to step onto their artist path, or their more soulful path in whatever form it takes.

Earlier, I had indicated that we can think of your transformation process as a sacred cauldron. It is important for there to be containment and the right amount of heat. We want to keep the process going, but we don't want you to feel like you're falling to pieces as you go through it. We want to keep the process hot and alive, but we don't want things to get to a rolling boil and start sloshing feminine mysteries potion everywhere.

Add to those elements of containment and the right amount of heat a plan for resistance and fear because resistance and fear will happen, invariably, and have the potential to pour sand on the whole thing. External circumstances and people who are not up to speed with the new, more soulful version of you will very likely begin to drop away, either of their own accord or because you may choose to extricate yourself. Are you ready for that? Be honest with yourself. This is why I continue to repeat that you need to make sure you are supported and that you have your self-care and spiritual practice locked down. If you do not, or if you are under a ton of pressure already as the result of preexisting upheavals or chaos in your life, then you may not be ready to follow the white rabbit of a feminine mysteries initiation at this time. Listen to your own gut, please, for the love of all things sacred.

Author Liz Gilbert shared an idea in an interview that the point is not to get rid of fear or kick fear in the face or anything silly like that. The point is to have a healthy relationship with fear because, I hate to break it to you, but fear will be coming along for the ride. It's just that fear does not get to drive. It doesn't even get to sit in the front passenger seat. Fear can sit in its little baby seat in the back of the car with a pacifier. We can thank fear for helping us to survive this long and for doing its best to ensure we do not step in front of any buses or get eaten by an alligator. *Thank you, fear! So glad to be alive!* But fear's job ends there.

It's important to remember that fear and resistance are both totally universal and totally normal. We just need to have a plan for them when they rear their heads, and they will.

Here's a fear plan: Think of fear as a dance partner. Once in a while, you are twirled across the dance floor into fear's arms. *Oh, hi, fear! I know you. We danced only a moment ago. Hello again.* And that's it. We often mistake fear itself with the thing we fear. Fear is not that. It has no teeth, no perilous chasms. Fear cannot hurt you. You have the power to let it burn through. *Thank you, fear! Thank you for keeping me alive! Now, are you securely strapped into your baby seat back there? Okay, good.*

It may be helpful to realize that courage and bravery would not exist without fear. Fear is baked into the very concepts of courage and bravery. You are courageous, and you are brave, when you feel fear, and you act anyway, doing what you know in your heart and soul needs to be done. If someone out there is truly "fearless," I don't know if I find that as compelling as the story of a human being who feels the full spectrum of messy human emotion, and who still does the shit that the most divine parts of them tell them to do anyway.

The Irish word for "fearless" actually translates more directly to "shadowless" (someone who has come to see and fill their shadow with the light of awareness). That's what this book is about: slowly filling the shadow (namely, the enshadowed feminine) with the light of love and consciousness (like Anandamayi Ma's name, which means light-filled / joy-permeated). Because once we've done that, then we really know what we need to do and have courage for. "Fearless" isn't as accurate as "shadowless."

Here's a resistance plan: Think of resistance as walls that your psyche throws up in front of deeper insight and in front of courageous steps into the unknown, or towards your deepest dreams and desires. Rather than trying to bulldoze that wall, we are going to say, *Oh, a wall! Wonderful! This is progress. We have met an internal part. This one is a wall. Let's love that wall, get to know it, see what is inscribed on it, and survey the type of stone used, all with love. This is where we are on our journey. We are at the wall.*

Fear might especially come up for women when stepping into their power and choosing a more soul-led life. It might have something to do with millennia of being killed for stepping out of line, or getting too big for our britches, or living in our passion. This is all part of the witch wound. But it doesn't mean we can't overcome it. We can. We can choose to be truly, deeply courageous, and leverage all the genius and magick in that choice.

NAMING THE NOTHING AND THE MOONCHILD

Within each of us there is a creative force that gets new, exciting ideas, nurtures desire and pleasure, and wants to run towards all that supports new life. This is the otherworldly part that "conceives" the idea for your next business venture, book, art project, or band. And within *most* of us there is a practical part that is concerned about making "reasonable" or "responsible" choices. This part tends to care deeply for the creative muse part, but sometimes believes it knows better. And within each of us there is a force that destroys creativity. It's the one that tells you your ideas suck, that no one cares anyway, and that you're embarrassing. This is what Steven Pressfield refers to (in *The War of Art*) as Resistance. The "practical" part sometimes makes deals with Resistance, thinking that what the little hobgoblin is selling might actually be some real, true stuff.

This universal internal dynamic is reflected in so many classic fairy tales. It can be hugely redemptive to apply this classic fairy tale configuration to your own inner landscape in order to track what's going on and who's running the show.

Recently, I applied the plotline of *The Neverending Story* to the same internal dynamic. Atreyu, the young warrior, must rescue The Childlike Empress and her realm from a destructive, faceless force called The Nothing. She implores him to give her a new name and to call it out, affirming the preciousness of her oracular wisdom over and above patriarchal, worldly, "practical" concerns. And he finds the internal gumption to meet the

206

challenge, running to the window in the form of the little boy reader, and shouting "Mooooooon chiiiiiiild!" into the storm. The Childlike Empress, Moonchild, is your feminine soul, your speck of the magnitude. She has been called by many names. It is time for all of us to say Her name and help to save the lunar soul of the world.

Think of Resistance and The Nothing as the same thing. Think of them as internal hobgoblins, if you like. Fear is certainly in cahoots with this internal force. But there's more to it because it comes with all kinds of messages about how you suck, how it's pointless anyway, how everyone will hate you, and how you should just keep doing the things that kill your soul. The spell is broken every time we are able to identify this internal force and name it for what it is.

Conversely, you call Moonchild's name every time you drop in and hear Her messages, the messages of the feminine soul. You call Her name every time you affirm Her wisdom, and put Her in Her rightful place as sovereign ruler of your internal realm. You call Her name every time you trust Her creative visions, which She receives like lilies from the otherworld, and which can only take life in Her hand.

You may find it helpful to unpack the most important players in the internal drama of creativity and what they've been up to lately in your journal. On a journal page, write, "Atreyu" with two lines under it, then do the same for "Moonchild," and, "The Nothing." Then, write what that part of you is saying, or has been saying to you lately. You could do the same using the characters of a story or fairy tale that resonates with you more. Here's an example.

Atreyu: You should keep revising your book since it's your first book and that's a big deal. Don't want to put anything out there that's cheesy, crumby, or slapped together.

Moonchild: This book has a beating heart and it's calling to the hearts of your readers. Let it be born. Forget yourself, and let your life flower open.

The Nothing: You're embarrassing, and you'll never be as cool as Patti Smith. People will probably laugh at you. They'll get mad at you. This whole thing was a bad idea.

THE GREAT TABOO OF DEATH, AND THE CONSPIRACY OF BUSY-NESS

I AM WRITING THIS BOOK BECAUSE WE ARE ALL GOING TO DIE.

-JACK KEROUAC

Death is one of the most taboo subjects in our culture, almost as taboo as sex was in the Victorian era. All things linked to magick, mystery, sex, the body, and our connection to the chaos and life/death/life cycle of the earth have typically been enshadowed in the West. This has been the case for at least the last two millennia, and maybe since around or before the dawn of agriculture.

Here is one of the Western taboos I will ask you to bravely bring back up from underground (no pun intended!) in this process. I, too, am writing this book because we are all going to die. And isn't that amazing?

Think about it for a moment. There will come a time, no one knows when, when you will cease to be. I know we don't love thinking about it. But no one knows what is on the other side of this life. It is as pure a mystery as mysteries come. It is the ultimate mystery initiation. The time will come, for each of us, when we must pass beyond that veil. I don't know what you, my lovely reader, believe about death or the afterlife. I tend to think of it in Walt Whitman terms:

"And to die is stranger than what any of us had supposed."

At the time of writing this book, I believe what it means to die is stranger than what any of us here in the historical realm of the living really *can* suppose. It may be the end of consciousness, kaput, forever. (And if so, time-bound words like "forever" are a mistake to use in the context of death, since time appears to be a construct inherent to our subjective consciousness. When that subjective consciousness ends, there is no "time" in the normal sense. So if death is simply the end of consciousness, it would be a mistake to think of death as dreamless sleep forever and ever. It would be more accurate to think of it as a blink, an eternal moment. The void.)

I don't know if that's what death is. But whatever it is, I know it is coming. The great public intellectual, Stephen Fry, once surmised in an interview that he believed one must absolutely live *as though* this is all there is, because it may very well be. In other words, taste every fruit, from every corner of the garden, because there may be nothing beyond the garden at all. I am inclined to agree with this *taste every fruit* mentality, combined with a dash of Whitman mystery. The garden may be all there is, so taste every fruit, *and* to die is probably stranger than any of us ever supposed.

As a bit of an epistemological anarchist (ready to entertain or destroy any theory), I also am deeply interested in the countless worldwide anecdotes of NDEs (near-death experiences) that have been documented for many thousands of years. And having become trained as a hospice vigil volunteer, I am well aware of the normalcy of interesting visions, dreams, and experiences occurring to the dying. These can include, but are not limited to, seeing and speaking to deceased loved ones, and sensing a place of great beauty, indescribable love and freedom they will soon enter. The NDE descriptions of Anita Moorjani are particularly compelling.

One of the first times I ever got really stoned, I leaned back in an erstwhile friend's darkening bedroom and caught a family member out of the corner of my eye carrying a basket of laundry into the laundry room. And I thought, "I suppose that's one way to use your time here on earth. Doing laundry." It felt like all this busy activity and sense of practical necessity is a defense against ever having to be with the endless mystery of being. I could sense that there was almost this vast conspiracy among the adults of the world to never contemplate or speak of death, and to live as if they would never die, to live as if they have all the time in the world. And they don't. None of us do.

I am bringing this up to give you a kick in the pants. Don't be afraid of living your life. The most fearful thing of all is to come to the end of your life and to realize you never took death, and therefore you also never took life, seriously. I don't want that for you or for anyone. Think of it now. You'll be glad you did later. It is actually a profoundly self-compassionate act.

If you forgo the challenge of facing your mortality and getting on your soulful path while you're still here, you'll be swimming in the soupy oblivion of a fear-led life with the best of them. This is not really living. This is staying asleep. It is profoundly unconscious, profoundly asleep, to just step in line with the seemingly frantic necessities of daily living and all the "normal," practical things you think you are supposed to do with your life. When the end of your life comes, you will be your own judge. No one else will be. Social media will not be. The Joneses will not be. Wake up. Get real about this now. Trust me, you'll thank me later.

Death is coming. It's useful to remind yourself of that whenever you notice that fear or resistance have found tricksy little ways to convince you they should be in the driver's seat of your life. But this does not have to be such a gloomy prognosis. Death is the end of a life, but maybe it is also the soul of life. It forces us out of artificiality, forces us to decide what we truly value at a core level and to live in alignment with that. It forces us to see each person and each living being around us as a temporary miracle with which we have the great fortune to overlap for a few very precious moments.

The red path of descent into your human incarnation, into embodiment and into the underworld is a choice to summon a wholehearted, brave, stupid-in-love yes to life. To choose to not accept the invitations that come to you from the realm of soul, the invitations into this precious process of soul-making, is to choose to dim your unrepeatable light. It is a choice to continue to experience low-grade anxiety and depression that you'll stuff, medicate, and numb in whatever way you can. It is essentially a choice to stay asleep. It may even be choosing illness and an earlier death. Sorry, dear loves, but life is a fierce journey. Not finding the courage to accept the invitations that come from the realm of soul will create a reality for you that is *ultimately* much scarier. I am personally terrified of reaching the end of my life and realizing I never accepted those invitations and it's too late now.

In the same interview series mentioned earlier in this chapter (*Sitting by the Well*), Woodman shares an anecdote about a deceased client who had an important dream as she was in her dying process. In the dream, she walked up into her attic and found an old shoebox. She opened it and found a tiny, beautiful yellow bird inside with an otherworldliness that would be difficult to pin down in words. The bird looked sick or weak, but it was still alive. She took it out of the box very carefully, and it asked her, *Why didn't you ever let me sing?*

Your life wants to sing. This otherworldly, instinctual part of you (like the little bird in the dream) wants to be fully expressed. There is a way to stay alive to the organic unfolding of your soul. It happens when you are led by the sublime spark that dances in your body, like a fiercely burning pilot light of beauty, joy, aliveness, and excitement. It usually also has some fear dancing around it. You might feel it in your gut, in the pit of your stomach, in your solar plexus, in your heart, or shooting down your legs and arms like divine, trembling electricity. You might feel it like butterflies.

As you stay true to that sublime, dancing star in your body, you will stay true to your continual unfolding, and you will continually make up your own rules. You may go on a no-drinking kick for a while. Another year, you may mix your cocktails like an ancient priestess at Eleusis. It's all good. It's your rules. It's your unfolding. Like the moon or the seasons, you are ever-changing when you follow the wild call of life, staying vital, open, and awake.

THE SECRET AFFAIR BETWEEN FEAR AND THE MYSTICAL

BUT I AM SHE WHO EXISTS IN ALL FEARS AND STRENGTH IN TREMBLING.

-GNOSTIC MANUSCRIPT, THE THUNDER, PERFECT MIND

Fear and anxiety cause us to cling to the most deformed and

far-flung ideological structures imaginable. And there's a whole hell of a lot of anxiety out there right now. Really, we all need to rework our relationship with fear and anxiety because fear and anxiety are underneath these perverted, distorted, dangerous ideological structures and conspiracy theories that seem to be growing by the day at the time that I write this book (2020). We all need to rework our relationship with radical mystery.

In some ways, the most powerful, important, and healthy thing anyone can ever say is, "I'm afraid." How honest! Bring it into the light! Frankly, there are good reasons to be afraid if you, like most humans, are afraid of death.

The great psychoanalyst Marie Louise Von Franze drew a connection between "fear and trembling" and the ultimate religious and mystical experiences, experiences of the sublime, and experiences of God. In some ways, fear, felt consciously, is divine. It is our responsibility as human beings to feel fear consciously. I know you can do it. Our ancestors have been feeling fear since the primordial soup, probably. It connects you to all humans, maybe to all life. Feel it. You have the power to be afraid.

Fear is felt near mystical experiences, near death, near God, near the awesome, the sublime, the new, the unknown, and this is all *real* life, *real* mortality, *real* juice, and *real* awe. The admonition over the doorway to the chapel of bones in Rome is: "Death is not the end. It is the soul of life."

We need to relate to fear consciously before we can

develop intuition or live instinctually. Fear lets you know you're onto something good, and you're hot on the trail of your unique unfolding, dark though it may be. You know the kind of fear I'm talking about.

This is what I am asking women to do: Follow the spark of the sublime in your body, even if it leads you to a life or a form that has never really been seen before. Good! No one has ever seen the likes of you before, nor will they again. Living a very full, very authentic life involves many great dances with fear, lots of sublime. That's what I want to help my clients do, is to *overcome fear*, ultimately, or master it. A tall order, one might say (rightly). Fear must be mastered on the artist's path, during big life pivots and all throughout them. This is why artists and anyone following the sacred call to authenticity blaze like such brilliant comets. They have done something that most people, frankly, are afraid to do. They are an incandescent happening.

Here's my final nugget of crone wisdom for you when it comes to the perennial topic of fear: The ultimately "fearful" thing (death) is coming for all of us. Embrace that and be fully alive! If you can choose to do that now, when the moment comes that you're going to meet your maker (the Great Artist?), I have a very, *very* keen intuition that the passage will be much easier for you.

But it's not all doom, my darlings. As the great mythologist Joseph Campbell wrote, "Follow your bliss and the universe will open doors for you where there were only walls." A fear-based life is like a Chinese finger trap. It continues to produce fearful things and may inadvertently nurture the insecurity it is designed to run from. On the other hand, jumping from faith cliffs can land us in feather beds.

The energy released when one woman speaks or lives her truth is medicine for the world, regardless of any visible, tangible outcome, how it seems to others, or your inability to ever fully see the ripple effect. Don't let fear deprive us of your unrepeatable medicine.

DAILY RITUALS AND OCEANIC LISTENING PRACTICES:

-To Begin to Master Fear and Resistance:

Use the "dialoguing with fear" (or the dancing with fear) practice outlined in this chapter whenever fear arises.

I watched a professional athlete speak in a Toastmasters meeting once. He explained how he applies his plan for athletic performance anxiety to public speaking. His message was, essentially: Embrace fear. You have the power and ability to hold fear and do what you need to do anyway. The thing is to bring fear into your window of tolerance so that it's not at a panic attack level. Implement whatever self-soothing practices bring it back down into your window of tolerance, and then embrace it as a friend. It is actually priming you biologically to do what you need to do and to give your best. Resist it, and it will grow stronger.

Try writing out in your journal what each of the characters within the Neverending story triad (Atreyu, The Nothing and Moonchild) have been up to lately. It doesn't need to be elaborate: just a check in of a line or two to keep your finger on the way the drama of the creative person is playing out within you. (Reference 'Naming the Nothing and the Moonchild' section.) This shouldn't take too long and you'll ideally want to do it daily.

-To Flip the Concepts of "Fear" and "Failure" on Their Heads:

The ideas that have a little fear dancing around them might actually be your best, most powerful current ideas. See that little dancing fear as an indicator that, yes, Mama, you're onto something good. Your gut will tell you when it's that kind of fear, and when it's the *this-is-actually-bad-news* kind.

What we're often afraid of is failure. Flip your concept of failure on its head. Strip it of all negative connotations. Failure is *good*. Each failure is a step toward actualizing what our souls are dying actualize. Each one is a learning experience worth its weight in gold. After all, it took Thomas Edison one thousand tries to invent the lightbulb. In an interview, he referred to each of those failures as "steps."

CHAPTER NINE

THE VISIONARY EYE THAT SEES IN THE DARK WOODS: CULTIVATING INTUITION

Go out in the woods, go out. If you don't go out in the woods nothing will ever happen and your life will never begin.
-Dr. Clarissa Pinkola Estes, *Women Who Run with the Wolves: Myths and Stories of the Wild Woman Archetype*

Doubtlessly, you are familiar with the fairy tale trope of the heroine, protagonist, or curious maiden crossing the border between her little village (or what is "known"), and whatever lies beyond. Generally, she goes on a strange journey where she meets strange people or beings, overcomes challenges, and ultimately returns transformed, and somehow more dissident and knowledgeable.

Usually, in the beginning of the story, there is an intrusion from the unknown side of life, or an invitation, something that destabilizes our heroine. Invariably, she answers the call, and with that first step into the other world, she is taking a leap. She's taking a risk. She's entering the dark woods, the initiation ground, and in some cases, she's entering the underworld itself. She had to go. She was always meant to, somehow.

While on those dark initiation grounds, she must meet a part of herself that is comfortable in the unknown. Often, she also meets internal dragons and allies. If she overcomes the challenges presented in the nether realm, hopefully, she returns home with alchemical gold in her arms, or even holding a fencepost with a glowing human skull on top. So, basically, like a glorious, renegade sparkplug.

Think of your own healing journey (or even your dark, difficult life transition) that way because it literally is that way. All of those old stories are allegories. They are teaching devices. They help us map universal processes of deep transformation. They are medicine.

Now, I want you to hold this fairy tale trope (of descent into the underworld) in your mind as we lay our scene. The transcultural and transhistorical myths and folktales that follow this trope are too many to recount here, which should tell you a little something about the universality of this alchemical approach to healing and transformation. This approach focuses on a descent into the unknown, the underworld, the lunar side of life, in order to become initiated as a fully credentialed badass. Persephone, Vasilisa, and Inanna are among them. So is the myth of Psyche, and many others.

We answer the call to our underworld descent in order to become more authentic, more whole, more naked before the world. In order to find that what appears to be a scary monster is actually a wounded, divine child, secretly holding the most precious treasure of our souls. All the world's old tales seem to tell us clearly that it is only by going into the darkness that we become permeated with light.

THE VASILISA FAIRY TALE AND SACRED SELF-ESTEEM

REJECT AUTHORITY. TRUST YOURSELF.

-TERENCE MCKENNA

In the Vasilisa fairy tale, which is an ancient ancestress of the more well-known Cinderella, our heroine steps out alone into the dark woods, as she must. Though we've already visited the basic outline of the tale, let's take a slightly more luxuriant dip here so that the lunar part of you can take longer drams of its archetypal imagery.

Of course, there is a wicked stepmother involved, and a lonely life of meaningless labor, suffering, and drudgery. Vasilisa needs to get the fuck out of there. She's alone, but she's got one thing going for her: She has a little doll in her apron pocket that was gifted to her by her lovely and kind biological mother before her untimely death.

And this is no ordinary doll. It's a little doll that speaks, in a quiet, subtle voice that Vasilisa must get very still to hear, as if she's putting her ear down to the earth of her body. Often the little doll speaks in very simplistic terms as Vasilisa wanders the dark woods, looking for something, anything other than the totally empty, boring, painful, and soul killing life she left behind. (Really, I think her wicked stepmother told her to go and get light from the crone's cottage after all their fires had gone out. But one has to imagine she jumped on the excuse to go.) Sometimes it just whispers, "Right," or, "Left," or, "Over there," or, "Time to rest now."

If Vasilisa isn't calming her indigent heart and staying still enough inside to listen, she won't hear, and she won't know where to go. She will have neglected her divine GPS. She'll be lost in the dark woods, rudderless and alone, rather than on a hero's journey, fierce and trying though it may be.

Another peculiar feature of Vasilisa's little doll is that she must keep it fed and watered. So Vasilisa saves a little crumb or nibble from each meal in her knapsack to spirit over to her tiny consort, and she looks for fat morning dew drops on the lower leaves of the forest to tilt down into the little doll's mouth. It seems to have a little life all its own.

Eventually the little doll leads Vasilisa all the way to the strangest cottage she's ever seen. It's up on giant chicken legs, and it has fence posts made of bones, each one decorated with a real human skull on top. "Holy shit!" she probably declares. "What kind of acid did I take back in the village?" But she didn't take any kind of acid. Rather, she has entered the realm of the crone, of Lady Death. (In this tale, she's called Baba Yaga.)

The Baba Yaga pushes the crooked, moss-covered door open with a low, creaking sound and stands before our young heroine as if expecting her, with a beak-like nose that seems to sprout wiry hairs out in all directions. Her hair looks like Albert Einstein mixed with elaborate modern art made with a mess of electric cobwebs. And her beady eyes shine with a wicked, ancient wisdom. She knows what's up. She invites Vasilisa in.

Often, in fairy tales of this sort, the crone has a question or a riddle for the protagonist that they must answer correctly before being granted entry into her domain. If they answer correctly, she may take a liking to them and assist them on their quest. If they answer incorrectly, they may join all the other skulls that round her house like a lush, macabre garden. And they'd better think fast.

The trick here is to answer in a way that shows you understand the crone's paralogical way of thinking, and that you do not approach the realm of Mystery with the arrogance of "normalcy" or the surgical knives of reason. If you say something "normal" or "expected," you're dead meat. She wants to see that you have what it takes to bring about the new, to speak from poetic instinct, to be one of Jack Kerouac's wild ones "who never say a single ordinary thing." She wants to see if you can hang in the realm of Mystery.

If she asks, "Do you come here by choice, or were you compelled?" you would be a fool to choose one answer or the other. An answer that would please the crone would go more like, "Dear madam, I am compelled by choice, and I choose sweet, savory compulsion." Give an answer like this and now you're in with the crone. For in her realm, all is paradox and paralogic. She scoffs at the Cartesian, dualistic, either/or world that you left behind, with all its silly rules about "what one does and does not do."

If you want to become initiated into her kind of wisdom, you must embrace that there are other ways of knowing, and other ways of thinking. You must be able to grok that there is a whole other side to life where all is paradoxical, taboo, and magical.

So, our brave Vasilisa gives a wry, unusual answer to the crone's question (maybe her little doll nudged her), which pleases the crone Baba Yaga, and Vasilisa is granted entry into the strange, whimsical, and unsettling little cottage. Once inside, the Baba Yaga has Vasilisa perform several tedious and seemingly pointless tasks. One is to sweep the entire cottage, and another is to separate out every little seed from a giant hill of mixed sand and seeds in the basement. Good Lord Almighty.

Once all the tasks are complete and the crone is very pleased indeed, she pulls one of her fence posts up out of the earth (you know, the ones made of human osseous matter) and hands it to Vasilisa to carry back through the woods to her little village. Once in Vasilisa's hand, the skull emanates a stark, otherworldly light from within, and Vasilisa's path back home through the woods is well lit. She makes her way through the twists and turns, overland and underland, with great confidence and sacred self-esteem. She's done it all before, so she walks more fiercely now, with proud hips and chin parallel to the earth.

I'd like for you to know, dear reader, that you also have a little doll that speaks to you in the dark woods. Okay, that sounds creepy. Let me rephrase. You have a soft, subtle knowing that speaks at the center of your life, and it will guide you step by step, breath by breath, through even the meanest of transitions, the darkest of woods.

In order for you to make your way through a feminine mysteries initiation, or any soul-quake in your life, you're going to need to learn to hear your little doll, the subtle voice of intuition, whatever you want to call it. So, you're going to need to practice getting still enough to hear it. And you're going to need to learn what her voice sounds like. You're going to need to feed her through practices that help you keep in contact with her and that help her grow and feel nourished. That little voice is, paradoxically, connected to a much vaster perspective. (It's no mistake it was given to Vasilisa by her true, deceased mother. I believe this gentle voice, the feminine soul voice, within each of us, is a speck of Holy Mother, a speck of the great magnitude of the feminine. Of course She'll guide you. There's no one better for the job.)

Once you've gotten through the most important challenges of this particular initiation, you will have developed even more confidence in this little voice, in your ability to see in the dark. That's when you'll have the skull-light of sacred self-esteem. And when you have that, you will walk through the dark woods like that is your fucking domain, like you are a wolf or a night bird. You already are. It's just that you probably don't know it yet.

Listening to intuition and to what your soul knows in any given situation will often feel like following a breadcrumb trail through the dark woods. Darkness, in the culture, is often associated with fearfulness, the unknown, even treachery. (I know. Don't even get me started on the ways this has contributed to the inconceivable suffering of human beings.) But that's only the way it looks from within the cleanly organized, scrubbed, structured, brightly lit village. That's what yin energy looks like from a yang perspective.

If you approach the dark from the part of you that knows it as kin, then it becomes a realm of mystery, magic, sex, pleasure, intuition, and the ultimate creative freedom. I think Lord Byron was looking at yin energy from a yin perspective when he wrote, "There is pleasure in the pathless woods."

YOUR NIGHT-SELF

A GOOD ARTIST LETS [HER] INTUITION LEAD [HER]

WHEREVER IT WANTS.

-Tao Te Ching

There is a lunar part of you, your night-self, a part of you that is comfortable in the dark. A part of you with an annual pass to the sidereal side of life where the mysteries live. I believe the poem "Woman Who Glows in the Dark" is based on the defiant waking of this lunar part. It's what Anais Nin was referring to when she wrote that poems are one of the ways that the night-self expresses. When we've reached an in-between place in our lives, we are on the night-self's turf. Surface-level identities and priorities may be melting away so that we can only be (and must be) anchored in something that is much more of the depths.

What is this night-self and how can we access it? This part is of the body and it is conversant in the language of symbol. It is the part of us that dreams. Its poetic wisdom can be accessed through deep imagination journeys and psychedelic journeys, through actual night dreams, and through creative inspiration and expression. We can also gain entry to its striking insight through the contemplation of art (in its various forms), through deep acquaintance with the body, and through deep internal listening and discernment.

This part is the poetic instinct that wants to find flow and make magick instead of conforming to rigid, externally imposed, machine-like structures or rhythms. It is the part that receives otherworldly visions and inspirations and allows us to reach beyond ourselves in the ultimate erotic position, the ultimate openness to life. It is the part that asks us to open and close like a flower, at one point introspective, finding "the mark within" (to use a Burroughs phrase). At other points, it asks us to bravely open ourselves to the radical mystery of this world, like an eye that opens and closes. If we can find this internal, visionary eye that sees in the dark, our life and creative projects blossom outward from it like an unrepeatable, otherworldly flower.

In this chapter, we will explore ways to tap into our night-self to find our way through this (and any) dark, liminal phase of becoming. These are different ways of seeing in the dark. We are going to practice getting very comfortable with this realm where intuition rules because it is often disdained, maligned, and shunned by the culture.

Why? Oh, fear, of course. People often feel safer if someone else is telling them what to do, laying out the instructions or steps, and flooding everything with fluorescent, sterile light. The challenge here is to get comfortable with the dark and your ways of glowing and knowing in the dark. These ways of knowing are the true secrets of strength, grit, and courage. And they don't only come in handy when you're in hell. No, no. This part of you is always showing you the next step, and then the next, if you'll listen. It will help you build your empire, write your book, be a fierce, independent renegade (or whatever your soul longs to be) and live a wonderful, rare, instinctual life.

People will wonder what your secret is. They will think you must have a plumb-like connection to some ore strength they don't know how to access. And it's not that you're not strong, because you are a daughter of the endlessly resilient earth, after all. That's some powerful shit. But it's really more that you trust yourself. Come what may, your heart, gut, and hips show you the way, and you trust that now. You listen.

INTUITION-FRIENDLY LIFESTYLE HABITS

The little doll spoke quietly, remember? Vasilisa probably wouldn't be able to hear that tiny voice very well at all if she was busy chastising herself or getting engrossed in racing thoughts about the seemingly frantic necessities of daily life. It would probably be drowned out completely if she was obsessing about things she did in the past or might do next week for dinner. She would need to have some degree of internal stillness in order to hear that voice.

That's why the number one lifestyle recommendation, if you want to hear your intuition, your soul voice, speaking to you, is to slow. The fuck. *Down.* A good way to set the tone for your entire day is to have some kind of morning practice for bringing yourself to a place of calm and stillness inside. It could be meditation, prayer, or something, anything, more elaborate that speaks to your spirit and soul. (You can do full-on transcendental meditation or a guided meditation using an app or a YouTube video or you might just pray or contemplate a holy book.)

If you don't currently have a practice, start simple. Don't overwhelm yourself. That's the opposite of the point. Try sitting somewhere reasonably quiet and private for five minutes each morning. Light a candle or burn some incense if you like. Add whatever speaks to you. The point is for you to allow the surface of your inner lake to be still, so small ripples are more easily discernible. And if you try to tell me you don't have five damn minutes in the morning, girl, please! The only person you're cheating with that kind of shenanigans is yourself.

You can use a mantra if that is part of your practice, and/or you can simply observe your thoughts like clouds passing in the sky. If your thoughts were cars on a busy street, the point is for you to get out of the middle of the street and to walk away onto a hill overlooking the traffic jam. That way you can observe the traffic jams instead of being stuck right in the middle of them going, "Oh my god, oh my god, oh my *gaw-ha-hawd,*" and pulling your hair out. You are so much more than your thoughts.

If you develop a meditation or contemplation practice for at least five minutes (or ten, fifteen, or twenty!) each morning, you'll notice that this calmer, meditative state seems to pop back into your mind throughout the day, like a song you've been listened to a lot. That's good. That's what we want.

The reason we want this is because when that still, calm, meditative state becomes a state you achieve more regularly, it is going to be a lot easier for you to be intuitive. If you have frantic anxiety programs running incessantly, or you have a severe superego constantly chastising you for this or that or for breathing, you will not be very intuitive. If Vasilisa had all that going on in the dark woods, she'd probably still be out there lost and wandering, or she'd have been devoured by wolves. Get real, beautiful souls. You need a practice for getting still if you want to hear the voice of intuition or if you want to live instinctively.

And our internal noise is not only reducible to our own internal crap-on-myself programs. It goes hand-in-hand with our internalization of the frantic clip of the modern world and its stimulation-bombardment. It's nearly impossible to hear your little doll speaking with all that going on. Therefore, try to reduce some of it or be more intentional about your engagement with it so that you are not constantly at the effect of ever-proliferated communication channels, pings, dings, and frenetic stampeding towards God-knows-where. If you have an iPhone, maybe turn all non-urgent notifications off and then check communication streams only at a specified time that works for you, perhaps once at the end of the day. And if you start your day getting grounded in stillness, in your depths, and in your own authentic values, you're less likely to get pulled into the vortex of rushed, rudderless activity. This chapter will give you more practices for doing this.

You may need to clear some emotional and psychological "gunk" before you can really deeply hear intuition, through therapy or another healing or growth process. (By that I mean unresolved emotional traumas, the ghosts of heartbreaks past, especially early ones. We all have them.) Sometimes intuition can finally break in at a particularly low point. But I want you to do the work so you don't have to get to that point. Start working with someone one-on-one who is hip to these concepts if you think you've got a lot of gunk to clear.

Furthermore, if your body is not healthy, it's difficult to be mentally or emotionally healthy, and it's difficult to receive intuitive signals. Your body is so inextricably connected to your mental health and your intuition that if you are flooding your body with crap, you are literally gumming up the channels. Also, your nervous system needs to spend a good deal of time in the calmed, rest and digest mode in order for you to be intuitive and to see your way through the dark woods of your life. Your daily relaxation practices will assist with that.

As a side note, I do not consider chronic health or pain conditions to be an impediment to cultivating the kind of health I'm talking about. You can cultivate the best health for the body you have now and for what you have available to you now. This does not mean intuition is only reserved for people who can afford to shop at Whole Foods for every meal. *Insert emotionally flatlined emoji face.* Just do the best you can with where you are and what you have. If you *know* in your heart of hearts that your overuse of nicotine products or your overindulgence in snack foods that are made out of essentially non-edible ingredients is a way to numb yourself, or to *not know what you know*, then give yourself permission to know that now.

And begin to lovingly ween yourself, replacing the sweetness of that soft addiction with the sweetness of love, or the sweetness of deciding to actualize your heart's true desires.

And continue recording your dreams. As you work with intuition and instinct, you may have dreams about animals, showing you the state of your instinct. Sometimes they are injured, forgotten, starved, or neglected. Don't let this dishearten you. It is very promising that the image would make itself known at all. It is *never* a hopeless situation. In fact, it can often be resolved rather quickly. And your dreams will immediately reflect that.

Now, a great deal of the internal noise and frenzy that are likely drowning the voice of your soul are related to what I think of as internalized patriarchy. We'll see how breaking the spell of internalized patriarchy goes hand-in-hand with developing sovereignty and remaining firmly anchored in your intuitive knowing.

BURNING THROUGH THE INVISIBLE SCOLD

FEMTHEOGENIC CONSCIOUSNESS CARRIES A PARTICULAR KIND OF KNOWING THAT OUR CULTURE HAS LONG NEGLECTED AND AVOIDED, ESTRANGING US FROM THE WATERY INITIATIONS OF FEMTHEOGENIC AWARENESS.

-MARIA PAPASPYROU, *PSYCHEDELIC MYSTERIES OF THE FEMININE*

According to the great Jungian analyst, Dr. Clarissa Pinkola Estes, women are usually sanitized away from their instinct.

They internalize the idea that they are wrong, that they know nothing, and that they have no firm ground to stand on within. They start to believe that other people's opinions and points of view are more valid, correct, and important. Sometimes women even internalize the idea that the most important thing for them to do is to please and go along with others, even when some strange alarm bell is going off inside, way down in the belly. This is how women get hurt and exploited. This is how they fall into the grips of people who do not have their best interests at heart.

Please don't misread this as a way of blaming the victim. No woman asks for any part of this. Some women find themselves in situations where it really doesn't matter whether they are hearing the voice of intuition or heeding it because that is exactly how cornered they are. That is not their fault. If it has happened to you, it is not your fault. Systems of oppression (based on race, gender, sexual orientation, and specific disabilities) are not your fault. You didn't bring it about, and you don't deserve whatever has happened in the moments when you may have heard or felt your intuition and didn't know how important it was to heed it. No one teaches us this stuff, not really. That's why we're learning now.

Remember that charming anecdote about the "wrong, wrong, wrong" voice? As a daughter of the patriarchy, I am very sorry to tell you this, but the odds are good that you have internalized a voice very much like that. Think of a time you got butterflies because you knew you had something wickedly relevant and original to say, but then you said nothing. Why did you do that? It's likely because there is a mean little voice inside you that says, "Wrong," about whatever you feel is *right*. You may have internalized the message that you don't really have anything important to say at all, and that if you worked up the gall to share your point of view or to tell your fascinating and poignant story (the real, raw truth usually *is* fascinating and poignant), no one would be listening anyway.

Rather than the proverbial tale told by a madman, signifying nothing, you may feel that your tale is one of blood-deep truth, the tenderness of the human heart and the strange mystery of life itself. And, in a Kafkaesque manner, you may feel you are telling that tale like a madwoman (if we continue to paraphrase Hamlet here), who paces and frets her hour across the stage, knowing that maybe her tale doesn't signify nothing, but no one is actually listening anyway. (Or maybe it *does* signify nothing, but you know that its nothingness *is* the lunar realm of infinite possibility. Still. No one listening.)

You may feel that if you stand up with a megaphone at a rally, if you speak up at a conference or board meeting, if you take the stage at a poetry reading, or if you work up the gonads to tell your story to the world in any format whatsoever, you will be shouting into the void. They'll cut the mics. Either your truth, your heart and gut knowing, are flat wrong, they don't matter, no one cares anyway, or worse. They could be intrinsically bad and could get you into some kind of dire trouble. The act of speaking your truth and creativity in-and-of-itself could be unwelcome and contemptible. So you allow yourself to feel bound, muzzled, wrong. You accept this. (Or, you tell yourself you do.)

It is our duty, not only to ourselves and other women, but to human beings of all genders, and indeed to life on the planet as we know it, to overcome this. If you want to smash the patriarchy, you've got to start on the inside. I'm not talking about doing any kind of violent, internal demolition. I am talking about burning through that internalized muzzle (back in the burning times, they called it a "scold") with the holy fire of your soul truth. I need you to. Please.

And once you've practiced that, work on replacing that internal "wrong, wrong, wrong" voice with a *loud* internal, "right, right, right" voice, okay? *Any* time you go with what you know in your heart and gut is right, I want you to imagine any woman you admire and trust overseeing your little revolutionary act and saying, "Yes! Right! Yes!" I want you to imagine that she is scrunching her face up with appreciation of the power of your gut knowing, the way someone scrunches their face up when someone puts on a really good funk record. That bass line is *so dank* that her face almost looks like there's a bad smell in the room. "Mmmm! YES! Right! Yes!" Imagine she's nodding rhythmically to put extra emphasis on the words, as if the power of your gut knowing is her favorite song.

Seriously. Practice this. It helps to surround yourself with other women who will *actually do this for you*. Regularly. So regularly that you can feel and hear them inside you when you are about to go with your gut or speak heart-and-soul truth. So regularly that you've internalized them, and they're much louder than the internalized "wrong, wrong, wrong" voice of patriarchy. This is how we burn through the invisible scold.

You might find this kind of deep validation in a women's circle, in female friendships, in a mentorship or coaching relationship, or even in your relationship with your therapist. This is what I try to always be for every woman I work with in any capacity. Someone who acts like I just tasted a *very* fine, stinky cheese of the highest caliber whenever she expresses what she knows in her bones. "YES! Right! Yes!" I do this to help fortify and solidify her own trust in her gut and in her heart. This is the most powerful thing that any mentor, teacher, or friend could ever do for you. It's not about *their* ego or them teaching you or demonstrating how much more knowledgeable or whatever they are. It's about them showing you that *you already know*, deep down.

REPLACING THE FRENZY OF "TOO MUCH" AND "NOT ENOUGH" WITH THE PEACEFUL STABILITY OF SACRED SELF-ESTEEM

Consider how you received shitty messages about your wrongness or inadequacy through culture, family, media, or any of the broader mezzo- and macro-level systems that helped to raise and socialize you. It looks different for each woman. A running theme, however, is some kind of pervasive sense of being "too much" and needing to shrink or tone it down, cut it off, pull it back, bind it up, tame it, or sanitize it. Make it "good." Another running theme for so many women is a pervasive sense of "not enough." Not smart enough, not pretty enough, not cool enough, not thin enough, not successful enough, not fertile enough, not desirable enough, not charismatic or funny enough. Not enough to be worthy of respect or to be heard or taken seriously or loved. Most women have a blend of "too much" *and* "not enough" as running themes in their internal narratives.

If you believe you're not smart or cool or beautiful enough, take a look at where those messages came from. I guarantee you'll be able to pinpoint a specific memory, or more likely several, when peers at school gave you that message, culture or the media gave you that message, or maybe an important adult in your life gave you that message. Seek help with doing deeper work to really pull this up at the roots if any memory associated with your "too much" or "not enough"-ness was severely traumatic or sufficiently damaging to cause ongoing, daily suffering in your current life.

When it comes to receiving damaging messages through culture or the media, it can be harder to pinpoint specific instances or memories because this influence is trickier and more serpent-like. The result is that women internalize aspects of popular culture that constantly tell them they need to meet standards they will never fully meet, probably not for one day in their whole lives. (Be really thin with big tits, amaranthine youthfulness, and undulating hair down to your shapely backside, while perfectly balancing being a multi-armed, magical dream-mother, and steamy, uncomplicated partner who can have multiple orgasms til dawn. If you can also be an earner, all the better! Just make sure to meet everyone's standards without ever making them feel threatened in any way. Whew! Pass me the Tylenol.)

And sometimes, what we internalize from the culture is more of a void than an actual thing we can point at. We internalize the yawning abyss where the people heralded as geniuses and great leaders from present day down the archives of history are almost always men. By causing women to feel they are never enough, we cause women to forget their terrific, inherent sexual and intuitive power. We sanitize them away from it. And their self-esteem suffers.

So we are going to vanquish these internal forces that have us so frenzied we can't even hear the voices of our souls. Because, I hate to break it to you, but if you think your self-esteem is going to be based on meeting all those harsh external standards, you are going to be frantically racing to meet them for your entire life. And you are going to miss out on the life that your soul is calling you to find. You see, developing intuition goes hand-in-hand with developing what Caroline Myss refers to as "sacred self-esteem." This is different from self-esteem based on conformity to external standards. It is self-esteem based on anchorage into something much, much deeper.

Myss describes sacred self-esteem as "managing the power of your soul." In order to do this, you must have some level of conviction that your soul and your intuition know more than you do. They know more than your everyday, egoic, rational mind. You have to believe they are somehow tapped into a vaster, more transpersonal knowing. I know this may require a leap of faith at first. But the more you live in alignment with soul and intuition, the more you start to realize they don't steer you wrong. This is why Myss says we develop sacred self-esteem "one unreasonable choice at a time." With each intuitive choice you make, you will begin to realize how powerful your soul actually is. You will begin to find terra firma within and realize you can stand on it with both feet firmly rooted. This is the very picture of sovereignty: Confidence in one's own conviction that comes from this firm, internal anchoring and trust, not from conformity to external standards.

The more sovereignty and sacred self-esteem you can cultivate, the more you will develop a feeling of peaceful stability within. That is a *much* more conducive internal environment to intuitive knowing. In the Rituals section of this chapter, we are going to love our "too much" and "not enough" parts so hard that it will be a little obscene. Think of it as quelling the internal frenzy in a deluge of rose petals. And we'll plant some seeds of sovereignty and sacred self-esteem, too.

KNOWING IN THE DARK

FOR THE PEOPLE OF THE ANCIENT CELTIC WORLD, SEERSHIP

OPENED WINDOWS INTO THE OTHERWORLD, AWAKENING THE

ESSENCE OF TRUE VISION AND WISDOM WHICH WAS KNOWN BY

THE POETS AS THE GLEFIOSA, OR "THE BRIGHT KNOWLEDGE."

-CAITLIN MATTHEWS

The soul is a liberator. You have to trust that the soul knows the way, one step at a time, especially when making big, scary life transitions. Your soul is a unit of selfhood that doesn't have anything to do with what you consume, what you do or what you don't do. It is tapped into vaster realms. Think of ego as the small self. The part that receives the still, small nudges is the soul, or the large self. (Paradoxically, the large self sometimes speaks in the quietest voice, while the small self sometimes seems to shout into an internal megaphone.) When we are being intuitive, we are listening to soul, to large self.

Spoiler alert: In this section we are going to get into the "clairs," or the different ways of being psychic. But don't pee in your pants yet. I'm going to pull you all the way down to the earth first, to the *real reason* for this entire exercise of finding our ways of knowing in the dark, because I'm a mean, mean Mama. Humor me for a minute.

The "clairs" are glitzier ways of "knowing in the dark." The only thing I ultimately want my reader (and any client of mine) to accomplish in this arena is the cultivation of a higher level of comfort with the *darkness of process*, what Keats called "negative capability." The darkness of process is where creativity and intuition live, both in art-making *and* in healing. When we get comfortable with the darkness of process, we are co-creating with Self. (By that I mean that we are leveraging our own large self, soul, or whatever you want to call it, that of any participant, and the greater-than-the-sum-of-its-parts field created between us. This field flirts with what might be called "divine ground.") I recognize that trusting the darkness of process may require a degree of faith, especially if my reader is not practiced at this kind of thing.

So let me take a moment to breathe a spark of faith into you because I *am* practiced at this kind of thing. As a therapist/healer and producer of the arts, I sit in the darkness of process all day everyday. And I'm telling you: You can trust the field (or the enchanted circle) of the creative space and the healing space. I know I may seem like a loo-loo-la-la fairy lady, but I've got a deep streak of practicality as well. Don't you want to be surprised? When you surrender into the darkness of process, you are brought into the present moment, and you may end up somewhere you could never have predicted. With that said, let's get into intuition, an aspect of the lunar part of you that knows, well, intuitively, how to dance with the dark.

Intuition has traditionally been scoffed at as something horribly "feminine" and unscientific. In my opinion, the main issue is (and continues to be) that not much is known (scientifically, anyway) about its workings. Perhaps there is also a valid wariness of giving credence to anything that any old Joe says is coming from their "intuitive knowing." That could have some pretty dangerous potentials. So let me be clear here that I do not want to perpetuate any junk science ideas that might give people permission to claim objective knowledge about any old bullshit they want to say. This is not what intuition is at all. It is far more subtle. It is a deeply personal, ongoing practice and way of being.

Let's briefly touch on how "unscientific" intuition really is. Mark Gober's *An End to Upside Down Thinking* compiles some of the staggering body of evidence supporting what might be called psychic or paranormal phenomena. These phenomena call into question the physicalist assumption that matter is the primary medium of reality and not consciousness. If it is the other way around (or if something even stranger is the case), suddenly these phenomena make more sense. The body of evidence is overwhelming enough that, were it any other kind of documented phenomenon, conventional scientific standards would be forced to acknowledge that, yes, *something* is going on here. It's the way these phenomena *work* that has not really been scientifically explored to my knowledge at the time of this writing.

I also hope to impart (before diving deeper) that these phenomena are deeply mysterious to the core. I don't know how they work. I only know, from my own experience, that psychic or "paranormal" phenomena do happen. Additionally, the nature of physical matter and the nature of consciousness are both unfathomably mysterious. It would be beyond the purpose of this book to try to illuminate those mysteries and their workings.

So let's dive in, shall we? I don't personally make a great distinction between the words *intuition* and *instinct*, although I consider *psychic* to have an area of overlap with intuition and instinct, plus a wider field of possibilities. Allow me to explain.

If a snake lunges at you, the odds are good that you would instinctively jump and maybe run in the other direction. This response is old, much older than you, than your mother and all her mothers before her. An instinct is a collective tendency. Generally speaking, humans and animals have a collective tendency to go towards that which promotes life and nourishment and to avoid, evade, or escape that which is perilous to the life force.

Your instinct tells you to get back in the car when you just parked somewhere remote at night by yourself to take a picture of the forest fire on the horizon. It's what tells you not to get closer when you encounter a bear in the wild. It's what allows new mothers to figure out how to take care of their brand-new babies who apparently never come with instruction manuals. Parents will also instinctively move to protect their young, springing to action at the drop of a hat.

Think of your baseline instinct as a basic fucking animal right. You can tell instinctively when you are in a situation (or nearing one) that will be harmful to your life force or to that of anyone you love. Things can get nuanced when we're talking about "life force." We could be talking about actual life-or-death situations (those certainly count), or we could be talking about situations that more abstractly suck the life force from mind, body, spirit, and soul over the years. These situations encourage the internalization of rage and have a corrosive effect on the mind, body, and spirit. Those abstract, ambient, and gradual threats to the life force also count. In other words, instinct certainly "talks" to us about those situations, too.

Now, where does instinct cross the line and become intuition? I would say at this point (though I am honestly still figuring this out because it is such a realm of mystery) that if instinct is one large circle, and psychic abilities are another large circle, intuition is the vesica between them. Intuition is firmly rooted in instinct, but it comes with extra details on the side. And the way those extra details come is unique to each person. Once you get into the *ways* those extra details can appear, then you start getting into the "clairs," or the different ways of being psychic.

Each woman is psychic in her own way. We are going to figure out how you are psychic. I would advise figuring out your top one to three ways and really owning and honing those (unless you're already quite advanced). And throughout this process, I want you to be very open to however it is that *you* know. Let it come to you.

Each of the most well-known ways of being psychic include the prefix *clair-*, which means *clear*. Clairsentience means *clear feeling*, claircognizance means *clear knowing*, clairaudience means *clear hearing*, and clairvoyance means *clear seeing*.

Clairsentience: This is the most embodied of the clairs, and it has a range of manifestations. It includes what we might call "gut" knowing, a literal feeling in the gut or in the pit of the stomach. It can extend all the way into the realm of somatically feeling what another person is somatically feeling. This happens sometimes in sessions with clients, and I am certainly not the only clinician-healer who experiences this. *Sometimes* voicing the shared somatic sensation can push the client's journey into its next phase, it can break a relational spell or freeze, or open a well of insight. Clairsentience can also manifest as an involuntary eyelid flutter or a sudden scratchiness in the throat during a client session or psychic reading.

The "subtle body" is very much implicated in clairsentience. This is a soulful, conscious awareness stretching from head to toe, cultivated through embodied soul work. As the subtle body is developed, it becomes easier to sense into the feeling of a place or situation. This way of knowing might be experienced as a pervasive, spectral sense that can stretch through the body or that seems to cover large tracts of the body.

Claircognizance: Perhaps the most difficult of the clairs to describe or pin down, claircognizance is when you "just know." The information comes in and you know like you know like you know. For example, you might just know who's calling when your phone rings. Or you might just know that a certain situation is not right for you. Oftentimes, things we know in our heart or in our soul are things we "just know." If this is your superpower, you may experience it as a "lightning bolt" of sudden knowing about a person, place, or situation. Or you may receive an unexpected intuitive "hit" about something, or have a sudden realization that you need to check something or call someone up.

Clairaudience: Most people "hear" their inner thought voice, right? (I hope so!) You hear it with your inner ear. And if you are sensitive to this internal hearing, you might notice a difference between your day-to-day internal thought voice, and another gentle voice that speaks quietly, unpretentiously, directly, wisely, and often with great compassion. This is clear hearing. Clairaudience may even be experienced as hearing the melody of a song with the inner ear, or a fire crackling or even the sound of an appliance as ways of receiving intuitive information about a given person, place, situation, or event.

Clairvoyance: Often the most coveted and misunderstood of the clairs, clairvoyance, or clear seeing, can occur in a couple of different forms. The first one is seeing with your inner eye, within your inner mental theater. Some people receive most of their intuitive information this way. Or they may get this kind of information frequently, but they don't pay attention to it, or they never share it, so they don't think it means anything. But you may receive the bulk of your intuitive and psychic information across the mental sky of your inner visual theater, with your "mind's eye" or your imagination.

Often people think of clairvoyance as the ability to see auras. It's true that some people appear to be naturally gifted in this way or to retain this way of seeing from childhood. Even people who do not identify as clairvoyant at all and who think it may all be a load of crap will take a dose of mescaline (or other visionary drug) and then! Suddenly, they're not only seeing complete, colored auras around anyone nearby, but they're doing full energetic healing work, finding ashy areas in the aura, and even seeing intellectual energy flashing around someone else's forehead like little red lightning bolts. I've seen it happen. However, it's not the kind of clairvoyance we're necessarily talking about here.

Your inner vision looks out on the imaginal world, a world that one might argue is real as this one. Whenever you imagine, you are doing magick, and you are a mage. There is a reason all those words share an etymological root! Guided vision journeys and deep imaginative journeys can allow us to receive images from our "large self." And it is often through the imaginative faculty that we receive psychic information. Yes, you read that correctly. *But aren't I just imagining it?* Yes, yes, you are just imagining it.

These might all sound much more normal and quotidian than you were expecting, and that's because they are. You've probably already been using psychic abilities much more than you realize. It starts to get really witchy and exciting when you start to notice and play with these forms of subtle awareness consciously. Because what happens then is you might start to notice dramatic shifts in your own life and in the lives of the people who are blessed to know you. So, let's explore some ways to deepen your clairs and know in the dark like a true heroine.

The sections that follow will offer practices and guidelines for getting a deeper sense of which clairs come most naturally to you. However, this is certainly not an exhaustive guide for opening your witch gifts. Consider it a beginning, an invitation. I will flesh out more fully my understanding of the ways that the subtle body (clairsentience) and the imagination (clairvoyance) play into this, because these are the ways of knowing that I've experienced and understand the most. Also, I consider the development of the subtle body to have particularly pivotal implications in a feminine mysteries initiation. However, please consider your ongoing dream recording practice to be a *profoundly important* aspect of your knowing in the darkness of this process, and your Oceanic listening practice with your journal as well. I hope you'll find practices and ways of knowing that work best for you. Each one is, ultimately, a communication from the realm of soul.

EMBODIMENT AND YOUR WAYS OF KNOWING

I THINK THAT SO MANY OF US STILL FEAR BEING FULLY PRESENT IN THE BODY BECAUSE IT MEANS OWNING JUST HOW POWERFUL

WE ARE. THE RESPONSIBILITY IS OVERWHELMING. WE THEN
ENTER A PLACE WHERE WE ARE HELD ACCOUNTABLE FOR WHAT
WE REALLY KNOW. WE HAVE AN IMMEDIATE SENSE OF WHAT IS
TRUE FOR US. REAL COURAGE IS SIMPLY SURRENDERING TO THAT.
THERE'S NOTHING MORE POWERFUL THAN A WOMAN WHO HAS
MET THE TRUTH INSIDE HER. NOTHING.

-MEGGAN WATTERSON, *REVEAL*

William Blake and others have suggested that, in some
mysterious way, the body is continuous with the soul, even that
the body itself *is* the soul (the visible aspect of it, anyway). It
could also be said that the soul is the animating life force of
the body, awake and alive in every cell; it is the indwelling light
(or Shekinah) in the matter of the body. The more embodied
you become, the healthier you become (because your body will
always tell you exactly what it needs and what *you* need), and the
more you actively develop your subtle body, which is the bright
awareness that stretches from the top of your head to the tips of
your toes.

Our body is the nexus of the only knowing to which we
really have access. James Joyce referred to the body as "Mama
Matrix Most Mysterious." It is the mystery matrix of our
ongoing, wordless conversation with life. In order for us to
become intuitive, our bodies have to become conscious. It is
very often with our fully embodied awareness, or the subtle
body, that we receive intuitive knowing. Woodman said this

kind of embodied consciousness is what we call "soul," a soul no longer in exile.

Authentic movement and ecstatic dance, both embodiment practices, are great ways to overcome ego (or small self) and get in touch with intuition (which speaks through the large self). Both practices involve letting go of whatever your ego is telling you about what you look like, and completely surrendering to the impulse that comes from the center of the body, completely surrendering to what you feel "moved" to do. I highly recommend you foray into one of the aforementioned embodiment practices at this stage in your journey. Your authority, your gravity, your original voice, your instinct, and your heart are all in your body. And look up Alexandra Roxo if you want to find additional, wonderful, deep embodiment practices.

Another thing you can try is just a regular old body scan. Sit quietly and slowly move your awareness from the top of your head through every part of your body, all the way down to your toes. Did you notice any standout sensations? Is your body talking to you in any particular region? Breathe into that area of your body, bringing your awareness there. Imagine that the breath is melting and loosening this area of your body just a little bit. Don't force it to change or go away. You're just loosening it up and bringing awareness to it so that it can talk to you.

Then allow yourself to intuitively receive any information your body may like to convey to your mind through this sensation. Don't grasp for the information. Just let it come to you. What you receive may surprise you.

Not only will regular body scans allow your body to speak to you and tell you what it needs, what it *really* needs (not what anyone else told you it needs), but it will allow you to access greater intuitive and instinctive knowing. Your body is your oracle. If your body tells you, *Stop. That's enough*, I want you to honor that wisdom as if it just escaped the lips of the highest spiritual authority in your life. I don't give a fuck what anyone around you is saying or what their title is or how spiritual their title is. Listen to your body. Your body is your shaman.

If we're afraid to listen to the wisdom of the body and move through any healing or lifestyle change our body may tell us we need, then we never get to experience the joy, bliss, wisdom, power, and ecstasy of the body. We have to make ourselves vulnerable and receptive to what the body speaks, even when it is uncomfortable, because that is the only way to be vulnerable and receptive to authentic joy. And of course, slowing down and relaxing increases our receptivity to the messages of the body.

HOW TO OPEN YOUR WITCH GIFTS AND RECEIVE INTUITIVE MESSAGES

What kind of oracular or anomalous experiences have you already had? We've all had them. They can point the way in terms of what to focus on as you open your witch gifts. You might not open them all until you're ready. You likely won't open them all in the reading of this book. You may have oracular dreams, or hands on healing gifts or you may be a natural midwife. You may be a musician or a science fiction author. Oracular dreams about clients come to me about five to ten times per year these days. And the instance of client-related oracular dreams only increased after I made the decision to share them. After a while, my by-the-book clinician tendencies were overwhelmed by my finding that my oracular dreams seem to propel sessions along and move my clients deeply. I consider them part of the dream-field cultivated by the healing dyad.

Notice what arises within you when you are on the phone with someone or sitting across from them. Notice what arises within you when you sit quietly and contemplate a subject.

There are myriad ways of being psychic, and the above list is by no means exhaustive. Some receive sympathetic body sensations, some have a penchant for knowing when their mother is about to call, and some can allegedly speak with the dead. There are almost as many ways to be psychic as there are people.

Does this mean that anything and everything you ever think of is a psychic "hit"? No. The more you drop in, do your inner work, and develop a familiarity with your particular ways of knowing, the more obvious it will be to you when something is a genuine intuitive hit and when it is something else. Keep dropping in, keep doing your inner work, keep getting still, keep listening deep.

Here's a very basic practice for receiving intuitive information while also getting a sense of your own witch gifts:

First clear your mind through a meditation or other practice for pausing and getting still. Then sit in silent contemplation with the intention of receiving information on a particular topic, ensuring you have your journal and pen on hand to jot things down. You may incorporate oracle cards or other forms of scrying or divination at this point, but you don't have to. Those are also just tools for opening up the knowing within the instrument of your own bodysoul. Take mindful breaths and just notice what arises within you in terms of images (clairvoyance), body sensations (clairsentience), thoughts or a sense of knowing (claircognizance), or even a thought or sound that you seem to receive with the inner ear (clairaudience). This is a process of simply noticing, trusting, and going with whatever is arising within you. Rather than trying to "grasp" for it, imagine that you are standing in a shallow river and just letting the information float downstream to you.

"Wait, but then am I not just making it up?" you might be asking, especially when it comes to images that may arise. Am I not just creating this "information" or "content" with my imagination? One *might* argue that you are. But my radical claim is that there is an overlap between the realm of imagination and the realm of psychic knowing that we have yet to completely understand.

You may notice mostly body sensations. For someone else, it may be more mental images. You may receive thoughts. It may be some combination.

There are formal processes for this. For example, some people work with angels and guides and verbally (or internally) ask to be shown information on some specific thing. I don't know what I believe, but I know this kind of intentional process can set things into motion powerfully, so I certainly do not discourage it. If you'd like to cast a circle beforehand, this should feel more comfortable.

A final word to the wise: Always stay tight with your own lived, embodied experience and the mystery of that. Don't succumb to the urge to reify and turn mystical, mysterious, anomalous experiences into the safety of rigid dogmas, concepts, or slogans. This would be yet another way to push the feminine, the realm of radical mystery, underground.

WRITING DOWN THE BODY AND RECEIVING INTUITIVE GUIDANCE FROM THE HEART

Remember the Moonchild activity from earlier? Out of all those different internal "parts" or voices that you unpack in that practice, the one I might deign to call intuition, or the voice of soul, is Moonchild. I sometimes experience her as located in the realm of my sacral chakra/womb, the great creative and oracular center in all of us (whether we literally have a uterus or not).

You may try another daily "unpacking" practice in your journal (after recording your dreams, of course!) wherein you write, each of these words, each with two lines underneath: Pussy, Womb, Solar Plexus, Heart, Throat, Third Eye, and

Crown. Then sequentially tune into each energy center and the wisdom it is giving you on a particular topic, jotting down two lines for each in your journal. Think of this as a Oceanic listening practice where you are learning to put your ear down to the earth of your body, just as Vasilisa was putting her ear down to her little doll. If you don't have time for all that, just focus on Pussy, Womb, and Heart. The lower centers are the ones typically neglected and maligned, especially in women who have become alienated from their bodies. And they are the centers of the kind of wisdom this book seeks to resurrect. We need to be rooted in the body, and the lower energy centers, in order to truly access the divine wisdom of the heart, the place where heaven and earth commingle.

In fact, your heart is so special that I am going to give you an additional practice for accessing its divine wisdom and knowing. Sit quietly and imagine your awareness sinking down into your heart, and just let it rest there for several breaths, or ideally, for several minutes. Then ask a question that's been bothering you deeply. Ask it into the dark stillness of your heart. What did you hear?

Thank the gods this kind of wisdom is available to us. I don't know if we would make it as a species if it wasn't. If you want to make this practice more elaborate, you might actively visualize your heart as a warm little cave that juts out into a tidepool somewhere where the water is warm and Caribbean blue. The water that moves gently within the safe secrecy of the cave is shallow and crystalline, but it opens out onto the vast ocean. So the very same water of the fathomless ocean is right there in the cave. And then you might see your heart as a divine child who lives inside that cave, maybe rocking peacefully on a little boat. You might think of the Smashing Pumpkins song title, "Porcelina of the Vast Oceans," when you see her.

You might build a shrine into the cave wall, complete with tall taper candles that somehow miraculously stay lit. (Mine is a Mary Magdalene shrine.) Sometimes you might imagine petals and spices somehow mysteriously falling all around the little child in your heart. (I like to imagine this because, as legend has it, when the early saint Thecla was sent into an arena to be devoured by a lion, the lion instinctually recognized the purity of her heart and laid down at her feet. The people in the arena recognized this as a miracle and showered her with flower petals and aromatic herbs.)

Since the child in your heart is a consistent miracle and vibrates at the frequency that caused the hungry lion to swoon and lay down peacefully, she gets to have flower petals falling all around her too. During your heart meditation, you might visualize all of this on your own, and spend some time with *Porcelina* (or whatever you'd like to call her). Finally, after you have sufficiently attuned yourself to her vibration, ask the question.

Feel free to add, subtract, or tweak any part of this visualization. Make it your own. You deserve to have stunningly gorgeous internal spaces, and powerful practices that you can bring with you anywhere and that no one can ever take away from you. You may be moved to tears by the wisdom of your heart-child. I sometimes am. Other times, it's like, *Oh. Yep. Can't argue that.* You deserve to know that this level of preciousness, divinity, and wisdom lives inside you, and that you can access it any time, free.

INTUITION-OPENING JOURNAL QUESTIONS

You do not need to consider the questions in this section as a necessary part of the transformation process offered in this book. Think of them instead as a quick reference for any time you want to have an intuitive journaling session. Give yourself all the time and space you need to journal out your answers.

- What would someone who loved herself do? (This question takes you right into your heart and soul, and into your ability to lovingly parent yourself. We've covered a daily practice related to this question in a previous chapter, but the question bears repeating because I believe it is a great way to find your way forward intuitively.) This question comes from Teal Swan's teachings on self-love.

- If I had a guardian angel looking over me, lovingly protecting me, and wholly invested in my highest good, how would they advise me in this situation? This question comes from Doreen Virtue's *Angel Therapy.*

- If a miracle occurred tonight while I was sleeping, and tomorrow morning I was suddenly in a different reality, the reality I would rather be in (regarding a particular situation), what would be the first indicators that would let me know? How can I make that real in my life now? This is called "The Miracle Question" and is often associated with solution-focused therapy.

- If this situation were to last forever, what qualities would I need to develop in order to have peace? I first heard this question in a Michael Bernard Beckwith sermon.

- What would the voice of grandmotherly wisdom tell me about this situation?

RITUALS & WRITING PROMPTS FOR YOUR OCEANIC LISTENING PRACTICE

-To Drown the Frenzy of 'Too Much' and 'Not Enough' in a Deluge of Rose Petals:

Take stock of the ways you might feel you are "too much" or "not enough." Journal it out. Then defiantly lean into that. Play with this for a while: If you're "too weird," then get weirder for a day. See what that's like. If you're too "macabre," then lean into your inner Morticia. If you're too sexual, find your inner porn star, your inner sex priestess. If you're too queer, stand on top of a car and shout, "I'm here! I'm queer! Now I'm over here!" If you're too transgressive, be more transgressive. Just give it a whirl, for a day or two. See what happens. See if you buzz, if you feel alive or energized. I have a feeling you will.

Give yourself permission to experience your "too much" or "not enough" sides as the very raddest and most lovable things about you. Your superpowers. They very likely are. What is the very most generous stance you could possibly take towards those parts of yourself? Thank fuck for them. Buy them roses.

-To Keep Your Little Doll Fed and Watered:

No practice will help you grow and nourish your soul quite like a regular creative practice. (A creative practice is also a good way to develop comfort with lusciously stretching out into the unknown. In other words, it helps you develop your lunar self, the side of you that is comfortable in the dark.) I know of *no better way* to feed, nurture, and grow your soul (the seat of your intuitive knowing) than a regular creativity practice. This is *especially true* during a dark transitional period or a feminine mysteries initiation.

What else feels like soul nourishment to you? A certain kind of music? A certain kind of person or food? You need it, especially now. Journal out your list and plan to make time and space for that soul nourishment in your life. You may have worthiness issues or calendar-cluttering "supposed to's" come up as part of this process. Seek support with overcoming those challenges as needed.

-To Plant the Seeds of Sacred Self-Esteem:

When was the last time you had a feeling (maybe against the odds or contrary to conventional wisdom) that something was the right decision? Did you follow through on it? If so, how did it go? (I'm willing to bet it went well.) Take stock of the times you made an "unreasonable decision" based on your intuitive knowing, and it went well. What "unreasonable decision" is your intuitive knowing currently asking you to make? (Remember to plan like someone who loves herself. You don't need to put yourself into the panic attack zone with your unreasonable decisions. Your internal Holy Mother, your soul, will nudge you to take the right steps at the right time and in the right ways.)

-To Do the Bidding of the Baba Yaga and Earn Your Skull-Torch:

How do you think Vasilisa was able to find all the seeds in that hill of sand at the Baba Yaga's cottage? She had to know the difference between seeds and sand, instinctively, infallibly. And she did. She did all that perplexing clearing, sifting, and sorting work that the Baba Yaga assigned to her until she was good and done. Everything was in its right place, and she could tell shit from Shinola. One of the glorious gifts of reclaiming your instinct is that it will help you sort out how much you've been motivated by external, patriarchal standards and how much you've been motivated by your own authentic values. Seeds over here. Sand over there.

So here's your practice: Look up a list of values and force

yourself to pick your top five. Then narrow that down to three. Then one. Are you living in alignment with those values? How not? How might you shift your current life to live more in alignment with your *authentic* values and desires (as opposed to someone else's values and desires for your life)? How have you worn the image of "femininity" or of your appropriate role in the world projected onto you by your family or by broader culture? Which pieces of that are yours? Which are not?

PART III

WHITENING AND YELLOWING

CHAPTER TEN

INTO THE SHADOWLANDS: INTEGRATING THE EXILES

A HUMAN BEING HAS SO MANY SKINS INSIDE, COVERING THE DEPTHS OF THE HEART. WE KNOW SO MANY THINGS, BUT WE DON'T KNOW OURSELVES! WHY, THIRTY OR FORTY SKINS OR HIDES, AS THICK AND HARD AS AN OX'S OR BEAR'S, COVER THE SOUL. GO INTO YOUR OWN GROUND AND LEARN TO KNOW YOURSELF THERE.

-MEISTER ECKHART

OH, SOCIALIZATION

In order to understand how the feminine has been buried in you, we need to understand a thing or two about the socialization process. As an extremely social species with a much longer than average developmental timeline (due to our large brains and the time it takes for us to become biological adults), we spend a long period of time highly dependent on our caregivers in order to have our love and survival needs met. We literally cannot afford to displease our caregivers too much, and we are biologically wired to be attached to them and to seek closeness with them, even if they are overtly abusive or even dangerous.

Since we as children cannot afford to not have the love— or at least the begrudging acceptance—of our caregivers, we will make our caregivers' behavior mean something *about us* way before we put two and two together and realize something like, "Oh, Mommy must've had a really hard day today and didn't mean what she said to me," or, "My caregiver isn't doing a great job today," or even, "My caregiver is being an abusive asshole."

No, children, at an implicit and powerful level, will make a caregiver outburst mean, "I am not worthy of love just as I am. I am not enough." Children may even make heedless caregiver behavior or communications mean, "I must be worthless. I don't matter. I deserve this kind of treatment." To complicate matters, children are making this kind of bunk meaning when they are laying the foundations of the internal working models they will use to understand reality in adulthood. So these kinds of beliefs usually stay with us, and these stories continue to spin in our unconscious in powerful ways that impact outcomes in every domain of adult life. (No cause for despair, however! As the result of neuroplasticity, we are able to alter these powerful unconscious programs through therapy and other healing modalities.)

In addition to the high-stakes game children are playing when it comes to winning caregiver approval, the situation is intensified because children spend almost all of their waking lives in an Alpha brainwave state. This, for an adult, would be considered a light hypnotic trance.

Adults spend most of their waking hours in Beta, which is the caffeinated, busy, tuned-in, switched on, narrow-focused state that you probably try to be in, at least for *most* of the day at work. Beta brain waves look tall and close together on a chart. Alpha brain waves are slower, so the curves flatten and lengthen a bit. As adults, we enter this state while reading, while zoning out, or while entering a light hypnotic trance.

The thing is, we are *overwhelmingly* more suggestible in an Alpha brainwave state. That's why, during hypnosis, your hypnotherapist will first induct you into a slower brainwave frequency. It's to ensure you are in a state of very high suggestibility and receptivity before they read the hypnosis script to ensure it does its job of reprogramming your beliefs at a deep, unconscious level. So, just think about that. *Children are constantly in a brain wave state which renders them far more suggestible than a typical adult brain wave state—up to 200 times more suggestible by some estimates.* They are literally soaking up every single adult and cultural message (both the implicit and the explicit) like a highly porous sponge with miraculous levels of storage space.

Now, since human children are biologically wired to understand that their survival depends upon caregiver approval, they are wired to want to do whatever it takes to remain in caregiver favor. (I know it may not seem like that when your kid is throwing a tantrum!) That means that kids are hyper-attuned to adult reactions to their behaviors and to their experiments with different ways of being. It's as if their ears are perked for approval. And kids amplify and play up the parts of themselves that win the most adult approval. They start to split off and relegate to their spiffy, new unconscious (we'll sometimes call it "the basement") parts that they are shamed for displaying or that garner adult disapproval.

For example, if you were brought up female, it could be that you were met with adult approval any time you displayed sweetness, kindness, prettiness, "being seen but not heard," helpfulness, helplessness, amiability, or caregiving behaviors. You may have been met with adult (or even peer) disapproval if you displayed "bossiness," anger, fierce boundaries, prioritizing yourself (your own needs, preferences, or desires) over others, any form of body shamelessness, fierce independence, or a penchant for smearing dirt on your face and calling yourself a witch. I'm not saying that this is the exact formula every time someone is raised female. I'm just spinning off some of the "greatest hits list" so that you can get a sense of what resonates with you.

It's important to mention that the behaviors adults approve of or disapprove of can be highly culturally dependent. Additionally, the whole socialization process is heavily informed by the specific personalities, preferences, and trauma histories of the adults involved. And make no mistake about it: teachers and other members of the "village" that raise a single child all participate heavily in the socialization of that child.

Each time we are shamed or met with disapproval for displaying some aspect of our nature, we split that part off from our conscious concept of ourselves. Where does it go? Well, it doesn't disappear. It goes down into the basement. This can happen in instances of actually being deeply shamed for being or acting a certain way, or it can happen when we pick up on some sort of chronic, low-grade disapproval of some aspect of the way we're showing up. It can also happen when we are traumatized or frightened so badly that a piece of our consciousness fragments off and remains frozen at the age of the trauma. It can even happen when we are constantly praised for one aspect of our appearance or personality, while other, really big, important parts go entirely unnoticed and unencouraged. These younger selves and exiled parts very often become part of our internal basement community. I sometimes affectionately call them "basement children."

Now, please do not read this section as an indictment of your parents, grandparents, foster parents, teachers, or any other wonderful people who may have played a role in raising you. In my experience, most parents are truly doing their best, and yet kids still create meanings about themselves in the wildest ways. Not only that, but most modern schools were not designed to call forth and develop the unique individual in each child. In one way or another, we were all scarified. We were all fragmented. And, as a result, we all have basement children. This doesn't mean you are a broken, damaged being. It just means you are very, very human.

ONGOING ADULT SOCIALIZATION

I'VE CREATED THIS CHARACTER, AND I'VE BEEN STUCK WITH HER EVER SINCE.

-PARIS HILTON, *THIS IS PARIS*

Our childhood socialization process gives us the psychic blueprint we bring with us to therapy (and to all our adult relationships). However, it doesn't stop there. We are each deeply, hopelessly ensconced in our cultures *and* in our historical period. So much so that it would probably be impossible to fully appreciate the ways our home cultures *and* home eras have formed (and *continue* to form) our personalities and even the way we are showing up in this very moment. Socialization continues every time we observe the behaviors, values, and concerns of others. It continues in our attunement to the implicit and explicit messages we constantly receive about who we are supposed to be, what we are supposed to want and value, what success looks like, and what kind of behavior is considered "normal" or "acceptable."

The particular expectations *still* placed on women in their twenties and thirties (although the culture is shifting in this area, thank the gods) create unique issues surrounding their full empowerment and integration at this time. If some part is deemed to be unattractive to a potential mate, further splitting and internal exiling can take place, leading to confusion, despair, and inner turmoil. Furthermore, there are very often internal parts *that do not want* whatever we are "supposed to" want at this stage of life. Sometimes women continue to exile their protesting parts because they believe that this particular desire or goal makes them "selfish," "weird," or "a bitch." Alternatively, we may experience freakish success at this life stage, but success that was built around an artificial persona, a strategic persona geared towards garnering the highest possible levels of approval, attention, or worldly success. And after we've reached the zenith of that success, we realize we feel totally empty and entirely homesick for our souls.

WHEN EXILES COME A-KNOCKIN'

From the perspective of your internal community, this process of exiling internal parts is not a malicious one. Rather, it's done with good intentions. *At the time that it happens*, it seems like the most loving, protective decision. To give an image articulated by teacher Artie Wu, it's as if all the parts have an internal committee meeting and unanimously decide that a certain part needs to go down into the basement so that the collective (that is, *you*) can continue to access love and safety. When it is *love itself* that is on the table, our internal parts are willing to do anything. Think about it. If you were told you needed to amputate your leg in order to have love in your life ever again, you'd probably pretty seriously consider doing it, wouldn't you? I imagine that the parts that go down into the basement do so with graciousness, humility, and great concern for the collective (i.e., you).

However, this may not always seem to be the case. Sometimes, when we meet these parts, they seem desperate for our attention and love, or they seem starved, injured, or neglected in some way. We can meet them during conscious Deep Imagination work or in our dreams. They are knocking on your door in any of the possible types of soul letters listed in an earlier chapter.

When the internal committee has been meeting with previously integral members exiled, at a certain stage in life, things start to feel really off. For lack of a better way to say it, we feel like we are living out of alignment with our purpose. Even if we do not language it that way, we feel an emptiness, a sadness, a longing for our soul. It is at this time that (again, out of love), the basement parts resort to their emergency tactics and start sending messages through in the form of soul letters. And when these soul letters fly in and we start to open them, we have accepted the call to adventure on the heroine's journey. We have taken the first step onto the initiation grounds, and the first step towards greater wholeness and integration.

SHAMELESS INTEGRATION OF THE
BASEMENT CHILDREN

WHEN YOU'RE WHOLE, YOU'RE HOLY, AND YOU'RE HEALED.

-DEEPAK CHOPRA

Imagine your psyche is a mansion with many rooms and an extraordinarily capacious basement. The conscious ego identity is the front parlor area, where the lights are always on, and guests are entertained. This is the part of the house the world is allowed to see. Behind that are all the other rooms, and of course, the basement. Parts of you that you are marginally aware of (or very aware of) live in the other rooms. They occasionally make their rounds through the front parlor, sometimes right under your nose. And the vast basement is the storehouse of all your unconscious material. Its deepest recesses conceal Narnia-like wardrobes that go even farther, seemingly into other worlds.

Think of your unconscious, the basement of your psyche, as your own personal underworld. It's just like the underworld or the dark woods into which all the heroines of the myths and old fairy tales must venture. It is the initiation ground.

Want a *very* general overview of what's down there? Complexes, wounded child parts, memories, unconscious beliefs and programs about yourself, others, life, and the world. In fact, I am going to streamline that even further by telling you that the wounded child parts *are* your complexes, essentially. (And they're always associated with certain memories and unconscious beliefs.) Often in psychology and healing, we find multiple ways of talking about basically the same thing. Another way to discuss this would be to call these basement parts "soul fragments" (the kind you would go in search of in a soul retrieval process) or shadow parts (the kind you would work with when doing any variety of "shadow work"). Now, good old Jung took the tack that complexes are actually wrapped around an archetypal core.

That may sound like fancy language, so let me explain. Let's say you have a mother complex. Maybe you have a hard time feeling safe around other women, especially women who represent authority in any way. Maybe you sense they are going to humiliate you, single you out for special torture, or devour your sense of self in one way or another. Maybe you didn't get what you needed from any kind of mother figure growing up. The outer edges of that complex will be comprised by layers of personal material, experiences, memories (traumatic or otherwise), internalized messages, and ingrained thoughts, beliefs, and behaviors. If you keep peeling back the layers, what you will find at the center of that complex is the universal archetype of "The Mother" Herself. From a depth psychology viewpoint, there is a gigantic archetypal energy animating that complex, making it dynamic and powerful, and (often) very tricky to overcome. This is why, in the grips of our complexes, we may struggle as fiercely as if we were in a battle with the gods.

Does this mean that our complexes are literally shaped like onions with a little archetype living at their center? No. This is more of a helpful, visual model than a description of the way anything is, say, physically organized in the brain. Don't worry too much about exactly what an archetype is right now. We'll get to that in a moment.

Now, you'll remember that, during the process of socialization, we learned that some parts of ourselves were going to be accepted, loved, and rewarded. Those become the front-facing, conscious identity parts. When we say, "I'm the type of person who _____," we are referring to those parts. The parts that are repressed, buried, or living in the basement, on the other hand, are the parts which cause our symptoms or may contribute to creating the life crises that bring us to therapy.

Integrating the rejected parts and bringing them into our awareness and love is not only an important part of any thorough healing path, but also of any thorough spiritual ascension path. In other words, if you want to go "up," first you have to go "down." Too often, there's a shadow intention hitching a ride on our quest to "ascend" or "awaken." Integrating our basement children and bringing them into the circle of our love, therefore, is sacred work. This is honoring the call to authenticity, in the deepest and truest way.

Integration is inside-out identity development, as opposed to outside-in. We engage in outside-in identity (and life) development whenever we look at social media and use that as a metric for our own worth, image, and "supposed to's." Integration, soul retrieval, and shadow work are about being shamelessly yourself. Because shame and fragmenting go hand in hand. They cannot be discussed apart from one another. (When we are shamed, we fragment, and split off parts of ourselves.) When you are shamelessly yourself, there is no competition. How could there be?

Here's a yummy anecdotal example of this: Poet and singer Jill Scott who performed after Erykah Badu at a concert was asked how she felt about following the goddess-like Badu's set, and she responded, "We all have our own thing. That's the magic: that everybody comes with their own sense of strength and their own queendom. Mine could never compare to hers, and hers could never compare to mine." Imagine feeling that way about *your* queendom!

Imagine getting so radical with your integration and shamelessness that you forget all about healing in order to be "all love and light" or in order to be "happy and blissful" all the time. For example, Our Lady of Sorrows has been one of the big archetypal energies in my life, and one that I have worked with through prayer and through art and embodiment practices. In fact, She's perfect to mention here because She represents the immaculate love and compassion that pierces all the way into our deepest agonies. So in a way, she represents radical alchemy. I embraced Her energy when it broke into some of my personal healing processes. And I've also embraced my sadness, my anger, my rebellious streak, and even my inner bitch. Each emotion is a sacred carrier of personal truth, and each part developed as a badass member of my internal queendom for a good reason. Each part can be exalted.

Because you know what? Life *is* sad. Tragedy is inexorably woven into everything. And yet life is also a riveting adventure and an unspeakably beautiful mystery. Not either/or. Both/and. The truly sad thing is to lose your soul and to be unable to recover it. When your soul has wandered far away, sometimes sadness feels like the closest thing to a connection to it. So don't exile your sadness. Sadness is of the soul.

FLIPPING YOUR PAIN INTO YOUR TRANSGRESSIVE PURPOSE

NOBODY CAN FALL SO LOW UNLESS HE HAS GREAT DEPTH. IF SUCH A THING CAN HAPPEN TO A MAN, IT CHALLENGES HIS BEST AND HIGHEST ON THE OTHER SIDE; THAT IS TO SAY, THIS DEPTH CORRESPONDS TO A POTENTIAL HEIGHT, AND THE BLACKEST DARKNESS TO A HIDDEN LIGHT.

-CARL JUNG

The great spiritual luminary, Krishnamurti, famously stated, "It is no measure of health to be well-adjusted to a profoundly sick society." In our frantic efforts to keep up and to be (or seem) well-adjusted to the profoundly bollixed society in which we find ourselves, we bury lightning bolts of radical and deeply needed transgressive potential.

For example, there is a glorious transgressive potential within depression. The depressive person often has some major problems with "the way things are," except, instead of doing anything about it, they are caught in the planetary gravitational pull of the depressive cycle, which saps their energy and leaves them feeling like even the laundry is as agonizing as the stations of the cross. It's not their fault. It's hard to figure out what is going on and put a wrench in the cycle if we don't have someone there to help us. Hell, I still haven't gotten to the bottom of figuring out all of my shit.

So, I want you to think of your symptoms not only as pointing to repressed parts (and their attendant archetypes) but also as pointing to all the ways that you truly long to be transgressive, a radical, a revolutionary, or even something you may have been told was "bad," impossible, or stupid. And I want you to bravely experiment with one more weird idea here: Your repressed parts (and their attendant archetypal energies) may have a lot to do with your purpose.

I know "purpose" is a tricky concept, so let me explain how I think of it: As far as the full ecology of you is concerned (including your divinity, your basement children, your conscious personality, and everything in between), your health and well-being are synonymous with remaining oriented towards your personal true north. For that reason, your internal queendom is wired to put you in pain when you've gone off course from your lode star. (I know, pain sucks. But it always serves a function. It hurts when you touch a hot stove because your system would like for you to keep your hand functioning and intact, if possible.)

Most of us have some element of "the rebel" within us. You've got to allow this part room to breathe. It's the part of you that kicks and screams underneath the surface when you plaster on an artificial smile and squeeze yourself into a situation or role that, in truth, feels like a prison to you. This is the part that probably causes your soul sadness, your restlessness and anxiety, or whatever other soul letters you're getting. And this is the transgressive part. Let her breathe. Speak to her, get to know her.

So, if you've ever wondered what your purpose is, your internal ecology is constantly trying to tell you. We are doing this work because *your life matters*. What you are compelled to do at a soul level matters. Period. Wake up and smell the hibiscus tea. This work stretches beyond just you and we need you now more than ever.

There's an important distinction to make here. We can shift disproportionate, paralyzing anxiety or sadness at the root by doing the kind of deep work this book proposes (usually in tandem with a trained guide). But we don't ever want to totally quell or numb it when it is a valid reaction to social and ecological realities. Also, *over*-focusing on deep healing work ad nauseam can become a form of disguised resistance to your art and your soul's true work. At a certain point, we want to honor the message that the anxiety or sadness offers about ways we could become more integrated while being careful not to extinguish the transgressive potential they may contain.

Ultimately, trekking down to the underworld of the unconscious is about owning what is down there and alchemizing it. Your rage, despair, and shame can be composted into a miraculous garden of creativity and purpose. The maenads would be proud. The mysteries of the great goddess and the work of her priestesses seem so often to be about the vital, transgressive potential revealed by flipping concepts on their heads and finding the mysterious consonance between death and new life.

And that miraculous garden of creativity and purpose will extend beyond you in more ways than one. The old occult saying from the Emerald Tablet of Hermes Trismegistus, "As above, so below," certainly applies here. There will be shifts in your outer circumstances as the result of your inner work. There will be shifts in your energy, mood, and perhaps even your physical health.

THE GIRL WITH NO STORIES

[Content Warning: The following section may be triggering to any current or former clients who have been traumatized by the drug use of people who were supposed to care about them. If this describes you, I would advise you skip this section. Otherwise, please bring any difficult feelings this may provoke into session, or contact me for a booster session if you are a former client.]

Sometimes we have to take several steps backwards, or so it seems, in order to fully understand a theme we've been working with all our lives. Often, we haven't really gone backwards. We've just returned to the same region, or the same season, on the ongoing orbit of our progress. It looks like hopscotch. It is not linear. It is a spiral dance. Let me hop backwards a few steps and tell you some of my secrets.

There's an old fairy tale called "The Girl with No Stories," considered to be the very old ancestress of *Alice in Wonderland*. In it, the heroine comes across a strange little cottage in the woods (of course!) and happens inside to see if she might find a place to rest and a bite to eat. A kindly couple greet her and ask her whether she has anything to exchange for such kindnesses. She replies that she does not. The couple inform her that stories are their very favorite form of currency and ask whether she has any of those. Puzzled, she scratches her head, shifts on her feet, and honestly replies that she does not have any stories either. The couple tell her to go out into the woods and collect a good story or two. When she has at least one good story to tell, she might be warmly welcomed into the cabin in the woods.

The girl wanders all over the woods, speaking to field mice, squirrels, dandelions, and rabbits, searching high and low for some good stories. Before she returns to the cottage, she is chased by a snarling, drooling, hairy monster who is about one hair's breadth away from eating her alive. Though old tales like this have a way of shifting, depending upon who's telling them, in most versions, she ends up back at the cottage, and she finds the same kindly couple, now old and gray. And boy, does she have a story for them.

Though I'd never heard of "The Girl with No Stories" when I was an adolescent, the grooves of my early wilderness years certainly did echo the shape of that particular fairy tale. You see, we are always interacting with the archetypal world, whether we are aware of it or not. And we may be enacting an archetype with a wealth of cultural treasure, story, and spiritual richness wrapped into it, and we'd never know unless we bothered to find out. The treasure a single archetype offers could not be fully experienced or researched in one lifetime.

I knew by the time I was about twelve or thirteen that I wanted to be a writer. But I thought, *Who is ever going to care about anything that a stupid little girl from Southern California has to say?* It was at that time I decided I would commit to giving myself every single kind of firsthand experience possible. I wanted to do this all so that I could eventually collect a sufficient number of experiences, or stories, to one day be taken seriously as a writer. I decided I would start with drugs.

What I didn't realize at the time was that I had already deeply internalized the message that, simply by virtue of who I was, I had nothing worthwhile to say. Nothing that anyone would ever care to read or take seriously, anyway. That was before I developed the conviction that the feminine soul voice is needed now on the planet like never before. But I won't let that get in the way of a good story now.

By the time I graduated high school, I had tried every single drug I could get my hands on, except for heroin. I would try that, only once, at age nineteen, while I was already on acid with a musician from The Brian Jonestown Massacre's side project band. By that age, I had already developed the conviction there were two entirely different classes of drugs: the psychedelic and everything else. And I already knew (thank goodness) that the "everything else" category was the truly dangerous and unappealing one. I knew it had the potential to deplete my vitality and pull me *off* the path of being a writer. Having dabbled was one thing. I had collected "the stories." But my gut feeling that I have a lot of work to do in this life was always strong enough to keep me from getting too deeply into any of the drugs in the "everything else" category. And the drugs classified as psychedelic, I thought, deserved a totally different classification. These, I already knew, were not addictive, nor were they particularly physically harmful. The idea of taking a psychedelic drug even one time per year for the rest of my life seemed like it would be a profound spiritual discipline.

Side note: Please be aware that times have changed and the likelihood of encountering fentanyl, a deadly synthetic opioid, in *any number* of common street drugs you might pick up anywhere is much, much higher now. Please do not do what I did.

What I failed to realize at the time was that so much of my behavior was based on a deep, deep disregard for myself. I often partied to the edge because, in a certain way, my connection to my own life was ethereal and sometimes paper thin. On a couple of occasions, I actually did not care what happened to me. I did not care if I was going to overdose. That is how little regard I had for my life, my body, and myself. I didn't even fully realize it at the time because I hadn't yet discovered any other way of being a young woman.

Later, I realized that my paper-thin attachment to this particular incarnation was, in many ways, the result of a vast shame about who I was. Sometimes suicidality is the ultimate expression of shame because dying would be the ultimate way to hide, to be un-naked. And this shame subtended later episodes of regular, intrusive thoughts about wanting to end my life.

From what I was able to observe, women are rarely great poets, musicians, writers, or artists, so if I wanted to create, if I had a fever to create, it might just feel like shouting into the void. And I had also drunk deeply (as we all have) of cultural messages about my value, potential, and purpose as a woman. But it would be disingenuous to say that these realities were the only causes of my shame and flirtation with suicide, though they certainly had a hand in it. Of course, a unique constellation of experiences and wounds contributed to the development of an (at times) abject sense of self by my adolescence.

My flirtation with death would weave in and out of my life continually, all the way up to the strange experiences of 2015 and just a bit afterwards in a slight halo. This is because my soul began to spontaneously heal the virgin/whore split in my psyche (inherited from the culture) and to offer to me what I needed in order to heal and to be whole: my inner artist, in the full flower of her tremendous horsepower.

It would also be a lie if I related that I am entirely free of this now. But it certainly happens less often. Whenever that malevolent jack-in-the-box thought of wanting to kill myself flashes across my mental sky, I take it as a sign that I'm allowing my soul to get steamrolled again in some area of my life. In this way, I've come to visualize my soul as an orchid-sensitive radio dial that starts to scream when her needle is getting pushed too far away from true north, almost as if she were actually being held over a fire. So in this way, my most acute mental health symptom (or soul letter) of suicidality lets me know when I am allowing the greatest oracle of my inner queendom to be burned.

In the same way, your most lurid soul letter may also point you directly towards the greatest oracle of your inner queendom. That's why I'm sharing this story. To show the mythopoetic dimensions of one of my blackest nights and how it pointed to my most important, hidden light. I now know that if I am not creating, I am not okay. What will you know about yourself when you open your soul letters?

You may not believe it now, but there are vast storehouses of treasure for you to uncover even in the darkest of nights, even in the most hellish descent into the underworld. *You* are a treasure. There is no one like you, and there never will be again. With courage, you can unfurl and develop the parts of you that are screaming, kicking, and crying, bring them to the surface, and give them air.

Showing up, having curiosity, and stepping into the unknown takes courage. When you've found that courage, you can access the tremendous, magickal potential of these initiation times in your life when you are called down into the underworld. This is the way of continual unfolding, continually staying open, and devotionally summoning a yes to life, like a ritual, rhythmic return to prayer. (That way, you don't have to *feel* a yes to life in a constant and unqualified way.) Paradoxically, you may find that whatever you are ashamed of, whatever you hide, or whatever makes *you* want to hide could point the way to the most glorious expression of your feminine potency, the greatest mystic of your inner forest.

RITUALS & WRITING PROMPTS FOR YOUR OCEANIC LISTENING PRACTICE:

-To Begin to Bring Your Shadow into Focus:

Pick someone in your family or in your social or professional vicinity who you really don't like. Write a list of attributes this person seems to possess that bother the hell out of you and that represent things you feel you are *not* and would never want to be. Just write a list of about 10-20 adjectives rather than a long monologue. So you might write something like, "narcissistic," "needy," or "pretentious." Circle the top three that you consider to be the worst offenses. Do that and don't skip ahead. After the next ritual, I'll tell you what to do with that list. No cheating!

-Journal Prompts to Identify the Exile:

Keep in mind: We're finding a sense of your exile(s) *for now.* Your understanding of this aspect of you will only continue to develop from here.

With that said, what themes did you play with in the "too much" and "not enough" ritual from a previous chapter? What were you constantly rewarded for as a child and/or throughout your life? How do you identify with that now and how does that leave you feeling off balance? What part did you have to dis-identify with in order to always put your "most rewarded" face forward?

Conversely, what were you consistently shamed or punished for? What (if anything) do you hate about yourself? What (if anything) do you consistently hate in other people? In what ways do you feel like you're wearing a mask? What would be underneath if you removed the mask? Answer each of these questions and see if you can identify any recurring themes. Circle or highlight them. What stands out to you?

Go with your gut about what is asking to be reclaimed at this time. It may already be clear to you based on recent dreams and current soul-deep desires, or you may go with a theme that has recurred in your Oceanic Listening practice so far. And keep in mind that this is not all about doom and gloom and accepting horribleness about yourself. The parts that are asking to be brought back into the circle of your love at this time are probably linked to your deepest soul hungers and your heart's fiercest desires. When we give ourselves radical permission to own these parts of ourselves, this process can feel exciting and delicious!

-And... Surprise!

The qualities you listed and circled for the first prompt in this chapter are some of your shadow qualities. Not to worry. Each of these qualities represents a neutral and very human energy with which we can play and adjust the volume. For example, if you wrote "idolatrous," that could be a low-side expression of "devotional." Even if you wrote, "judgmental and gossipy," you could refine that energy within yourself to, "discerning, highly perceptive, and yes, even sometimes bitchy." Any time you ask yourself what really gets under your skin about other people, this can point to parts of yourself that are deeply enshadowed, and their attendant archetypes, of course, but more on that shortly!

-To Ritualize Your Deepest Intention with a Little Seasoning of Magick:

Now that you probably have some sense of the part of yourself to be reclaimed, feel into a color that seems like a good vibrational match for the part you will be reintegrating. Find a candle of that color. Carve a small emblem or symbol for that part into the candle. Dress it with an essential oil that feels like a vibrational match to the part you are integrating. Write out your deepest intention or prayer for this process (in only a line or two). Now go wild and write your heart's truest desire for this process (in only another punchy line or two)—something that would make your heart sing.

Light the candle and read the intention and your deepest why (from an earlier chapter) *out loud*. Make sure you're in a time and place where you won't feel weird about summoning the deep feelings of joy, gratitude, and aliveness associated with the intention and desire, and to let those beautiful feelings carry on your voice. And then, for a final dash of magick, go ahead and read it all two more times out loud and state, "By the power of three times three, so mote it be!"

-To Deepen Your Insight Into the Exiles While Inviting Them Into the Circle of Love:

I have included a proprietary Shadow Alchemy deep imagination journey on my website at https://deeperwelltherapy.com/ enchantments for this process. If for any reason you are unable to access the process on a laptop or computer at this time, I've included a simplified version here. If at *any* point during the inner journey, things seem dark, menacing, or scary, please pause the activity right away and seek the support of a trusted therapist, coach, shaman, or healer before proceeding further. If you have a specific trauma history you are aware of, this may be more likely to occur. Please trust your own gut and be gentle with yourself.

If you're doing the simplified version, please get comfortable wherever you are seated and bring your awareness to your breath, allowing the breath to draw you into the present moment on every inhale and every exhale. Once you feel centered, calm, and present, imagine you are sitting in a forest clearing, and that the forest clearing is a gigantic circle of love. Imagine you are going to invite a part (or parts of yourself) forward into the clearing from a dark part of the forest where people rarely go. Imagine there is a river of light that cuts through the clearing between you and the side of the clearing the exiles will enter. And just keep breathing and allow them to come forward. Trust whatever images come to you, not grasping for anything.

They may appear dirty, hungry, ragged, or deformed in some way when they come forward. It's okay. You can invite them to step into the river of light to wash away all the dirt and cobwebs. Take as long as you need. Notice how the parts seem different when they step out of the river of light. How did they change? If you feel ready, you can invite them to your side of the river for a hug. You can tell them they are always welcome in the circle of love, and you are grateful for the role they play in your internal queendom.

Journal about what you saw on your inner journey, right away if possible!

-To Identify Where the Wound Lives in Your Body:
We've already done a body scan together in this book, but it's an important practice to repeat, even as part of your daily rituals. Each time, you will notice emotional and energetic imprints shifting, changing shape, size, and color, offering new information. That's a good thing.

Do a body scan after you complete the Shadow Alchemy meditation, setting the intention to notice any places of pain, tension, tightness, stuckness, discomfort, holding, or any other unusual sensation as you guide your awareness from the top of your head to the tips of your toes. Give yourself a few moments to breathe into the sensation(s) in your body and to allow your body to offer up any information or wisdom that is being communicated through this sensation.

Describe what the body sensation looks or feels like in your journal poetically, giving it a shape, texture, color, temperature, size, and any other qualities that you sense with your interoception. Think of this description as the most accurate photograph you're likely to get of an energetic/emotional tangle that's been living in your body.

-To Find Out All You Can Directly from the Exile:

You can journal out a dialogue with any internal part in an interview format, using your own initials and a set of initials you come up with for the part. Feel into the part and invite it to write through you as you ask about its role, fears, desires, needs, concerns, how old it is, when it had to split off and why. Ask about the degree to which it feels appreciated or understood. Alternatively, you can set an internal intention to allow this part to step into "the driver's seat" and write through you, and then allow it to speak to each of these questions in its own way. Continue until there is a mutual understanding of what is needed in order for integration to occur. You may even ask the part directly: *What is needed in order for integration to occur?*

291

-To Let Some Magick Begin:

Commit to meeting the needs of the formerly exiled part in your actual, daily life, and to going after its desires, assuaging its fears, and tending to its concerns. *Putting this into practice in your lived experience* is where the rubber meets the road. Talk to your community and/or your healer about anything that seems to get in your way. If you feel safe, supported, and ready, you may even experiment with swinging the pendulum even more deeply into this aspect of yourself for a little while until a healthy synthesis is found. Write a short letter to the exiled part. It could be an apology letter. And place it on your altar.

-To Invite *Extra* Magick:

Engage in your preferred form of creative play inspired by this part. This can reveal even more to you about the deeper dimensions of the part and the magickal energy that's been stowed away with it. You could write a poem or a song or make a visual artwork. Don't worry about creating an ingenious work of deathless beauty and unremitting societal value. Just worry about allowing the part to reveal more of itself to you through your chosen creative medium.

-To Invite the Deeper Love Alchemy to Begin:

Place anything else on your altar that represents this part, whether an object or artwork (current or from childhood), or simply the letter from the previous step. I love Marianne Williamson's statement that whatever is placed on the altar is altered, because the altar is simply the intention to see through the eyes of love, which is a miracle in each instance. By placing this part on the altar, we are allowing it to be altered into its high side, loved expression. The way to express this part on the high side is to keep it in the circle of your love and awareness. It may sound like a bit much to you to *love* this part (or parts) that you've completely disowned until now. Okay, fine. Try starting with neutral acceptance and place them on the altar, anyway. Let love work its magick behind the scenes.

Try to always find ways to deeply embrace these parts of yourself that you've been told are "bad" or undesirable. Even the "bitch" part, even the "too much" part and the "not enough" part. There are treasures in *each of these parts* if you dare to look. Bitches will never allow anyone to walk all over them. Women who feel they are "too much" are bright, one-of-a-kind transmissions who happen to have been born in a culture that tells them women should be pretty, well-behaved, mostly closed-mouthed sidekicks. Women who feel they are "not enough" are completely natural, human babes who have been fed a whole truckload of bullshit all their lives about who and what they are supposed to be, look like, do, and have.

Use your journal to dream up ways that these "shadow" qualities could be adjusted into your greatest gifts, your wildest transgressions, your brightest internal star. This will prime you for the next bit, which is all about finding the mythopoetic brightness and power underneath these rejected shadow aspects.

CHAPTER ELEVEN

SEEING THROUGH THE MYTHOPOETIC LENS: A MAGICKAL PERSPECTIVE ON ARCHETYPES

—————•┼•—————

THE HOPELESS WEIRDNESS OF ARCHETYPES

ARCHETYPES ARE INHERITED PSYCHIC SYSTEMS THAT ARE DEEPLY
BURIED WITHIN THE COLLECTIVE STRATA OF OUR UNCONSCIOUS,
SERVING AS PRIMAL INNER MAPS OF OUR HUMAN NATURE.
THESE COLLECTIVE PSYCHIC ENTITIES ARE PRIMARILY EXPRESSED
THROUGH SYMBOLS AND METAPHORS.

-MARIA PAPASPYROU, *FEMTHEOGENIC CONSCIOUSNESS*

In some ways, archetypes are really a secular term for what were once called the "gods" or "powers." Archetypes are hopelessly weird and, therefore, the task of defining them is ineluctably tricky. Let's go in this way. We are all born with an inherent recognition of the mother-baby dyad. When you see a representation of the Virgin Mary, for example, there is a deep recognition of *something* that the image represents: "Mother." This transcultural *something* that stands behind the representation is the archetype. The representation is not it. Rather it stands in front of, or in the basic shape of, the inherited psychic structure of "Mother" in its great magnitude.

The magnitude of "Mother" stands outside of conventional time, while its representations belong to the realm of linear time and history. In this way, it could be said that, when we sense "Mother" behind a historical representation of a mother (in art or in life), we are sensing the realm of the timeless intersecting with the realm of time. And these nodes (in art and in life) where the realm of the timeless shines through the realm of time can seem almost like little stitching points where time reveals its secret, cyclical nature.

And, like a Medusa or a blinding brightness from Plato's World of Forms, the timeless magnitude behind the representation can never be seen, sensed, or known by us in its fullness. Representations (in art or in life) give one small window on the magnitude as it can be perceived through the human apparatus. But the thing in-and-of-itself, what it is *for* itself, can never be fully disclosed. Its vastness can only be sensed. And when the realm of the timeless is sensed within the realm of time, and this vastness is sensed through our small window on the magnitudes, we are having a *numinous* experience.

Sometimes I refer to the archetypes (and even "the masculine" and "the feminine") as arcana ("secrets, mysteries") or as *mysterium tremendum et fascinans* in the Rudolph Otto sense ("awe-inspiring mystery"). We can get at their most superficial layers with different definitions, but there is always a stratum at which they drop out into pure mystery. Even the things and people nearest and closest to us will ultimately be unknowable at their cores.

But not to worry! We don't need to fully understand the archetypes in order to work with them in art, occult practice, and depth psychology. We don't need to thoroughly flood their realm with fluorescent light. We can let them remain mysteries. Remember the crone's riddle? In order to cross over into the underworld, you must demonstrate that you are able to hang in the realm of Mystery. As a sufficient working definition for now, think of archetypes as a sort of collective, inherited, non-physical museum of universal themes that are found in art, fairy tales, mythology, poetry, dreams, and magick. As we go along, I may alternately refer to them as archetypal energies, arcana, magnitudes, or even just Mysteries.

You'll develop your own way of relating to them and sensing them. You may sense them most distinctly when you stand before great artworks, in a cathedral, or under an ancient tree. You may relate to the realm of the Mysteries as the realm of the gods, as the unfathomable glittering darkness from which all great artwork is born, or as the occult practitioner's palette. I consider these to all, essentially, be the same stuff, and it's the stuff we're working with in this process.

SHEDDING SOME MOONLIGHT ON THE MYSTERIES

Here I'll offer a list of archetypes, as they've been enumerated by some Neo-Jungian authors, so that you can read through and start to get a sense of what might be active for you now. Understand, however, that we all have access to each one of these energies. It's just that some of us will express or be "tuned to" some energies more strongly than others. We are each a unique blend. And one specific energy may be "breaking through" and much more present for you all of a sudden when you start going through a period of profound transformation. Now that you have a sense of the exiled part you are bringing back home in this process, try to get a sense of the archetypal energy standing behind it as you peruse these lists. Let the lunar part of you make the discernment, the part that knows in the dark.

Also, understand that these lists are not, by any means, exhaustive. Consider them a way to get a clue, and an invitation to further exploration. First, I'll give a couple of general Neo-Jungian lists, and then I'll offer some of my own examples of specifically feminine archetypes.

First, Carol Pearson and Margaret Mark came up with the following three groups, organized according to fundamental driving forces:

- Ego types:
  1. Innocent
  2. Orphan/regular guy or gal
  3. Hero
  4. Caregiver
- Soul types:
  1. Explorer
  2. Rebel
  3. Lover
  4. Creator
- Self types:
  1. Jester
  2. Sage
  3. Magician
  4. Ruler

Margaret Hartell and Joshua Chen, listed twelve archetype groups, each with a subset of five archetypes:

- Caregiver Family:
  1. Caregiver
  2. Angel
  3. Guardian
  4. Healer
  5. Samaritan
- Citizen Family:
  1. Citizen

2. Advocate

3. Everyman

4. Networker

5. Servant

- Creator Family:

  1. Creator

  2. Artist

  3. Entrepreneur

  4. Storyteller

  5. Visionary

- Explorer Family:

  1. Explorer

  2. Adventurer

  3. Pioneer

  4. Generalist

  5. Seeker

- Hero Family:

  1. Hero

  2. Athlete

  3. Liberator

  4. Rescuer

  5. Warrior

- Innocent Family:

  1. Innocent

  2. Child

  3. Dreamer

- 4. Idealist
- 5. Muse
- Jester Family:
  1. Jester
  2. Clown
  3. Entertainer
  4. Provocateur
  5. Shapeshifter
- Lover Family:
  1. Lover
  2. Companion
  3. Hedonist
  4. Matchmaker
  5. Romantic
- Magician Family:
  1. Magician
  2. Alchemist
  3. Engineer
  4. Innovator
  5. Scientist
- Rebel Family:
  1. Rebel
  2. Activist
  3. Gambler
  4. Maverick
  5. Reformer

- Sage Family:
  1. Sage
  2. Detective
  3. Mentor
  4. Shaman
  5. Translator
- Sovereign Family:
  1. Sovereign
  2. Ambassador
  3. Judge
  4. Patriarch
  5. Ruler

Now for the specifically feminine archetypes. The most basic breakdown must include Maiden, Mother, and Crone, branching into various subtypes, such as the Ingénue, the Muse, Holy Mother, the Fierce Feminine, Holy Whore, Lady Death, the Creatrix, the Queen, the Femme Fatale, the Oracle, the Wise Woman, the Medicine Woman, the Witch, the Sorceress, the Sex Priestess, the Mystery Priestess, the Scarlet Woman, and the list goes on. You may relate to these magnitudes in your own way or have your own, poetic names for them.

For a deeper exploration of the feminine archetypes, look at the fairy tales, the myths, religion, and the arts. Look at your own dreams. Behind each of these emanations is the great goddess Herself, Sophia (Living Wisdom), Shekinah (the light in matter), She of many names. She is the crystal that breaks into the rainbow of the many feminine archetypes.

THE MAGICKAL PERSPECTIVE ON ARCHETYPES

THERE IS SOMETHING THAT HAPPENS WHEN YOU START PAYING ATTENTION TO SYNCHRONICITIES—YOU SUDDENLY START GETTING A BUNCH OF THEM. WHEN YOU START PAYING ATTENTION TO DAEMONS OR INCORPOREAL INTELLIGENCES, WHATEVER, ALL OF A SUDDEN, ALL KINDS OF WEIRD, FAIRY-LIKE PHENOMENA START HAPPENING IN YOUR LIFE.

-PHIL FORD, WEIRD STUDIES

When we hold a magickal worldview, we interact with everything as if it had its own life force or indwelling spirit. Maybe we even interact with everything, from plants to cats to radiators, as if each one contained the mysteries of the very universe. Within this magickal framework, we interact with a tree as a fellow being, not as a technically living but ultimately insensate, meaningless concrescence of matter. If we are interacting with archetypes within a magickal framework, then we are ritualizing them and interacting with them as if they are tremendous beings. We are interacting with them as if we can have an actual *relationship* with them.

Since the archetypes are tremendous energies that are much bigger and older than us, I tend to advocate for the magickal framework. Also, I have noticed a couple of things about these energies. One is that it's vaguely psychedelic to be held in the thrall of an archetype. We might say each god is a visionary lens through which a different perspective on the world can be glimpsed. Another thing I've noticed is that there can be a certain volatility about energies of such tremendous voltage, both in my own life and in the lives of my clients. In other words, this kind of stuff has the potential to feel like it's blasting your circuitry. That is why I do not recommend playing with archetypes or tapping into them as part of your healing process without reverence, or without a healthy lifestyle, adequate community, and one-on-one support.

If interacting with archetypes is such a full contact sport, why would we ever consider bringing it into the delicate container of the healing process?

First of all, keep in mind that none of these archetypes are "inherently good" or "inherently bad." They are neutral. But they tend to have high side and low side expressions through human beings. By identifying the archetype underneath a complex or a rejected aspect of ourselves, we can consciously switch from having a "battle with the gods" to recognizing and activating the exalted form of the archetype, and thus, of the part of ourselves we've disowned. Then we can employ all the energy that's gone into keeping ourselves stuck in the service of our next soulful adventure or creative endeavor. To give an example, when the Warrior archetype is pushed into the unconscious or rejected (on an individual or collective level), it doesn't just go away. Rather, it comes out in its "shadow" forms. When it is brought to consciousness and exalted, it can express as discipline, training, and gritty strength employed in the name of a greater cause.

Second, a Jungian would tell you that you are interacting with the energetic spheres of the archetypes whether you like it or realize it consciously or not. Better to relate to them consciously. Also, it brings a depth and a dimension of transcultural sacredness and consequence to the work, making it easier to absolve these rejected aspects of ourselves. When we see they are a tiny little expression of a neutral archetype, we might be inspired to imagine how we can learn a thing or two in our own lives from the ways a particular archetype can be expressed in a conscious, healthy way. Furthermore, the archetype and its attendant stories provide points of reference for our own processes of transformation. We'll get more deeply into that, and into ways to relate to an archetype within a magickal framework, in the next chapter. It's important to first realize that you don't ever need to actively obsess over this or try really hard to relate to any archetype. It seems these spheres *want to connect with us*. And they will continue to do so through dreams and synchronicities.

SYNCHRONICITIES AND PRACTICAL MAGICK

"*Acausal, nonrational, relatedness* are words associated with the feminine. These words are not quite yet respectable in the West. But the scientific discoveries of the past several decades are forcing us to take seriously the ideas they embody. Scientists have begun

TO ACKNOWLEDGE THAT CERTAIN PHENOMENA IN THE QUANTUM WORLD IMPLY ACAUSALITY, AND THEY HAVE EVEN CONSTRUCTED COSMOLOGICAL THEORIES THAT *REQUIRE* IT."
-MARION WOODMAN, *DANCING IN THE FLAMES*

Jung posited that archetypes are an inherited tendency to form certain representations, and these representations occur cross-culturally and throughout history in religion, art, literature, myth, and dreams. Funny enough, that's also what an instinct is, isn't it? An inherited tendency? I suspect that the realm of instinct, and the mystery realm of archetypes (of the gods), are intertwined in more ways than one. There is a big vesica between them. Not only do we need to be in touch with our instinct in order to navigate the realm of Mystery. It also seems to be the case that, once you begin to live instinctually, you are more likely to call forth powerful mythopoetic initiations and transformations. The kind we are talking about in this book. The kind that put you in touch with the transpersonal realm of the goddess, with all her many faces.

So, by living from the poetic instinct (from "the mark inside" to use Burroughs' phrase), we may be activating more synchronicity in our lives. By creating from the poetic instinct, we dance with the gods.

In this way, living from our mysterious, lunar, instinctual center becomes a magickal way of being. I believe it literally activates the dreamlike, storybook face of reality. It re-enchants the world. It brings about more incidences of acausal connectedness. (More on that in a second.) So centering into the poetic instinct, moment by moment, *is* practical magick. It turns life into a poem, a novel, with its own symbolic themes that recur in the most uncanny ways. And living by poetic instinct is not reserved for privileged housewives who never have to work. No, it can be activated by anyone at any time. It's ready to go no matter where you are, what your life circumstances are, or what you are doing.

So how does this translate into the kind of practical magick we're doing here? A commitment is a magickal act. So is shadow work. So is playing with archetypes. Therefore, making a commitment to do this work *is* practical magick. My weird claim is that some kind of power is released in the intention to work with an archetype–power that organizes synchronicities. Synchronicities are strange, acausal occurrences which happen when we notice outside of us what is active within us. We might refer to them as "coincidence." Classical Western psychotherapy pathologizes the act of noticing seemingly synchronistic events under the category of "thoughts of reference," a characteristic of Schizotypal Personality Disorder and other pathologies. But doing away with them is too easy. Reality is weird. No one actually knows what is going on here.

Something happens when we interact with archetypes, in art, divination, or magick. They somehow dip our toes into this strange, acausal aspect of reality. What does that mean? Acausal connectedness is when, for example, you pull The Tower card first thing in the morning and then, somehow, the theme of communication breakdown runs through your day like wood rot. I know skeptics will respond, "Well, you were just noticing communication breakdown more after pulling the card, possibly even unconsciously contributing to it yourself." So let me give you another example.

Imagine an electrical fire starting in the home of a witch's enemy after she places a hex on him. The hex did not directly *cause* the electrical fire in the traditional sense. The outlets were already faulty, and some of the appliances were already old and outdated. Rather, the witch's hex reveals (or unveils) a strange, dreamlike, storybook aspect of life. By casting the spell, the witch has engaged the acausal face of reality, summoning it.

Interacting with archetypes summons the "diviner's cause." Let me explain. There is an African tribe, the Azande, who propose five different types of causality. Those include the four classic Aristotelian types of causality, plus a fifth one, which they call "the diviner's cause." It's the cause that accounts for the weird results magickal workings actually seem to yield, and for the weird accuracy of various divination systems that so many "rational" people can't help but notice.

Causality is one of the fundamental principles of classic rationalism. But causality, as a principle, is entirely derived from experience alone. (Just ask David Hume.) And I would say it's largely derived from the highly contained, structured, shrunken lives of modern people. When we use divination systems, engage the creative process, or get into the storybook flow of life (what our poetic instinct usually nudges us to do) in any number of ways, this acausal aspect of reality suddenly becomes a part of our experience as well.

This points to a connectedness that requires paralogical understanding. Both/and thinking as opposed to either/or. Femtheogenic, lunar consciousness more readily accepts this. These occurrences seem to point to a relationship between psyche/soul and matter that is stranger than we ever supposed, or, as logician Bertrand Russell wrote, "the truth about physical objects must be strange." It could be that the world soul subtends these occurrences so that when we activate them, we are walking through a moonlit All Soul's Night.

I'm not smart enough to fully understand or explain this. There is something really weird going on here. Let it be a mystery. And have fun with it! (Oh, and please don't cast any hexes. The hex anecdote was only an example. My hope is that you will activate poetic magick that brings previously undreamt of levels of meaning and richness to your life.)

LOVE, EROS, AND MAGICK

SYNCHRONICITY AND ACAUSALITY ARE THE GODDESS IN ACTION. SYNCHRONICITY RISES OUT OF THE COLLECTIVE UNCONSCIOUS OR THE WORLD SOUL, WHICH CONTAINS ALL POSSIBILITIES, THE PROLIFERATING WOMB OF SOPHIA.

-MARION WOODMAN, *DANCING IN THE FLAMES*

The great modern magickian, Damien Echols, has stated that love and magick are really the same thing. I believe that's probably true. The Eros, the erotic desire, that makes grass grow and makes the earth spin on its axis and holds the stars in place is the same as your own erotic desire, or your any kind of desire. Whatever compels you beyond yourself, whatever dissolves your defenses, breaks you open, and causes you to fix your eyes on Beauty. It is all Eros; it is all love. And when you live in alignment with that, you are seeing the life force inside of everything, and you are living inside of real magick.

In other words, love and magick exist on the same channel or within the same stream of consciousness. They are similar *realms*. Some people have the kind of intellect that does not easily accept or grant access to this. But all those people need to do is remember the first time they fell in love or the moment their first child was born to get plugged immediately into the realm of love and magick. In love, and in magick, anything is possible.

The medieval philosophers and mystics wrote of an interconnecting love that is implicated in synchronicities. If they were onto anything, then perhaps this interconnecting love is unfathomably intelligent and is implicated in the mathematical perfection, the knife's edge on which the possibility of our lives in the universe hinges. And maybe that unfathomable, interconnected perfection somehow orchestrates or is implicated in what we experience as synchronicities, coincidences, and acausal connections. So this one, interconnecting, intelligent love is the real magick.

FINDING THE ARCHETYPES THAT ARE CURRENTLY ACTIVE FOR YOU

THE GODS HAVE BECOME DISEASES; ZEUS NO LONGER RULES
OLYMPUS BUT RATHER THE SOLAR PLEXUS, AND PRODUCES
CURIOUS SPECIMENS FOR THE DOCTOR'S CONSULTING ROOM, OR
DISORDERS THE BRAINS OF POLITICIANS AND JOURNALISTS WHO
UNWITTINGLY LET LOOSE PSYCHIC EPIDEMICS ON THE WORLD.

-JAMES HILLMAN, *GOLDEN FLOWER*, P. 37.

There is a Gnostic idea that the psyche reflects the emanations of God. Each psyche is especially attuned to a unique gallery of archetypes, or emanations. That means *you* have a personal gallery of archetypes. Whatever those key archetypes are for you, they have a lot to do with whatever you feel, at a deep level, you need to do with your life. If that is disowned, it will bubble up through some of the symptoms and other soul letters discussed earlier.

When I say that you have a personal gallery of archetypes, I do not mean that, literally contained within the basement of your psyche is a certain number of archetypes (these tremendous, universal energies), and that those *belong* to you and literally *are* different facets of you. What I mean is that we are, each of us, *tuned* to certain magnitudes, like a tuning fork vibrating in mirror-like fashion to a much larger, more powerful musical note. The tuning fork and the grander musical note are not one and the same, although it might be said that the energy of the grander music *is* indeed coursing through the tuning fork. One might even say, *channeling* through the tuning fork. Each of us are uniquely tuned to certain kinds of grander music.

There are a number of ways you might discover your personal gallery of archetypes. But an important caveat before we discuss them: You may not discover the full gallery to which you are uniquely attuned within the content of this book or the practices offered here. This is because your psyche knows what is best for you, and it will only usher you through one integration experience (with its attendant archetypal energies) at a time. I would not recommend trying to completely excavate or illuminate the entire gallery with one fell swoop of your internal flashlight. Remember, these are tremendous forces, and they can have delicate, even volatile, personal material wrapped around them. Even working with one at a time risks becoming overwhelming. (There is only so much light we can shed on the underworld at a time.)

The primary indicators an archetype is active are appearances within your dreams, synchronicities, and a new kind of energy surging forward consciously. There can also seem to be a strange overlap between these three main features. For example, you might dream of a beautiful, goddess-like woman one night who tells you her name is Sophia, and then the next day, someone tells you that Sophia means wisdom. A week or so later, you may discover that a prayer associated with the Black Madonna indicates nothing is more worthy of desire than wisdom. At the same time, you may notice that a humble, yet utterly dignified, wise energy seems to surge through you in new ways, especially when walking under very old trees. This great-goddess-as-Wisdom archetype may be active within you.

MAIDEN TO MOTHER

Many of my readers may be passing from Maiden to Mother at the time they read this book. (You don't literally need to be pregnant or becoming a biological, adoptive, or foster mother in order to make this archetypal transition.) As we transition to taking more responsibility (hopefully for our gifts and for actualizing them in the world), we are integrating a new archetype, that of the Mother. She is *vastly* creative. She is plugged into the creative matrix itself. She is best personified, perhaps, by The Empress card in the classic tarot deck, the Queen of Life. The "nevertheless" of wakeful creation in the face of the ineluctable tragedy of life. A sort of mysterious "yes" (like the one you've been finding for yourself in the pages of this book).

Maiden energy will always remain accessible and a part of you, but you may come to embody Mother energy in a new way during this initiation time in your life. Archetypally, this transition is drenched in a feeling of liminality simply because this transition was often so much like a death and often held the potential for actual, physical death. For most of the agricultural era, across world cultures, women were often "given away" to their new husband's family. They would lose their name, their former home, their previous roles and relationships, and transition fully to a new home, new family, and new name. Surrounded by new people, they were forced to forge new relationships.

This was very much a death process. Women had to die to their former Maiden selves. Often, this transition involved pregnancy and childbirth which, for much of our history as a species, brought with it unavoidable peril. A woman could *literally* die during this transition.

I believe this is why there are so many death motifs around the "happily ever after" endings of fairy tales, like riding away on a white horse. Death and marriage are very connected in the collective unconscious. So, in more ways than one, there is a deep connection between the passage from Maiden to Mother, and death or the other world. If you think about it, a new mother brings a new being into this world from the other side, and in the process, she may be whisked away to that other side herself. Throughout this transition, she is standing with one foot in the other world.

Also, the twenties are typically a time when we reflect on where we've come from for the first time. Perhaps we begin to heal some aspects of our childhood, deciding which parts of our upbringing we'd like to carry forward, and which we'd like to leave behind. Often, this process involves reclamation, with all the otherworldly, archetypal potential inherent to retrieving lost parts from the basement of the psyche.

It is for this reason that reclamations occurring in the twenties can really feel like strange, otherworldly initiations. Collectively, this passage from Maiden to Mother is already associated with a nearness to the other world. These archetypes, along with their associations to various fairy tales, may be active in our psyches. In addition, we may do some adjacent healing or integration work along the way, which is very specific to us, our backgrounds and our psychic makeup. This work, of course, can come with its own archetypal flavors.

Remember that the archetypes will come *to you*. The following exercises may send a signal letting it be known that you would like to connect. But this requires a feminine, receptive way of being. Synchronicities and dreams are *received*, not sought after or actively created. The dream section is by far the most crucial. Follow the other suggestions and writing prompts to your taste, remembering that when you enter an initiation moment in your life, the archetypal energy flowing through you will make itself known anyway.

RITUALS & WRITING PROMPTS FOR YOUR OCEANIC LISTENING PRACTICE

-To Find the Active Archetype Through the Avenue of Dreams:

DREAMS ARE THE CHURCH WE ENTER AT NIGHT, AND THEIR IMAGES ARE AKIN TO THE STAINED-GLASS NARRATIVES, LIT BY A NUMINOUS LIGHT FROM WITHIN, THAT WE CAN MEDITATE ON,

AND THUS DRAW OUR MINDS TOWARDS HIGHER THINGS.
-ANDREW MCENEFF, AUTHOR, SCHOLAR, AND FRIEND

Your soul is always trying to push into the next stage of its unfolding, integration, and healing. And just like your body knows how to give birth (ideally, with some deft support!), your soul knows how to give birth to the next stage of your unfolding. Each dream image is another big push. Dreams truly are the most organic, gentle, Mother Nature-approved method for zeroing in on the archetypes that are currently active within you. Dreams are always letters from soul-land, showing you exactly what kind of balance is needed.

For that reason, continue your dream-tending practice. If you do not follow any of the other suggestions in this book for digging deep into your internal landscape, this (with sufficient support) will be enough. So let's talk about how to deepen your dream-tending practice now.

Each morning, give yourself at least fifteen minutes to write your dreams down, weird details included. Don't get totally bogged down by every single last detail, though. If you're a vivid dreamer, you may end up filling reems of notebook pages and this can actually be a clever way of avoiding ever going deep with any of the dream themes. So just include everything that seems crucial, including the feeling of the dream.

This should be the very first thing you do, maybe after peeing, brushing your teeth, drinking some water, and making your morning beverage. Then take your morning beverage and sit right down (or cozy up in bed) with your journal. Light a candle or burn some incense if you like. But just do it. The more you make this into a practice, the more vividly you will remember your dreams. It's important to do it as soon as possible after waking up, because dreams have a way of curling away from us like ethereal little wisps of smoke only moments after we awaken. The sooner you write it down, the more juice you are going to capture, directly from the lunar realm. We all wake up with the other world still hanging all around us.

Then go through and circle each noun in the dream narrative. You'll probably find things like, "sister," "mirror," "shit," "twins," "road," "spider," etc. After you've circled, see which one of those circled nouns really jumps out at you as a theme or image that carries a little jolt of electricity within it. Play with that image. Free associate from it. Dialogue with it. Research it. See how, where, and whether it appears in any world mythologies or fairy tales. I'd bet $1,000,000 that it does. See if you notice patterns or themes emerging with this practice. Your healing images will appear repeatedly in your dreams. You might notice repeat appearances of a specific feminine archetype or some other archetype, or it could be a color, an image, a number, an animal, or some other symbol. And remember, it might have a journey to take you on before it reveals everything to which it connects.

You may often find artistic, musical, poetic, or other creative inspiration from your dreams. Follow it, and the avenue of inspiration and insight will only continue to open before you.

Some words to the wise: Alcohol and marijuana can interfere with our ability to remember dreams. I've *heard* B vitamins and peppermint tea will help you to both dream vividly *and* remember your dreams. I've also *heard* that blue lotus tea can produce vivid, sometimes strange, even lucid dreams. If you're going to try it out, drink it with reverence. Blue lotus was considered a sacred teacher plant in ancient Egypt. Though it is considered vaguely psychoactive and it contains apomorphine, you can obtain it legally in the United States and order it easily from vendors online. It is super dreamy and tastes vaguely like violet flowers. But you didn't hear it from me! Suggestions like this are considered to be beyond my scope of practice, so consider this an invitation to look into it for yourself.

-To Find the Active Archetype Through the Avenue of Synchronicities:

WHEN AN ARCHETYPE IS ACTIVE WITHIN US… SYNCHRONICITIES REPEATEDLY ARISE THAT BLATANTLY SHOW US THIS ARCHETYPAL FORM.

-ALANNA KAIVALYA, PhD

Synchronicities will show you what archetypes or symbols may be active within you. Continue keeping a log of them (as well as your dreams and your relationship to the moon cycles). And be prepared to encounter more synchronicities when you begin to notice and log them.

What have you been noticing over and over again lately? Any weird coincidences or numinous moments (when the timeless realm seemed to intersect with the realm of time)? Any name, person, book, institute, tradition, school of thought, or idea that's been mentioned to you two or three times in the last couple of weeks, to the point that it seems a little weird or unusual? Write those instances down.

-To Find the Active Archetype Through the Avenue of Shadow:

Remember that the parts of ourselves we deny, reject, and disown are often related to, or vibrating with, a certain archetype. (For example, Caregiver, Angel, Warrior, Hero, Liberator, Ambassador, Alchemist, Storyteller, Reformer, Martyr, etc.) Return to your answers to the journal prompts from the previous chapter and ask yourself whether any of those exiled parts seem to correspond to any of the archetypes listed in this chapter. Here are some additional journal and exploration prompts, which might deepen your sense of that exiled part and its attendant archetype.

What energy, if you were to give in to it now, would contribute to your highest expression of who you are at this moment of your life? (This could point to the myths and/or archetypes that you are dying to embody now.)

What did you gravitate towards as a child? What were you passionate about? Were you at any point shamed for being magnetized towards a certain activity, theme, or way of being? What was that?

-To Find the Active Archetype Through the Avenue of the Stars, the Tarot, and Other Oracle Systems:

Have you ever looked at your natal chart? If not, I encourage you to pull it up for free now on Cafe Astrology or Astro.com if you have access to the internet. If you do not, see if you can plan another way to have your natal chart read. Each of the "planets" in astrology point to archetypal energies that live in all of us, but your unique intersections of planets, signs, and houses might point to more specific archetypes that could be prominent within you. An experienced archetypal astrologer will really be able to help you hone in on this.

If you're exploring on your own, start with your "big three" (your sun, moon, and ascendant). Look up the signs those big three are in, and associations, myths, and stories related to them. They often point to an archetypal energy you will be working with in this life. When you do your own sleuthing on this one, go with your gut. If you find something in a book or online and you're getting a big intuitive hit on it, then go with that.

Similarly, the classic Rider Waite Tarot or other oracle systems can be great tools for relating to arcana, including whatever arcanum (or archetype) you are working with throughout this process. If you feel compelled, grab a deck and begin a practice of pulling a card each morning to start to develop a relationship with it and the archetypes that stand behind it.

You'll be ready for the next chapter once you feel pretty certain about the archetypal energy (or energies) you're working with. The next chapter will guide you in squeezing even more creative and magickal juice out of your relationship with the archetype.

CHAPTER TWELVE

RITUALS FOR WORKING WITH ARCHETYPAL ENERGY

———•••———

EVERYBODY'S LIVES, ORDINARY PEOPLE'S LIVES, ARE TOUCHED BY

DEEP MAGIC.

-TERENCE McKENNA

ART ALTAR

Once you have a clearer sense of the archetypal energy that has been active in this moment of your life, you can place images, artifacts, or found objects that represent it on your altar. You might place them near, or in relationship to, any altar additions related to the exile part you've been resurrecting from the basement of your psyche. And understand that you will

323

continue to unfold to yourself, and life will continue to unfold to you, as long as you live. Whatever you put on your altar now may not represent the full story. That's okay. You contain (and are attuned to) multitudes. And remember, if you work with more than one or two archetypes at a time, you risk missing the richness and the deep teachings of the archetype that is most relevant to this particular moment of your integration, living, and creating.

You may even sit before your altar (after prayer or meditation one morning) and silently ask the archetype to please come through at a level and pace that makes sense for you at this time. Only one time will do. There is no need to obsess over this.

If you don't have an altar, or that's not your thing, a wonderful alternative practice would be to make art (in any form) inspired by this archetypal energy. If you're a poet, write a poem and allow the archetypal energy to course through you as you do. If you're a musician, compose a song with the archetype you've identified as your great muse. If you're a visual artist, roll up your sleeves and let your arms become paint encrusted in a deep, visual conversation with your archetypal inspiratrice. The creative medium doesn't matter. It only matters that you open yourself to this vast energy through the act of creative expression, and that you remain embodied as you do so, noticing in each moment how you feel in your body and allowing that to continually breathe through the artistic work, laced by the greater spheres. Don't worry about creating a masterpiece.

Consider this a practice of liberation and play, allowing it to be a conversation between you (and *only* you!), the archetype, and your chosen medium.

Then, if you feel so moved, let your creative work decorate your altar in any way you please. Whatever you do with your creative work, try not to ossify its meaning. Let it be a charged hub with multifarious energetic spokes, reaching out to myriad possible, layered meanings and interpretations. The ones that speak to us most immediately tend to be the ones that are alive or active within us at a given moment of our lives—the ones for which we currently have the deepest hunger. This is how your creative work can be like a medicine wheel.

If the idea of creative work makes you squirm, then just stick with an easy way to find a visual representation of the archetype for your altar. Or if you like both, then do both! Either way, think of the creative work, or the new altar addition (or any creative work that *becomes* a new altar addition) as being sort of like a Yantra, which in the Tantric traditions literally means a "machine, contraption," or a mystical diagram. It reminds you of the energy while simultaneously focusing it and deepening your understanding of it in an ongoing conversation.

If you've found this process a little too spooky or difficult thus far, and the idea of channeling the archetype through creative work feels emotionally or psychologically daunting, then please listen to your gut on this one. Any simple visual reminder, like a simple found object, is certainly enough for now. Because once you allow the magnitudes to inspire creative work through you, it can start to feel like a portal has opened. Then, the synchronicities and uncanny connections that will seem to show up everywhere may become too overwhelming. For that reason, whether or not you have an altar, I advise making the same internal petition of the archetype before you bring it into your creative practice, or any of the practices in this chapter. (Ask it to please come through at a pace and frequency that make sense for you and your current projects.)

Now! Take a deep breath, roll up your sleeves, and get ready for a crackling, new energy to infuse your practice, projects, and life!

DEEP INQUIRY INTO THE ARCHETYPE

Way before I ever suggest you look up the archetype in an encyclopedia, in your local library, or in an internet search, I am going to challenge you to do a much deeper kind of investigation through a form of active imagination.

Close your eyes, slow down your breath, and bring yourself into a deeply relaxed meditative state, using your preferred method for doing so, journal in hand. Once you are very deeply relaxed, bring to mind an image that represents the archetype. And from that deeply relaxed state, silently ask the archetype any questions you may have for it as if it were a real, living entity standing before you within your imaginal world. Jot down anything the archetype tells you about itself. If you're brave, you may even allow the archetype to freely write through you during this exercise. It doesn't matter whether or not you do. What matters is that you get an intuitive sense of the textures and dimensions of this energy through your own wild knowing before going to other sources. You may be amazed at how consonant your intuitive knowing is with any information you can find through other forms of investigation.

Depending on the archetype, there may be elders in your family or community who could tell you a thing or two about the religious significance of this archetypal energy, or maybe some stories or myths associated with it.

Now! Feel free to do more conventional forms of "research" into the archetype, using whatever resources are accessible to you. Use the public library, the internet, or any books you can get your hands on (keeping in mind that there's a lot of crap on the internet these days). Look for its representative in world cultures, mythologies, and fairy tales. I guarantee all of this will be a fucking *goldmine* for you at this stage of your unfolding. Just trust there will be a lot in there for you that you don't even know about right now.

You are likely to find the archetype making cameo appearances in mystical, spiritual, religious, mythological, folk tale, artistic, and literary traditions. As you explore the ways this particular archetypal energy has been represented throughout these traditions, you will deepen in your understanding of it. You will also deepen in your understanding of yourself and your unique journey and work in this life. Listen to the songs that were written for this archetype. Read the poems, prayers, and incantations out loud that were written with this archetypal energy as inspiratrice.

Next (you guessed it!), journal about this. Ask yourself how you can integrate this archetypal energy more into your way of working, loving, and being in the world. After all, this is the goal of this stage of your individuation (or awakening) process: For you to fully integrate this part of yourself and the energy it contains and to fully express that. How might this archetypal energy allow you to be more fully expressed, more brave and authentic in your work, and more balanced in your relationships? You might allow this archetypal energy to continue to inform your creative work in some form, whether you're starting a business, making art or music, writing, acting, or gardening. Spend some time really contemplating this and taking steps to actualize all the ideas you generate.

And as you do this, be aware that, like a dream or a great poem, this archetype will never be "finished" with you. You don't just integrate it and then you're done and you move on. Heck no. We are talking about a vast, unbelievably rich, and multi-layered collective tendency as old as our species (and probably much older), which has played across the screens of all the world's artistic and spiritual traditions.

Quite frankly, even if you devoted your life to exploring and deepening your understanding of a single archetype, there is no way you would ever get to the bottom of it. This is one reason why this practice is so unbelievably enriching and life enhancing. You have uncovered a power, a vast energy, and an endless treasure trove with which you have a unique and one-of-a-kind relationship. Let this deepen you in your work and in every level of your expression. Let it also remind you that there *is* still some magick and mystery to be found in the world, no matter how bleak things can seem.

As you research, you will likely at some point encounter other cultures' mythologies, religions, and spiritual or folkloric traditions. You may feel inspired to investigate deeper, or to integrate your findings into your life in some way. For that reason, it's important to offer a quick word on the difference between cultural appropriation and cultural appreciation.

If your seeking brings you into contact with a spiritual tradition or practice from a culture other than your own, that's wonderful! Approach it respectfully and as a student. Seek reputable sources and actually speak to people for whom this is their home culture. People will usually let you know if it would be offensive, tone deaf, disrespectful, or wrong for you to use a certain religious item, practice, or other cultural symbol in any certain way. Make sure you find people who are *eager* to talk to you about the tradition, not pressuring anyone into educating you.

Keep deepening your knowledge, understanding that this subject is yet another bottomless well. Whatever it is, you could probably devote your life to learning about it and still not know everything there is to know. Maybe it is part of your journey to become a student of this culture or tradition. This kind of cultural interface and dialogue represents another step in the direction of the kind of world we'd all like to live in: a peaceful world of humility and respect for all peoples, journeys, and traditions. If we are so afraid of appropriating that we never go near another culture, then we are unwittingly participating in another form of segregation. Don't do that. Appreciate.

Also, listen to your gut about dosing. You can find yourself going down all kinds of arcane rabbit holes forever with even one archetype. Often, creative people have a bit of an obsessive streak, and they can just run with one idea and go so deep with it that they start to see it everywhere. *Leverage* that obsessive streak in your creative practice or on your artist path, but be careful it does not get hijacked by an inner (perhaps unconscious) proclivity for escapism.

EVEN DEEPER INQUIRY: PRACTICES FOR EMBODYING AN ARCHETYPE

The great Jungian analyst Marion Woodman was a big proponent of embodying your dream images. This takes dream journaling one step further. Don't just free associate from the eagle image or go into light trance states to dialogue with the spirit of the eagle. Spread your wings, ah-hem, I mean your arms. What does that kind of expansion feel like in your body? Dreamt of a lioness? Get down on all fours and let her move through your body.

Do you feel self-conscious? Good. Interacting with big energies should always take us beyond our ego.

If your ego is saying, "Er, um, wait, what are we doing?" that is a very good thing. The ego only holds your current idea of yourself, and you are expanding and growing. The archetypes offered to you by your dreams are the perfect balancing expanders for your current idea of yourself.

There is a reason so many of the world's spiritual traditions have involved some form of ecstatic dance, from the Sufis to the maenads and beyond. Look at the roots of that word. *Ek* comes from the Greek *outside*, and *stasis* means *to stand*. So ecstatic dance and movement is any dance or movement that causes you to *stand outside of yourself* or to be *beside yourself*. Think of this as standing outside of the nice, neat, easily defined persona that your ego likes to present to the world. If you feel a little stupid when you begin an archetype embodiment practice or ecstatic dance practice, even when you're at home by yourself, know that you are already well on your way to ecstasy.

Let me give you an example of how powerful this can be. In 2107, I attended a week-long workshop hosted by Dr. Clarissa Pinkola Estes in Loveland, Colorado. There was a giant pink box at the back of the room, next to little slips of paper and miniature pencils. Since the workshops always began early in the morning, participants were encouraged to walk bleary-eyed straight to the pink box upon entering the workshop space and to write a dream on a slip of paper and place it inside, if they liked. CPE (as she prefers to be called) would occasionally stir her hand through the little dream slips, but she never said exactly why or what she was going to do with them.

Finally, one day, she chose a dream. She read it to the group, and she had some participants come to the front of the room to play each of the dream characters in a mini psychodrama. The power that surged through the room in that impromptu exercise was palpable. There was not a soul present who did not clearly recognize it. Everyone knew an archetype had passed through. There was a soft, collective gasp and hush. Some people had tears in their eyes.

This kind of dream re-enactment can be another way to embody the archetype speaking through the dream. And this might be the very best form of "research" into the archetypes. You have to feel something with your body, you have to experience it, to really know it.

Actors play with this kind of practice when they're getting into the energy of a role. If you do it, you'll be able to tap the energy more easily for any creative project or other purpose at any time... And I believe this is nothing short of magick.

Here's a delicious example. I believe most women have used the energy of "gorgeous" at some point. Come on. You know what I'm talking about. There is an energy that you can turn on when you want people to look at you, and you can turn it off when you'd prefer they didn't. The odds are very good that you've done this before.

A friend of Marilyn Monroe's took her out for lunch in New York City one day. Marilyn wore a hat and sunglasses and very "normal" clothes. The friend recounted that a waiter took their orders and people were passing them by as they sat in this sidewalk cafe as if she was just a regular old person. No one recognized her. Even as they walked down the street after their lunch, there were no stares, no adoring fans, no recognition of who she was.

Then Marilyn turned to her friend and said, "Want me to turn it on?" The friend said, "Sure," not exactly certain what she meant. Just then, Marilyn's posture changed, the way she carried herself in every cell of her body changed, and the energy emanating from her grew into a delectable, highly magnetic, golden aura of gorgeous. Suddenly, people were gawking, ogling, and recognizing her everywhere.

When Marilyn said "it," I believe she was talking about the tremendous voltage of the sex-alicious side of the great goddess Herself, as this energy expressed through the unique vessel of Marilyn. Marilyn knew how to embody that.

And you can embody that, or any other archetype, too. After you've done a private, at-home practice, you might try practicing with a friend or healer, or in a group setting. There might be laughs and defenses. Maybe for quite a while. Then, hush. Oh, wow.

FIND THE RIGHT FAIRY TALE MEDICINE FOR THIS STAGE OF UNFOLDING

"Something inside you is always telling a story. I believe every single thing that you see and hear is talking to you."

-Jim Carrey, *I Needed Color*

As you conduct your inquiry, the odds are very good you will find a story or two, in the form of a cultural myth or a folktale of some kind. And it is at that point something very surprising might happen.

You might find a fairy tale with strange parallels to your own life, or more specifically to this moment of your life. When I first noticed this, I described it as the realm of fairy tales breathing its uncanny breath onto our side of the veil. That's one way of looking at it, to be sure. All I know is that this happens, and your fairy tales are out there. You'll know you've found the one if it feels wonderfully redemptive to read it.

Why? Because reading the fairy tale or myth that pertains most to this moment of your life will feel like a whimsical, somehow edifying breath has been exhaled over the comparatively drab landscape of your days. It will also feel like meaning and perhaps even purpose has suddenly been injected into what might seem like pointless hardship. Not only that, but it will seem like you now have some intimation of where this moment of your life might lead you, and what the points of reference are along the way. Though things may not be going exactly "your way" right now, the right fairy tale for this moment of your life might bless you with the redemptive feeling that life really does have other plans for you. And maybe some larger part of you has always been in on those plans.

Stories, originally, served as medicine, as currency, as instruments for conveying wisdom poetically. Wisdom that might be good medicine for a given person at a given time. Not only do people *want* to hear stories about travel to unknown places, heroes overcoming challenges, and the triumph of the human spirit, but often, stories served (and still serve) as allegories for processes of inner transformation.

The use of allegories as maps for processes of psychological transformation is an incredibly ancient practice. It was used by the Gnostics, and probably for a very, very long time before them. Fairy tales are snapshots of the collective psyche, woven together by people without psychological knowledge or terminology, making them a stark composite of reference points for processes of inner growth and sea change. The reference points they provide allow us to see where we are on the journey. That is their psychological and religious function.

If you consider each character in the story as a different aspect of one person's psyche, then you are getting closer to the money. Look how the parts interact with each other. What are the warnings? What happens if the heroine overcomes the challenges? If she doesn't? Now, consider this entire drama is playing out inside one person: you. Because I guarantee you, if you've found the right fairy tale, it is.

Consider this an invitation to find the fairy tale or myth that is perfect medicine for this moment of your life (if you haven't already). Follow the archetype you've been working with to get there. When in doubt, refer to Vasilisa the Beautiful. The images in that particular fairy story apply universally to feminine initiation, and also (in many ways) to the creative process, and the creative life itself.

During some life transitions and trials, it might feel immediately redemptive to view your hardship as the lessons of the dark woods. However, depending on the pain level implicated in a particular passage of life, it may seem glib to suggest that you can redeem the whole experience by just telling yourself you are doing your sifting and sorting work in the house of Lady Death. If you, dear reader, are currently experiencing such deep bereftness, I pray you find a moment of grace in your dark night of the soul. Perhaps even the original John of the Cross poem, "Dark Night of the Soul" could be your best medicine now.

If you just keep breathing, if you stay alive, you *will* glean some treasure from the underworld. Like Inanna, you may remove all of your clothing (your pretenses and masks) in the process. Your heart may completely break open. You may return, in Vasilisa fashion, like a flaming Roman candle. Or like the Maiden Persephone, you may come back turning the world green again with your every footstep. Maybe all three. Either way, if you keep breathing, you will make a return. (And the gold you bring back may be something entirely different from what you ever expected. It may blow all your old theories apart.) And the wheel will continue to turn.

Understand a lot of the deeper instructions will come through dreams.

Continue your dream-tending practice. To get instructions from a dream, free-associate from each of the main images in the dream. After you have a good sense of your personal associations with each image or character, look at the storyline of the dream and how each of the characters are interacting. Then apply that to some of your most important or charged associations, and to different parts of your own psyche. What is the dream telling you? The feeling of the dream should give you a clue. During this process it is not uncommon to have wedding dreams, baby or pregnancy dreams, and wounded or lost animal dreams. Dreams will show you *exactly* where you are on the journey and *exactly* what is needed next.

Then put the dream and fairytale wisdom into practice in your life.

If your dreams are offering instructions to you, heed them. If you are having trouble deciphering the messages contained within your dreams, guess what I'm going to say, my darlings? That's right! Consult with your healer, whoever they are.

THE DANGER OF OVER-IDENTIFYING WITH
AN ARCHETYPE

THERE ARE MORE THINGS IN HEAVEN AND EARTH THAN ARE
DREAMT OF IN YOUR PHILOSOPHY, HORATIO.
-WILLIAM SHAKESPEARE, *HAMLET*

Each archetypal representation has the actual archetype standing behind it, and behind that is the Great Mystery. We will never fully grasp, own, or "know" these energies. That's the point. That's why they're so endlessly intriguing. We are on a journey of refining our questions more so than finding answers and sticking with them. The point is not for you to own, master, or fully understand any archetype. You never will. You're just a unique blend of resonances. A little song comprised by multiple notes. Maybe that's why we're here, so that these greater forces can sing through us.

You've been given a wonderful instrument (you!) and the best way to enjoy that instrument is to learn different songs and really see what it can do. All the while, you must remember that even if you devoted your life to only playing one note, you would still never be able to fully encapsulate it in any intellectual concept. When we try to do that, we stymie the flow. We contain and box in what is vast and wild. It seems we must relate to the Mysteries *as* Mysteries in order to keep the magick alive.

Here's another very important thing to note: The archetype is not you. You are not the archetype. Rather, you are tuned to a unique constellation of archetypes. When you are practicing embodying an archetype, for example, you are just playing the unique keyboard that is you like a master. Over-identification with any one archetype presents the potential for using that archetype as a means of ego inflation. Humility is required in this process. If you have a hard time with humility, think of how wonderful it is that *human* and *humus* (soil, earth) share the same root. Humility brings us closer to the earth and to our humanity. And maybe that is the most sacred task of all: To be fully human.

There was a wonderful *Onion* article that came out recently entitled, "Writer Miranda July Called before Congress to Explain What Her Whole Thing is About." It delighted me to see that because the most wonderful thing about Miranda July is that it's not entirely easy to encapsulate her in a sentence, or even a paragraph. And that's what makes her such an authentic artist. There's so much pressure to define "what your whole thing is about," in a nicely packaged, easily digestible way for others, especially in this age of branding and making sure your Instagram page follows a color scheme. You know what? You can go through phases! When you over-identify with a certain "thing" or "phase" because you read in a blog somewhere that's what you need to do on your Instagram, you're actually being less authentic. It's okay to be difficult to classify or categorize. In fact, that is (largely) what this book is encouraging.

In short, don't try to over-identify with anything except the full, authentic, one-of-a-kind spectrum of you. No one else is doing it! There's no competition. The pressure to be someone else, to sell out in some way, or to have a brand that can be explained in four words is tremendous. You are robust and rare and there is no one quite like you. Fully enjoy your instrument, your humanity. Honor your fullness and defy classification.

HOW THIS RELATES TO BADLY-BEHAVED FEMALE MYSTICS

Some daytime TV show about Joan of Arc came on once when I was a kid. During the opening sequence, a barrage of words used to describe her flashed across the screen, each with question marks: "Saint? Witch? Warrior? Heretic? Madwoman?" I was so intrigued by the idea that a single woman could embody each of these archetypes (or have each of them projected upon her). Being brought up Catholic, naturally I wondered how in the holy hell she could be a saint and a witch and a heretic all at once, let alone all the other things.

Before they burned her at the stake in 1431, she famously stated, "I die for speaking the language of the angels." She was a woman who was completely guided and directed by the weird divinity at the center of her life, regardless of how you might judge the actions or consequences of her life. And it caused her to bust out of every box, defy every norm, and to mystify and bewilder her contemporaries and people even today.

We think of people, and women especially, as belonging to one specific box. She was either a saint or a heretic. Which one was it? And this can contribute to the internal splitting, bisecting, and burying that takes place within the psyches of women: this pressure to identify with a convenient, safe, simplified package. It contributes to the ongoing burning of the witches of our psyches.

We do this because, in a certain way, our brains are lazy. Our lazy brains would like people to fit into simple, neat little boxes. That way, we can categorize them and tuck them away in our comforting understanding of life, the world, and people. But life, the world, and people are children of Great Mystery, and we are as nuanced, mysterious, paradoxical, sacred, profane, and complicated as She is. We have seasons. We have internal regions and internal weather. And for some weird reason, we can call on these vast energies that are sometimes called archetypes. And not just one, but many. Each of them, to some degree.

There's a reason they say well-behaved women rarely make history. It's because well-behaved women are being what their families, institutions, husbands, and societies want them to be: good little girls. And what do good little girls do? They fit into boxes for ease of categorization and understanding. You either fit the snowy virgin bill or the sultry whore bill. Not both. Choose one. You are either a monastic or a radical, not both. Choose one. And if we direct our lives from the outside, rather than from our own mythopoetic depths, we might unconsciously agree to conform to that oversimplified, ill-fitting projection.

This manifests for so many modern women along the lines of the Virgin-Whore split, and it also manifests regarding their role in their family and their professional identity. Once people decide which neat little box you fit into, they tend to keep telling you that is your box, over and over and over again. And when people tell you something about yourself over and over, it's pretty easy to start to believe that about yourself. Don't do it. You are so much more than your box. You are a marvelous, one-of-a-kind occurrence. I want to see you brazenly busting out of boxes, guided and directed by the sacred mystery teacher of your soul. When women make the decision to do this, they truly become forces to be reckoned with.

Besides, our categorization of a woman as a "heretic" or as a "saint" depends upon our understanding of what those terms mean and the institutions within which we apply them. When the institution is sick, conflicted, or confused, someone deemed a heretic could very well be a saint. In fact, in such a situation, I would argue it is a saint's duty to become a heretic.

Mostly, Joan was considered a heretic because she was one in a long line of women who believed she could speak to the divine in her own heart, without need of any institution or intermediary (usually a male representative of said institution). I encourage my reader and anyone I ever work with to make a similar move. You can call it the divine in your heart, you can call it your soul, your depths, or feminine consciousness. Or you can take after me and call it Moonchild. Just make a U-turn back towards that and away from external measurements of you or your worth. And consider that internal power, whatever you call it, to be your greatest creative counsel, and your surest way of relating to holiness, Mystery, and Beauty with a capital-B.

Modern mystic Andrew Harvey states beautifully, "I just continue to follow the one in my heart who loves." Keep following the one in your heart who loves, calling it whatever you want, and believing whatever you want about it. I believe, in some strange way, this beloved, this force in our hearts that wants to choose love and keep loving, is divine. Perhaps it is "the divine" itself. Concepts fail at a certain point.

The mystic Saint Teresa of Avila, in her spiritual classic, *Interior Castle*, wrote that the heart is where the most secret things pass between the soul and God. Call this whatever you want. I consider it no small coincidence that the ultra-sexed, ancient Queen of Heaven was a "Holy Whore" in the sense that she was crowned with love for all. The one in your heart who loves is crowned with love for all. The greatest aspiration of my life is for my heart to become a Holy Whore, a temple where all are welcome, where there is always food, and the doors are always open.

I hope you'll join Joan and me in our soiree of heresy. And know that you are joining a bright constellation of holy women who rebelliously declared that their relationship with the divine was closer than blood and breath and was not under the control of any institution. This form of heresy is also rather divine and saintly. Let it be all the above. Let's no longer flatten it.

Let's no longer flatten *you*. Let's bring back the beautiful otherness that you had not yet learned how to conceal as a child.

And when you do that, you will always transcend genres, and you will be utterly unrepeatable. You will be holy and badly behaved, divine and transgressive, sacred and profane, all at the same time.

This is why we need to "stay tight with [our] instinctual nature," as CPE wrote, because this is what will show us when something new needs to unfold in us. It will show us when we are too squeezed into too tight of a box, when we've been forced into a shape that is no longer natural for us. Your gut knowing, your spark of the sublime, will tell you when it's time to move forward, unfold, turn the page, fold your cards, close shop, set up shop, shed another skin, or put your old soul skin back on. Listen.

Understanding the archetypal dimensions of this personal unflattening work connects it to the level of *collective* shifts that are currently needed on the planet. It also connects the work to the collective, very poignant fact that the feminine has *literally* been buried in the West for millennia. We can embody and give life and airtime to the feminine archetypes not only for ourselves, but for our communities. These energies are universally recognized and craved. The balance is needed everywhere. By doing this work, we are helping to earth Her and make Her more present and more awake in the world, in all of Her paradoxical glory.

WRITING PROMPTS FOR YOUR OCEANIC LISTENING PRACTICE

-To Deepen Your Relationship with the Magnitudes and Let Them Crackle Through Your Life and Projects:

Which archetypes are you *dying* to embody in your life these days? It could be something from the list above or something else entirely.

Choose a day to allow that archetype to influence the way you decorate yourself. Make a plan to sort of "role play" that archetype for the day.

How can you publicly own and embrace this energy more? It's okay if your plan only involves baby steps for now.

How can you invite this energy into your life *even more* from now on? How can you allow this mythopoetic texture to influence the shape of your life and where things are going from here?

How has this energy been expressed or repressed in your past?

PART IV

REDDENING

CHAPTER THIRTEEN

WHAT DOES THIS HAVE TO DO WITH MY WEIRD TRYST WITH RED?

———•———◦———•———

THRESHOLDS AND TRANSITIONS ARE ZONES OF MYSTERY AND

RIDDLE—HERE, THE ATOPIC *OTHER* BEGINS.

-BYUNG-CHUL HAN

IT STARTED WITH AN INEXPLICABLE CRAVING

The archetypal energy that was becoming conscious for me (during that strange chapter of my life beginning in 2015) had a distinct flavor of redness. I did not entirely understand at the time what was happening. Any understanding I have now is only partial and is mapped on in retrospect. I believe the reason I entered a depressive state was that I had activated powerful integration processes within my own psyche simply by reading a Marion Woodman book (and by being ready for it on some level), but without adequate guidance or containment. As you make your way through your own archetypal initiations, integrations, and shadow work, I hope you'll do so with support, insight, self-care, and some understanding.

My current understanding can really only be told in narrative form. I'll play it from the beginning. I remember reading in *The Pregnant Virgin* that one of Woodman's analysands was going through her own integration journey, shedding skins, and giving herself permission to honor instinct and desire in new ways. Woodman shared that, at some point, her analysand knew she absolutely must have a cherry tart! This activated something within me: What did *I* suddenly know I must have, if I allowed instinct and desire to flow through me unabated? The first and only thing that came to mind was the color red.

The first way I made sense of this was that I had identified as a "cool colored person," probably since kindergarten. I distinctly remember the day I transitioned from telling everyone my favorite color was "rainbow" in preschool (as my first little rebellion against what girls are "supposed to say," i.e., pink), to opting for the cool colors in the crayon box: blue, purple, and green. It was a moment of identity formation. I had already decided or internalized something about myself: That my energy was, or should be, in the softer, darker, more muted, or dreamy spectrum. I was not going to pop or be too loud or bold.

So my first instinct was to understand my new red craving as simple balance. A resurgence of an energy that had been buried, shoved into the basement, underappreciated, and ignored. Somehow, by welcoming red back into my life, it seemed I was welcoming back a bold, rebellious streak. The psyche is generally trying to balance itself during these growth phases. It was an infusion, like water and vitamins, to a part of me that was deeply thirsty and malnourished. A blood transfusion for a weary soul.

THEN, THE SYNCHRONICITIES

Then, strange synchronicities started to happen, more than usual. They didn't necessarily all involve the color red. Most involved immediate echoes in the following day of a dream I'd had or a recent oracle card reading I'd done. Lady of the Well had come up in various forms, as had the theme of "two sisters." And in numerous other ways, it seemed the movie genre of my life at that time had suddenly switched to "weird realism," where the strangeness of dreams seeps into waking life through some unseen border.

Then, about one year past reading *The Pregnant Virgin*, another bright red synchronicity sent a vibrant frisson through my subtle body. This was right around the time I was beginning to practice self-love in earnest and was getting ready to leave a relationship that was not working. I was scrolling through the long list of *Sounds True* interview titles on my iPhone, a spiritual podcast featuring interviews with psychologists and spiritual thought leaders. After a quick swipe of my thumb that caused the reel to race down, down, down, and then slow to a halt, my spiritual spidey sense suddenly lit up like a motherfucker. (It often feels like an electric chill in my thighs or even my full body). A title appeared at the center of the screen. It read, *Red, Hot and Holy*, an interview with feminist spiritual author Sera Beak. This strange synchronicity, accompanied by this electric, embodied chill, told me that the magick of the *Pregnant Virgin* chapter of my life was still active.

Of course, I listened to the interview immediately, and I promptly devoured any and all content I could find that had ever been produced by Sera. Sera's work largely centers around the archetype she calls "Red." This archetype relates to a buried feminine spiritual lineage in the West, which Beak sometimes calls "the red thread." She largely focuses on Saint Sarah-la-Kali, the apocryphal daughter of Jesus and Mary Magdalene, who is supposedly connected with an ancient priestess lineage.

Saint Sarah is considered to be the patron saint of all Roma people and outsiders, and she has an underground shrine in the south of France at Les Saintes-Maries-de-la-Mer (Saint Marys of the Sea). Under Beak's care in her beautiful books, Sarah-la-Kali comes to life as a fierce, forgotten feminine archetypal force who has been kept underground within modern Western spiritual traditions. (If we understand "modern" to refer to the past 2000 years!)

Stumbling upon Sera Beak in this incredibly kismet way deepened my understanding of the archetypal energy that was pouring through me during the spontaneous integration process of 2015. Or, it started to open a portal through which Red could reveal more to me. Oh, and guess what color Saint Sarah's cape usually is, when she is carried from her underground shrine to the sea on her yearly feast day? Red.

Sera's work also led me to the work of modern mystic, Andrew Harvey, who, incidentally, discusses the "red path" and the "white path" of spirituality in his work. The white path is the path of transcendence. It is the more classically masculine, intellectual approach geared towards transcending "gross" spiritual matter, including the body, and seeking more blissful, spiritually "pure" realms elsewhere. This approach can be found in both Eastern and Western traditions.

Harvey contrasts this white, transcendence-oriented approach with a... well, a more red path. This can be called the path of the heart, of the passions, of the body, or even of "descent" (as opposed to transcendence or ascension). It is an equally valid (though frequently maligned, misunderstood, or even ignored) approach to spirituality, which seeks to sink all the way down into this human, embodied experience, both feet on the earth. It finds the light in matter (Sophia, or Shekinah) and the sacred within the profane. It finds the path to mystical experience through embodiment, through the body itself, and through being all the way *here, now.*

This approach can be found in the vast, pluriform traditions of tantric yoga, even in ancient Sufism (case in point:

the ecstatic poems of Rumi) and it has also existed in the West, though much more frequently buried, ignored, maligned, or misunderstood here. I think of the saying from medieval alchemy, in sterquiliniis invenitur, "In filth, it will be found."

In this way, I now connect my red-clamation to a balancing or healing of my root chakra. This energy center of the body, located at the bottom of the spine and around the groin (so basically, your whole "no-no" area) is typically associated with the color red. Most spiritual traditions considered "serious" or "real" spiritual work to mostly be the province of the higher chakras, the chakras of spiritual transcendence, cosmic insight, and oneness.

It is not my intention to disparage that. We need experiences of oneness, and connections to more transcendent realms, and we also need to roll around in the mud and come to know this realm of warm, messy, dirty incarnation. We need to enjoy our animal bodies and reverence the wisdom of matter, and we also need to chase the great, ineffable Gnosis. We are the incredible intersection of heaven and earth: They meet in our hearts. So really, we need to be firmly *rooted* in order to fully sink into the heart. Philosophies, traditions, and cultures of transcendence, without heart, can be dangerous.

Wanting to come to understand this archetypal energy, Red, even more deeply, I found and read voraciously *The Red Goddess* by Peter Grey, a book which deserves to be an occult classic. In it, he urges the reader to entertain, at least for the duration of the book, the magickal fact that Inanna and Ishtar are the same goddess, and She is the red goddess. She is also the Scarlet Woman of Aleister Crowley's occult system of Thelema. This goddess is wantonly gorgeous, and usually draped in intricate, delicate, latticed lapis jewelry. She is wickedly sexual, the ultimate force of "animal magnetism," and in ancient Sumer, She (known there and then as Inanna) was also called "The Queen of Heaven."

Interesting, I thought. The little Catholic school I attended as a child was called Our Lady Queen of Angels, referring, of course, to the Virgin Mary. She, also, was the Queen of Heaven. I started to think of the Red Goddess as an ancient, electrically sexy ancestress of the Virgin Mary. Mary with a labia, before she became so snowy, ethereal, and pure. When she had weight, blood, and heat and was all the way here, on earth, in the body, in blood, in sex, in food, maybe even in the mysteries of the land, animals, and elements. When she pointed (perhaps down, with her left hand) to a path of sex, drugs, and rock'n'roll as a path to the spiritual summit.

Let's take a step closer to the dim sanctum of a Red Goddess temple. Did you know that the priestesses of Inanna were sacred sex workers? Peter Grey goes into depth in *The Red Goddess* about what the Holy Whore archetype means to him, especially with reference to the great Red Goddess, the Queen of Heaven. He writes that to be a holy whore does not mean to fuck indiscriminately, with an empty heart. On the contrary, he writes, it means to be "crowned with love for all."

This is where I sense a strong overlap with the Holy Mother archetype. As the mother of all, She is crowned with love for all. All. No exceptions. No discrimination. All are welcomed into Her healing waters at Lourdes and other holy wells and grottos of the goddess. It doesn't matter how messed up, unusual, uniquely wounded, crooked, or smelly you are. You are fully enveloped, embraced, and welcomed into Her shining waters.

This is the energy that heals people. This complete, unconditional embrace. It is a redemptive release into divine love. It is the exalted energy of sex and of the holy whore that redeems all. There *is* a cleansing at the heart of sex, isn't there? When another demonstrates complete acceptance (or even adoration) of these parts of our bodies that we've been told since childhood are filthy and shameful? Similarly, it is the energy of the sensual alchemy suggested in these pages that redeems whatever it is about yourself you find unlovable, shameful, ugly, or bad. Again, my darlings, *In filth it shall be found.*

In a quirky, delightfully vivid example, Grey invites the reader to imagine that, instead of Jehovah's Witnesses knocking on the door, we had the steamy, sexually switched on priestesses of Inanna paying an unexpected visit. *Have you accepted sexual ecstasy as your personal lord and savior?* I believe the archetypal energy of the Red Goddess and Her priestesses are connected to the modern phrase, "red-light district." At this point, I'd begun to find the "red-light district" of healing and spirituality.

MARY MAGDALENE AND THE HEALING OF THE VIRGIN-WHORE SPLIT

Then I found Meggan Watterson, in my Beak-inspired further explorations of Red, Mary Magdalene, and what I began to privately think of as the West's buried feminine lineage. She is a fabulous feminist theologian whose work focuses mostly on the powerful, poetic Gospels of Mary Magdalene, which were *literally buried* for the better part of the past two millennia. They only entered print and a tight, initial circulation in the 1950s. Before that, they were hermetically sealed in a clay vessel somewhere near Akhmim in Upper Egypt.

At the Council of Nicaea, when it was being decided which Gnostic and original Christian texts were to be included in the official canonical Bible, it was decided that these and other (more specifically Gnostic, radical) texts were to be excluded and destroyed. A group of radical monks protected the Gospels of Mary Magdalene, and buried them in secret. I hope those monks have a cushy place in heaven alongside the sexy priestesses of Inanna!

Through Watterson, I learned that Mary Magdalene was sometimes referred to as "Red," and is often depicted with long red hair and/or a red veil. Scholars debate whether or not Jesus and Mary Magdalene were historical personages who actually lived or whether they were character motifs in a powerful set of allegories created by the Gnostics as devices for spiritual transformation. Whatever your leanings, it has been surmised that Mary Magdalene was connected to an ancient lineage of priestesses that may have practiced or been connected to sacred sex.

Ultimately, Red came to represent the healing of the Virgin-Whore psychic split that I, as a denizen of Western culture, had inherited. Red came to represent a feminine, embodied path that embraces the body, sex, emotions, and the mundane *all* as sacred. It also represents the path of descent, both in terms of healing and spirituality.

I do not see the path of descent as separate from the path of transcendence at all. Instead, the path of descent (doing your shadow work, and not skipping out on the course your soul is currently taking called "being a human") is a much more thorough spiritual path. It does not negate the path of transcendence. Rather, it completes it.

And since it's been buried in the West for the past 2000 years, we need it now like sacred jump cables. (Funny enough, Mary Magdalene, or Red, is the one who presides over resurrection.) This spiritual imbalance has contributed to the rapacious exploitation of the earth, which has pushed our planet to the point of collapse. If the ultimate reality is not here (on earth, or in the body), then who cares, right? Wrong. We need to arrive here, fully, now. Not just for ourselves, but for future generations and for all sentient beings.

Later on, I learned that the myth associated with bright Inanna, the Queen of Heaven, is one of the oldest underworld myths we have. It is one of the original maps for the spiritual path of descent into the underworld. Inanna is the archetype, the deity, who shows the way through the underworld, the darkest night of the soul, who shows us how to keep getting more naked. Just like Our Lady of Sorrows, Inanna's grace pierces into even the deepest of agonies, seeping like honey all the way down, down, down.

How could there be a greater love than this: the love that sinks all the way to the bottom of the shadowland? This myth, and all of its cousin and descendent myths, are some of our greatest cultural treasures. What deeper kindness is there than the kindness that accompanies us all the way through hell, saying, "Look honey, I am right here with you, even as we pass again and again through the flames." And like Mary Magdalene, maybe Inanna also presides over resurrection: our own resurrection from any descent into hell.

Because ultimately, Inanna finds and brings back treasure from the underworld. In Her case, it is the treasure of her newly birthed self for, throughout Her descent, a secret part of Her has been in labor. She represents the perennial rhythm of the festival of innocence that springs up like a miracle from the ashes of our deepest hell. This is a love that represents hope even in the darkest of nights. And if we can't feel hope, she represents hope that, eventually, hope will come. She is the fierce resilience of life itself, the rebellious resurgence of wildflowers through asphalt, and the inevitable tearing down of all walls.

This aspect of Inanna/The Red Goddess is connected to the Black Madonna. Deep, emotional adoration of the Black Virgin, at any of her hundreds of shrines across Europe, continues to this day with devotees summing up their adoration in this phrase: "She has been through the fires. She knows our pain."

It felt like Red was revealing Herself to me one coincidence, one synchronicity at a time, like a trail of red velvet cake crumbs someone had laid out in the dark woods, walking backwards and winking. It seemed this tryst with Red connected me to a deeply feminine, mostly buried spiritual lineage, which I could hardly find any information on, but which kept unfolding before me in a sequence of synchronicities and uncanny connections. It was almost as if Red *wanted me to keep following the thread.* This is usually what it is like when we are interacting with an archetype. We call in information and representations of that archetype's energy throughout time and cultures everywhere, so that a thread or a breadcrumb trail seems to become clear before us.

AND THE RED CRUMB TRAIL CONTINUES

Red connections continue to appear on my path. The magnitudes, like great poems or important dreams, will never really be finished with us. Some seem very arcane, or unlikely. Some almost blow my hair back with the sheer level of connection and coincidence. For example, I recently learned that feminine deities in eastern cultures are sometimes pictured with a bowl of blood, representing raw, feminine, embodied, creative power, like menstrual blood or the blood of childbirth.

In the ivory-white Virgin Marys I grew up with I sense the same feminine archetype, but with all of Her blood, heat, and secrets drained from Her. If you think about it, pink, the color classically associated with girls, is a red that's been bled of its rawness and gaudy ferocity. The "acceptable" feminine color, pink, retains some of this essence, but not fully alive. Not fully awake.

Looking back now, I suspect my initial craving for the color red was the beginning of my unwitting interaction with the Red Feminine. She was, after all, the kind of balance, the kind of step towards wholeness I needed. No one represents the healing of the Virgin-Whore split quite like the Red Goddess and Her priestesses. Since I was also reclaiming my inner artist, I believe I was particularly attuned to the Red Feminine in Her creative aspect, as the representation of a woman's primal urge to create. In this aspect, perhaps she is consonant with the Creative Matrix itself: what we all interact with when we create art, books, poems, babies, businesses, and music. *Poiesis.*

Oddly enough, the first known author, Enhueduanna, was one of Innana's priestesses who wrote heartfelt hymns to the Holy Mother. I suspect maybe this archetypal energy has a particular affinity for writing and authorship, at least in my case, since it inspired a book!

Devotion to this deep, red mother feels so ancient and familiar to me. I don't know how or why. I don't know how past lives or ancestral or collective memory or soul groups work. All

I know is that some things feel ancient and familiar, and She is one. So does the aroma of mistletoe at the holidays, and the embodied certitude that the land is holy. Maybe it's because I sense a more ancient, incense-drenched, fully human, and sexual Mary in Her.

THE BLOOD-HONEST TRUTH OF WHERE I AM NOW

At a certain point in my surrender to the depths of Red, it seemed I reached a threshold, a sort of decision point. By the time I reached Crowley's Scarlet Woman, I was sure enough that there was some kind of magnitude behind all these connections I'd found. And then I learned the basic mythos surrounding the Scarlet Woman in Crowley's Thelema system. She asks the initiate to cross a sort of chasm to get to Her, and in so doing, they must completely surrender their ego. They must offer every last drop of blood to her chalice, which contains the blood of the saints. By meeting this challenge, the initiate becomes a weird kind of Crowleyan saint.

One night at a bar, I told one of my little brothers about this. And I indicated that I *had to* surrender everything, didn't I? I didn't want to be the sort of chump who doesn't go all the way! He responded, "Anna, it's okay to get really far out sometimes as long as you know how to bring yourself back." And that broke through.

At a certain point, I had to cool my heels when it came to Red. I sensed potential psychological unsafety in proceeding further. And maybe that was wrong. Maybe I should've gone for it and crossed over completely into the strange sainthood of the Scarlet order, whatever that even means. Maybe one day I will. But this time I chickened out. And I like where I am now just fine.

Now I view my tryst with Red as an interruption, an intrusion, of the atopic Other (in the Byung Chul-Han sense) in my life—something from the other side. An eruption of lunar consciousness which was to ultimately have the salvific effect of pulling me out of the torpor of depression and out of myself. Anything that pulls us out of our whirring, involutional narcissism and opens us to what is radically Other keeps us open to life and Mystery. It keeps us in the Erotic position, reaching beyond ourselves to touch the Other. This is the opposite of the modern, melancholic, narcissistic position. In the Erotic position, we must make art, we must fall in love, we must forget ourselves. We must keep reaching out for Beauty.

Red should be, to this book, like the bucaro at the center of the Velazquez painting *Las Meninas*. An otherworldly, central axis. It is a meditation on life's little invitations, portals to the realm of "anima" (pleasure, magic, mystery, paradox, taboo). It is a realm where the rules of productivity, logic, and cause-and-effect thinking fall away–the rules that typically govern our ordinary, waking lives in this productivity-oriented culture.

When you've been enchanted, invited to see the world in another way, or invited to fall into the eternally powerful portal of sex (and it could be *right* in the middle of your work day!), you are in the lunar realm of anima, the Feminine, goddess. Committing to a soulful life, a life of expression, can feel like foregoing the rules of normal day-to-day rationality, productivity, and Cartesian dualism. At a certain point, we are so in love, so bewitched by the tender, enchanted, beautiful realm of soul, we recognize that a life ruled by logic and fear, even if it *is* the only way to stay safe, must be abandoned. Soul becomes our princess, and we are willing to slay any dragon for her, and to trust that her continually unravelling spool of thread will keep leading us somewhere through the forest. And it will probably be the meandering, scenic route that doesn't make a lot of immediate sense.

Somehow, I believe my interactions with Red helped to seed this book from the other world, and I believe the creative process always carries with it this entirely otherworldly potential, welcoming synchronicities and all manner of anomalous experiences. The part of me that received the red otherworld seed of this book like a lily was my Moonchild, my night-self. It is only she that can allow the otherworld spark of any creative project to take life in her hand.

Portals to the lunar realm could be anything at all. Prussian blue has been calling to me lately...

WRITING PROMPT FOR YOUR OCEANIC
LISTENING PRACTICE

-To Welcome More Mythopoetic Texture into Your Life:
What would *you* suddenly know you must have, if you allowed instinct and desire to flow through you unabated? (It could be a color, a flavor, a new experience...?) Challenge yourself to fill up to three journal pages if you can! See what really stands out.

CHAPTER FOURTEEN

AWAKENING YOUR SLEEPING BEAUTY

I WILL STAY AWAKE FOREVER IF I HAVE TO.

-ELENA AVILA, *WOMAN WHO GLOWS IN THE DARK*

DEEP SLEEP

In the Gnostic gospel, *The Book of Secrets*, Eve utters the cryptic words, *Beware the deep sleep*. These apocryphal gospels often have a deep, poetic, even pagan feel to them. They seem to point to deeper wisdoms and esoteric mysteries without directly enunciating them. In that way, they really are great poems, or works of art.

There are so many ways that this gospel, and those words alone, might be interpreted. I am not a theologian and I lay claim to neither the training nor the time spent in exegesis that this line deserves, but I often get a big intuitive hit when I am in the presence of great art or a great poem. Great art and great poems hit us with some kind of deep, universal, even ancient wisdom without directly saying it. However, some deep part of us catches the tail of some oceanic strain of meaning, the part of us that dreams.

There is a concept in depth psychology called *psychoma*, or "the sleep of the psyche." Another way to say this would be *the sleep of the soul.* And Eve warns us against it. Don't fall asleep, she says. There is a very tempting, yet ultimately fearful trance that the world can cast upon us. Beware of that, she says. You may need to fight to stay awake at some points.

This is not for the faint of heart. There is a ferocity in this wakefulness. There is a joining of spirit and soul in it. You must have a fierce prize fighter spirit that is in love with the treasure of your soul. Your fighter spirit will keep the realm of soul from being sealed off forever, leaving you in a state of psychoma. This is the state most modern people walk around in. Most people are asleep. The temptation is great.

e e cummings was aware of this, and I believe it's what he was speaking of when he wrote:

To be nobody but
yourself in a world
which is doing its best day and night to make you like

everybody else means to fight the hardest battle
which any human being can fight and never stop fighting.

An integral key to working with fear and resistance during this process of soul-making is the recognition that soul-sleep is a far worse fate than taking a risk and "failing," or stepping into a more soulful life. This is all part of learning to have faith in the conviction of your soul by making one unreasonable choice at a time. Different parts of you may come up during the process that are resistant or afraid. But you've been flipping the concepts of "failure" and "fear" on their heads during this process. The maenads would be proud.

It's important to acknowledge that feminine awakening is not some permanent state of spiritual transcendence. Rather, it is a process, a spiral dance, of refusing to go to sleep over and over and over again. Taking off masks, shedding skins, and getting naked, sometimes as regularly as the seasons. Ultimately, it's about finding the voice of the feminine soul at the center of your body and letting that be the ultimate spiritual queen of your life.

Once you complete this book and your current transformation, the wheel will continue to turn, and you may find yourself no longer feeling quite so alive in some aspect of your life. Listen to that. Continue unfolding. Continue following your butterflies. Fight to stay awake if you have to. The sleep of the soul (dreaded since the time of Eve) is what's at stake if we can't overcome fear. This was her way of saying, "Don't join the living dead."

DEEP WAKEFULNESS

WHO LOOKS OUTSIDE, DREAMS; WHO LOOKS INSIDE, AWAKES.

-CARL JUNG

When I was driving to the SF Office of the Treasurer and Tax Collector to register my psychotherapy private practice, my first business, I felt like a pregnant woman whose water had just broken. If I had been taking the bus, I imagine people would've given up their seats for me, somehow intuiting the gravity of this huge, metaphysical pregnancy. Though I still had not entirely decided on a name for my baby yet, the time had come. The creative matrix has her own law that must be respected, as much as it may oppose or shit all over the agendas of our ego. Women's waters often break at what seems like an "inopportune" moment. When *would be* an opportune moment?

At any rate, I was crossing the bridge from Oakland to San Francisco, the one that sits next to the original, crumbling Bay Bridge that Hunter S. Thompson once crossed on acid in the 1960s, certain that once he got to the other side, he would find people who were just as "weird" as he was. Different names for my baby flitted through my thoughts. *This one? Ugh, no. Not quite right.* The word "Awake" kept playing through my mind like a broken record, trying on different iterations. I thought, *Awake Feminist Therapy? Ugh, no.*

Anyway, I got there, and I still didn't know. I bungled my way through the process of registering the business, and... I still didn't know. When it came time to declare the name and bring the registration to the Hall of Records, I wrote, "Awake Therapy Space" on the form. Later, the name would change to "Deeper Well Therapy," because I realized that my associations with the word "awake" are pretty arcane and unusual, and that the initial face of the business did not quite trigger the immediate sense of feminine mysteries initiations in the general public.

Let me explain what "awake" meant to me in that birthing moment. I'm sure you're familiar with a little fairy tale we know as *Sleeping Beauty*. If we are faithful to the depth psychology approach to interpreting fairy tales and mythos, we must view each character as a different aspect, or "part" of one individual, of one psyche. So think of Briar Rose, Aurora, the sleeping beauty herself, as your soul. And consider this: There is something native to a woman that wakes her up from the inside, from psychoma, from "the deep sleep," and it's not any external Prince Charming.

This is her own prize-fighter spirit; a transgressive, revolutionary, fierce, and feisty part of her who is *not* going to stay asleep like a good girl. This part will fight to maintain a deep wakefulness in her. And I don't mean "awake" as some permanent state of spiritual transcendence. I mean a process of (and a fierce commitment to) refusing to go to sleep over and over again.

You might call the part of a woman that wakes her up from the inside her spirit, or you might even call it her inner masculine. Remember that we each contain a blend of what we might call the "masculine" and the "feminine." A complete feminine mysteries initiation involves an internal marriage between your healthy inner masculine and your feminine soul. He must be devoted to her, and willing to fight for her. All of his energies must be leveraged in service to her (not to any external standards or agendas). When this internal kiss happens, this internal wedding, a woman wakes up from the inside. In this way, the Sleeping Beauty fairy tale is about a woman kissing herself awake.

There is a Tibetan Buddhist feminine deity called the Vajravarahi, and she is always pictured with a staff held crosswise against her chest. Now, I trust my reader will continue to follow me here, since we've already been talking about some things that are punk as fuck. At the top of the staff are three human heads. One of them appears to have been freshly severed, one appears partially decomposed, and one of them, the product of a decapitation of the more distant past, presumably, is a clean, naked skull.

According to Marion Woodman, the staff represents her complete integration of her own inner masculine, and the heads represent her transformations. Each transformation is, after all, a death, if we are to follow the crone logic of the life-death-life cycle. The fact that there are three of them, in different stages of decomposition, seems to indicate that, with the help of her fully integrated inner masculine, she has completed not one, but numerous past transformations. And this is the nature of feminine transformation. It's not a one-and-done type of deal. You will be invited on another transformational journey again in your lifetime, and likely then another, and another, until the final, radical transformation of death.

As you stay true to these transformations, accepting the soul invitations when they come, you stay awake, fiercely, defiantly, proudly. Like fuck will you be going back to sleep.

Not surrendering to this process when it comes to you in the form of soul letters (and seeking community, support, and spiritual practice) will mean that you'll likely have to come around to it again. And it might come around more fiercely next time. And if you say no to it again, you'll have to put your soul to sleep even more fiercely than the time before. Remember my darlings, *Beware the deep sleep*, says the mother of us all. (Whether or not there was literally an Eve who is literally the mother of us all is beside the point. The archetype, the collective idea, of the mother of us all, speaks through these perennial words of wisdom.) There's a fairy tale that warns of this, of course. It's the tale of the wish-granting fish.

There once was a man and a woman who were very poor and who eked out a living, getting by however they could, and trying to scratch out meager harvests from the arid land. The husband would sometimes go out fishing and would once in a while bring home a catch that sufficed for a tasty and satisfying dinner for both himself and his wife.

One day, out in the tidepools, he glimpsed a special, silver fish darting past in the water below. He couldn't take his eyes off of it, so otherworldly was the sheen of its scales, and so hypnotic the way it moved. To his surprise, it rose to the surface and it spoke to him, telling him it actually had the power to grant him one wish, any wish he might have. The man wished that he and his wife might be rich, and live in a fine house with fine things, and never want for anything again. "Granted," the fish said and then disappeared again beneath the billowing sea.

The man and his wife were bedazzled by the miraculous change in their circumstances, and the wife declared that if the fish could grant a wish once, surely it could grant further wishes. And she urged her husband to go back out to that same cove in his little fishing boat to try to find that same, uncanny fish. And, wanting to please his wife, the husband did so, again and again, until he and his wife had risen in wealth, rank, and societal station to such a degree that the wife finally declared she wanted to be made pope. Granted, granted, granted again.

But all was not as well as it seemed, for each time the man went out on the water, he noticed the fish grew weary. It swam more slowly in the water, seeming exhausted, weakened, even perhaps sickly compared to the most recent time he had seen it. In accordance with his wife's wishes, he went out yet again to look for the otherworldly little fish. "Oh fish, oh fish, where are you? I have just one more wish! My wife sends me out to find you!" This time the fish rose to greet him very slowly, and it was bleeding in the water. It informed him it could not grant another wish for him... ever... again. And it sank beneath the waves, leaving a little trail of red behind it. The man did try to go out to find the fish once, twice, and three times more. And it never again appeared.

This story seems to warn that it may be possible to offend your soul so badly that it wanders away from you, never to return. Every time you shove down, dismiss, or numb the soul letters (in whatever form they take), you are shoving down, dismissing, and numbing your soul. You may no longer even be able to discern whether or not your lifestyle or activities are offending her anymore. The story seems to indicate that there may come a time when it is no longer possible to accept the invitations, when you have become wedded to your sleep instead of to your spirit. I'm not sure whether I believe that. But I'll heed the warning nonetheless.

We offend our soul when we misdirect its true energies and harness them in service to our egoic desires and plans, or in service to external, patriarchal standards. Ego cares about keeping up with the Joneses. Ego cares about how you are being perceived on your social media profiles. And ego is often in cahoots with fear. And when our inner masculine is much more on board with the agenda of the ego (i.e., externally imposed agendas, mostly), it might accidentally stomp on the butterfly of your soul. When your inner masculine bends the knee to your soul, as delicate and otherworldly as she might seem, all is right in your inner queendom.

Ego may want you to stay in your nine-to-five job, and to continue binging on Netflix and Cheetos whenever your soul speaks to you and tells you of its sadness. Ego may love for you to continue using those numbing agents. Think of those numbing agents as soul-sleep agents. They are putting your soul and its messages and invitations to sleep, keeping all of its treasures buried underground.

Remember? The best self-soothing is to turn off the TV and make a plan to follow your bliss, or to sit with that emptiness, sadness, or anxiety in emotional vipassana, or journal it out. Find out what it is telling you. Then, start making a plan based on the messages the emotion carries. You may feel some flickers of defiant life and excitement in this act by itself. You may even feel that sublime, alive, awake feeling in your body that you are onto something good. You may even love fear, in the right doses, and consider it to be your indicator that one of your ideas is getting really warm. You may even associate it with life, with the butterflies in your tummy that you are going to follow. And in this practice, you may just bring forth the voice of your soul.

There is another dimension to psychoma, to the sleep of the soul. We do not just put ourselves to sleep when it comes to the true longings of our souls, our true desires, yearnings, and interests. We also do it when it comes to the deep hungers and crises of our times. So, soul-sleep also becomes attractive to our egos as a way to turn off our awareness of the suffering and destruction currently taking place on the planet.

Your soul won't *stand* for this. Holy Mother does not stand for this. She does not start wars or shoot people for resisting arrest or wipe out entire peoples or ecosystems. FUCK no. This is not the way. She prizes all life, without exception, especially the voiceless, the vulnerable, and even the fragile, tender life of new creative ideas. In the realm of Holy Mother, all of life is loved, and all of life is nurtured, including the creative lifeforce as it lives in you.

And I'll tell you a little secret: I'll be good goddamned if your soul's true desires, yearnings, and interests do not align in some hidden, magical way with the yearnings, hungers, and needs of your time. You don't need to see how it aligns right in this moment. It's not possible to see that in its entirety, nor to see all the doors that will open for you. It sometimes seems very much to be the case that there is a greater intelligence or pattern that is urging us along for some greater purpose. Your soul is the through line to that realm, and I believe that you *can* turn her navigational system back on anytime. It's never too late.

By creating wakefulness and peace within, you help to create wakefulness and peace in the world in more ways than one. Even if that statement is patently untrue, won't your life be more interesting if you experiment with believing it, even just for one day?

If we choose to stay asleep, we choose to kill off the transgressive potential in our emptiness, our sadness, or our anxiety. By waking ourselves up, we wake Her up, in all of Her transgressive, salvific, and sacredly profane glory.

Perhaps by waking your own sleeping beauty, you are actively helping to awaken the great goddess. Perhaps by calling out to your own Moonchild, your own inner through line to Beauty, you are helping to save the lunar soul of this world. Dostoevsky did famously write, "Beauty will save the world." By living and speaking from your feminine soul, your inner wakeful beauty, you are letting Her live and speak. And Jesus Christ Almighty, do we need Her to speak now. Listen.

WRITING PROMPTS FOR YOUR OCEANIC LISTENING PRACTICE

-For Wakeful Beauty:

Where have you been asleep in your life? How were you keeping yourself asleep? How did you wake up?

Where are you asleep now? How could you fight to stay more fully awake in that part of your life?

What's your plan for staying awake?

CHAPTER FIVETEEN

LIFTING THE VEIL

APOCALYPSE

According to some of the world's great spiritual traditions, enlightenment (or liberation) involves a process of continual removal. The more we listen to and follow instinct, the more we peel back the layers and become more naked, alive, authentic, and free. We become the women no one else could be. It has been my intention to write this book in a rhythm that serves as a sort of sympathetic magick; to write it like a belly dance, with rhythm and consequence at the end of each stanza, a slow striptease, a removal of one veil, and then another, and then another, like Inanna making her way through the underworld until she stands completely naked.

Though, as I come to the end of writing this book, I am beginning to appreciate more and more the virtues of concealment. It may not be possible to ever be fully naked. It's certainly not possible to ever be fully known. Even the rawest memoir transfigures real experience into a sort of fiction, while fiction may inadvertently make the author even more skinless than memoir does. Partial concealment itself can be a beguiling invitation to the imagination, even a portal to the lunar realm.

Still, the uncanny connections that have to do with peeling back the layers, shedding skins, lifting veils, and getting naked, continue. The goddess Babylon is considered by many scholars of Western esotericism to be the Red Goddess, connected in magickal fact to Inanna-Ishtar. And I believe it's no coincidence that Crowley's Scarlet Woman was interchangeably referred to as Babalon. She is also the force referred to in the Old Testament Revelations in descriptions of the coming apocalypse, in those instances as The Whore of Babylon. Well, let's get radical and look at the root of that word, "apocalypse." It comes from the Greek *apokalupsis,* which literally means to uncover, to lift the veil, and originally referred to the shearing of a sheep's wool. The apocalypse is the lifting of the veil.

There are all kinds of weird roads we could take with just that little gem, but for our present purposes let's take this one.

Every single process of transformation you will go through in your life involves the lifting of a veil, the removal of a mask, the shedding of a skin. And it also involves death, in some sense. It involves the end of a world. You must die to the world you inhabited before. The caterpillar dissolves into sludge in its cocoon before it gets to become a butterfly.

That might sound like some scary shit, I know. But I bring in these rich etymological connections in order to shed the light of magick and hope on even the roughest transitions. Remember the Vajravarahi with the three human heads on her staff? Those represent the deaths, the transformations, she has completed. She holds them proudly. To complete even one initiation, as a woman in this world, is a dazzling accomplishment. She should hold those heads like the dissident firebrand she is. And, oh, weirdly, like Vasilisa holding her skull torch on the return from the Baba Yaga's cottage.

By transitioning from being a traditional, safe, Apollonian psychotherapist to being my own kind of wounded healer (in various capacities) who is completely "out" as a highly weird artist/writer, my soul is being threshed from one husk. This will continue until the final, big threshing. I am removing a mask, lifting a veil. The paradoxical thing is that you become more and more alive each time, if you just continue to unfold, unfold, and unfold again.

Remember that internal "board members" have to be exiled in order for you to keep your mask on. By integrating the exiled "board members," which is what you've been doing if you've followed the process outlined in these pages, you will find yourself, inevitably, removing a mask of some kind. How might you be removing a mask now? What mask were you wearing? What is underneath? Whatever it is, I guarantee it is more naked and human. And people love to see that. (Not in a perverted way, ya dingus!) How will you commit to your ongoing shedding of shame-skins? The more you do this, the more refreshing and magnetic you will be. It may feel scary while you're doing it, but it will pay off, big time. And remember, when you are bold, "great forces will join you." The great forces we've been working with throughout this book.

Underneath the layers of false personas and the din of internal "board members" is always the little doll of the Vasilisa tale, the soft voice of the soul. It's a bright energy at the center of the belly that speaks through butterflies, poems, and dreams.

FINDING SOUL-SKIN

Let's take one last little dip into storyland. I know that the best way I can help to midwife feminine consciousness in others is by telling my story, as honestly as I can. And I know that one of the best ways to bring a message home to your night-self is to tell it in a fairy tale. May this story be a guiding image for staying in touch with the mysterious guidance of your soul, now and always.

When I left mental health agency work, I wanted to be in the flow of life, living by instinct, not according to the pumping of any machine. I recognize this may sound totally nakedly privileged. While I have lived a very blessed life, I sincerely believe that a life guided by the depths of the belly is available to all. My life has demanded the removal of one mask, then another, getting freer and freer and freer. Your life demands the same of you. May you be free.

This book began to be written in 2015, and as I sit here completing it, I am in another growth phase, removing the wooden, good-girl clinician mask I've created, and revealing the wounded healer-artist underneath. Each growth phase is about reclamation, becoming freer and freer. And so each growth phase for you will be about reclamation, becoming freer and freer.

After becoming licensed and starting a private practice, I felt like the young girl from a novella I'd once read when I was about ten. In this fantastical tale, a young girl ends up living in the ocean after she loses her entire family in a boating accident. A pod of wild dolphins takes the girl under their "wing," and she learns to swim as fast as they swim, and to live her entire life in the rhythms of the ocean with the protection and love of her pod. She even learns to drink dolphin milk and perhaps live off of wild caught fish, if I remember the story correctly. And when she is finally found, she weighs 100 pounds, and ten of those pounds are all hair, which would trail around her down to her feet like seaweed when she swam. A feral girl.

As the story goes, she was brought back to "civilization," and learned how to speak, read, write, and solve math problems.

The tale itself is told in the voice of the feral girl. And as it progresses, her writing gradually regresses, becoming more childlike. The sea beckoned to her, and one night she slipped away and returned to her true watery home.

Like the girl in the story, I felt the call of the sea, and I gradually became more and more feral. I felt the call to return to what I always was. And you too shall feel the call of the sea and become more feral, returning to what you always were.

The preteen novella that struck such a deep chord with me when I was younger mirrors (probably intentionally) an old folk tale (of Ireland, Scotland, and the Faroe Islands), the selkie story. I have been exposed to differing versions of the tale, but the basic gist is that there was a lonely man, a fisherman, who wanted a wife more than anything in the world. He went out to the seashore for some early morning trawling in the wee hours while the veil of the night was still over everything. And the silver moon still shone down onto the surface of the water, which always looked to him a bit like a mermaid's tail.

He thought he could hear chanting and singing in the distance, and when he drew nearer to the source of the bell-like laughter and celestial singing, he saw a group of women dancing, as naked as the day they were born. And their skin in the moonlight gave off the luminescent glow of a fish's belly, and it seemed to shimmer somehow, as if there were traces of silver in it.

Stunned, the lonely young man was magnetically drawn to these women, for they were the most beautiful women he had ever seen. He had to go to them, to learn their names or take their hands. He really didn't know *what* he wanted to go to them for because when a man falls in love, he gets so confused that he doesn't know *what* on earth it is that he wants or likes at all anymore. Only that he must have his love.

And so he drew even nearer, and suddenly, one of the beautiful ladies gasped, and quick as a flash, they all threw their skins back on, which were seal skins, and hopped back into the dark water one by one. All but one of the beautiful ladies, who lagged behind.

Somehow, the lonely young man turned on his charm, and maybe he took her by the arm, and promised her the world on a stick, if she would only do him the great honor of marrying him and becoming his wife. He must've turned on some world-class charm because somehow, she acquiesced. As soon as he got her back to his humble cottage, he hid her seal skin away in a locked chest in the attic, because he knew that if she were ever to see it again, "neither chains of love nor chains of steel" could keep her from her true home, the sea.

In no time, they were married, and she bore him handsome children, each with a love of the sea. And though she seemed to dote on her children and love them dearly, as the years wore on, her beautiful face grew more pale and wan. She grew thinner. The light went out of her eyes. Her undulating hair grew coarse, and she became more and more weak and fatigued. She started to spend a good deal of her days in bed.

The versions of the tale differ as to the lengths that the *Selkie*, the seal-lady, went to get her skin back. The point is that it was the key to her vitality, her light, and her very will to live. It was her true self. Eventually, she had to be returned to it, or she would die. In all versions of the tale, she is eventually returned to her seal-skin, and to her true home in the sea.

As I've journeyed on in my life, I've always tried to find my seal skin, my soul-skin. I've always tried to return to the sea. And I want you to find your soul-skin as well and to know the wild joy of the ocean and the lyrical air. How could you do that now? What is the key to your vitality, light, and will to live? How can you be returned to that?

FOLLOWING THOSE BUTTERFLIES

Another process of metamorphosis is upon me because no matter what my official "title" is in the modern world, I am a woman who walks in both worlds, alternately called a priestess, a witch, an oracle, or an artist. Does this sound like fanciful thinking? I would implore you to check in about which part of you says that it is. You may be one of us, too, *especially* if you have a judgmental reaction to that statement. Remember that the things that irk us about others are often indicators of our own exiled parts. We've had many names in many times and places. We don't really have a tradition in the modern West. I believe we exist in a myriad of fields in the modern world, connected by an invisible thread of love.

There is a need in me to love people, transcend genres, share my weird art, my blood-honest stories, my eldritch poems, my oracular dreams. Adhering perfectly to the mold of traditional, by-the-book psychotherapy flattens me. I'm busting out of the set of monk's robes I've been wearing. And I finally decided to honor this. Which set of monk's robes are *you* busting out of? How can you honor that?

What do you do, and what are you about, that is just a bit beyond the box of the caricature that the world uses to define you? How is there so much more to you? How might this "so much more" point to your real work, or the next big "thing" for you? Understand that your great work could be raising a child or being a wonderful friend. What great works do you feel you are here to do?

I call it the spark of the sublime in the body, the little doll, the soul voice, the lunar self, Moonchild, or just plain butterflies. Others have called it the still, small voice within (Marianne Williamson). SARK calls it your "best wise self." Julia Cameron calls it "the benevolent something." Some of the most interesting and successful people make a practice of listening to it. And we're talking about success in terms of the way *you* define it, not anyone else, not your parents or your friends or your social media feed. Often that *something* (whatever you call it) takes you on a journey. You may arrive somewhere you thought was "it," and then you hear that voice or you feel that spark, *again.* Oh no! And you keep journeying. This is the heroine's journey of life.

You may be fascinated by your current life situation or even deeply compelled by it, but if you feel you are constantly being corrected, pushed down, or constrained rather than pushed to your personal growth edge (where you feel that healthy, growth-oriented sense of correction), this may be something to look at. Perhaps this specific arena never fully fit your form and you've always known that on some level, which has always caused you some level of pain. This is a special journey for women in particular, as we are just now learning what it looks like when a woman is fully integrated, fully herself, *and* fully empowered. Just keep following those butterflies in your tummy and you will become something the world has never seen before.

When you're willing to lift the veils and keep lifting them, you open yourself to see and feel the numinous. When you keep lifting the veils, the world gets more naked before you, too. And often, things that previously seemed unattainable suddenly reveal themselves to be ripe for the plucking in your own backyard.

It's because your butterflies, the truth underneath all the bullshit, point the way to your biggest life. I'm not talking about the butterflies you might get when you think about crossing the red tape of the inevitable complications and pain that would result from you fucking some hot, unavailable dreamboat. I'm talking about the butterflies you get when you daydream about who you might one day become. I think you already know the difference.

RETELLING YOUR STORY

We are constantly telling stories, whether we mean to or not. Even when we're not consciously aware of it, our unconscious is always looping on the same old narratives. Stories are *made of symbols* (even if we're only talking about the words that comprise them), and with our stories we are constantly making our world. It seems to be the case that, in some mysterious way, when we interact with symbols, we are harnessing the diviner's cause and magickally summoning acausal connections in our outer world. In other words, it seems to be the case that we invite the world to correspond with that story, or to continue showing us that story.

Our souls/bodies/unconscious hold our stories, our family's stories, and our ancestor's stories. We can begin retelling the story of who we are, going as far back or being as thorough as we like. Even one sentence can retell the story. Or you can rewrite the entire narrative of the past that brought you to where you are now. And this can retell the story of who you are, from this day forward. By telling a new story, we are doing practical magick. We are harnessing the constant story-telling aspect of who we are. This can free you from the shackles of stories that don't spring from your own depths.

So, what's your new narrative? Retell the story of who you are with your new awareness of the preciousness and badassery of the part (or parts) you had previously disowned. And fully own the new story that comes from your own examined depths. There is a solidity and magnetism to the presence of someone who has done this. It's as if people who hide under shame cloaks, under the belief that they contain "bad" parts, inadvertently invite others to perceive them in the same way. Conversely, your own deep acceptance of yourself seems to invite others to want to deeply accept you, too.

PIVOTING

If you've been putting each of the new insights you've received into practice in your daily life throughout this process, bravo! In any case, there might be another way you could enact this new level of soulful integration in your actual life. As the result of becoming more integrated and getting deeply honest with yourself on a variety of topics, what do you think you might like to change about your current life?

If you gulped or felt a little shimmer of fear when you read that, it probably means there's something you know, at a bone-deep level, you need to change. It could be a job, a relationship, or some unhelpful, addictive behavior you've been engaging in on and off for years.

Ask yourself what you truly want here. Ask yourself what your soul, your deeper self wants, what your heart wants. And ask yourself what pain or scary unknown you cover up and avoid by continuing this behavior or lifestyle. Get whatever help might be most appropriate for making a plan to transition, depending on the situation. And be gentle with yourself. Plan like someone who loves herself.

It's important to recognize that self-sabotage can actually sneak in with a plan that is *too* daring. Would someone who loved herself undertake that plan? Or a different plan? That is the litmus test. Remember, love is the first and the last in this process. Jenny Blake's *Pivot* offers a wonderful system for preparing for a career pivot and for ensuring that you plan in a smart way. It's often best to aim for meaningful change within a feasible timeline, not massive change within a panic-attack timeline. With a practice of deeply listening to your soul, your confidence in its nudges (whether to move to Prague tomorrow, or to make gradual, gentle changes) will only continue to grow.

A word to the wise: You would do well to maintain a community of soulful people who keep you true to your path. Because the temptation to go back to sleep is sometimes *so* large and *so* looming and *so* hypnotic. Just know that. We all struggle with it.

HOW BEAUTY SAVES THE WORLD

Let's walk out into the garden to pay one last visit to the Empress, the Queen of Life. She seems to suggest the whole adventure of life might still be worthwhile, despite death, drudgery, pain, and the thread of tragedy woven into all things from the very beginning. Her Mona Lisa smile, therefore, captures the strange soul of art. It shies away from neither the tragedy nor the unspeakable beauty of life. It makes *both* plain and puts a drop of the fathomless invisible oceans of tenderness in a vitrine. She is Ginsberg's vision in the garden, when he saw the mystery at the heart of things, and returned to the tenement flat crying.

This is why dewy rosebuds spring up all around her feet, and (like Inanna-Ishtar, Queen of Heaven) twelve stars shine over her head. She does not deny the tragedy of life. But her smile says, "Nevertheless." This is the "nevertheless" in the conscious decision to become a biological mother, or just a good mother to yourself, and in all great works of art.

We live in a world of terrible beauty. I have been deeply tempted to write that when we can muster a "yes" to that terrible beauty, we are showing up to the sacredness of what it means to be fully human, both feet on the earth with an open heart despite everything. However, it would be wrong to suggest that resistance does not also have its place. Resistance in the face of whatever would destroy the creative lifeforce, or whatever we hold dear. Maybe saying "yes" to our inner Moonchild and shouting her name from the window are the most vital acts of resistance any of us can do. She is Beauty with a capital-B. Maybe by calling her name in our own ways, we let a wakeful Beauty save the world.

Did you know Anandamayi Ma used to sing "Jaya Bhagavan" every morning? *Jaya* means victory, and *Bhagavan* means divine/love. Let Beauty save the world. Let love win. Even if it's a "lost cause" to maintain an open heart and to do what your butterfly-soul compels you to do, you can do it anyway as an act of beauty. If you can do that as an act of beauty, in a weird way, beauty has always already saved the world. This is how you can make your whole life sing,

Really, I am an artist, and I work for Her.

AFTERWORD

Something within me is resistant to tying things off into a neat and satisfactory conclusion. My sincerest desire is to make books as works of art that are never entirely finished with the reader, always resplendent with new applications and new meanings to be found. Whether or not I've accomplished that here I cannot yet know. What I do know is that the upending of my understanding of reality, womanhood, and sanity implicated within the strange experiences of 2015, and the intuitions I began to develop about those experiences, will never be finished with me. They will haunt my future works, flashing some great mystery but ultimately revealing only that the world is like a woman who might get totally naked before you, but whose essence remains completely occult.

The deep symbolism of that moment of my life did not come to any neat close or point of final resolution anywhere.

Nor did my journey of healing, unfolding, and becoming. It seems, from the lunar vista, that perhaps the process is the point.

I wish I could part the final veils and disclose to you the great secrets. That would not be honest. I wish I could write that the synchronicities have pointed me to some specific result or destination. Really, they've just opened avenues of inquiry. And they've deepened my intimacy with my own soul, with life, and with this mysterious world. Ultimately, they led to the birth of this book.

So if there is anything to be concluded, perhaps it is that the great magnitudes revel in creative expression. Perhaps they moonlight as muses.

While we're being honest, I'll disclose here that the strange experiences of 2015 were not the only anomalous experiences I've ever had in my life. There have been others. Some I haven't been brave enough yet to share. Perhaps I failed to make myself sensitive to the ways they could have fueled other creative projects.

Perhaps we can also conclude that, from the vantage point of femtheogenic consciousness, it appears obvious that by bringing ourselves back to wholeness, we bring the world and others to wholeness. By filling ourselves to overflowing with love, we fill the world with more love, and we become more loving beings. It becomes obvious that our densest lead could become the alchemical gold that could help to usher in a new golden age. So much of that lead is buried transgressive potential. And it's never been more important in the history of our species for us to salvage the subversive lightning hidden underneath sadness, emptiness, and even clinical-level depression and anxiety. Maybe, by offering deep listening to these parts of ourselves, we are speaking the language of the angels, the burned books, the witches. We are breaking the silence of the oracles. We are bringing the feminine back up from underground to unfurl Her scarlet radiance in the light of the sun.